BUSINESS REVISION FOR LEAVING CERTIFICATE

BUSINESS REVISION

FOR

LEAVING CERTIFICATE

SECOND EDITION

JOHN F. O'SULLIVAN

GILL & MACMILLAN

Gill & Macmillan Ltd
Hume Avenue
Park West
Dublin 12
with associated companies throughout the world
www.gillmacmillan.ie

978 07171 4137 1

Print origination by
Carrigboy Typesetting Services

The paper used in this book is made from the wood pulp of managed forests. For every tree felled, at least one tree is planted, thereby renewing natural resources.

CONTENTS

PREFACE

The aim of this book is to provide pupils with a comprehensive summary of the Leaving Certificate business course, both Ordinary and Higher level. It contains many fully worked solutions to examination-style questions and a list of the more important terms at the end of each unit. The end of the book contains useful advice on examination structure, examination timing, and outcome verbs used in examination questions.

I hope this book will be of assistance when revising business in the months before the Leaving Certificate examination.

I would like to thank the editorial staff at Gill & Macmillan for their help and assistance.

John F. O'Sullivan BComm HDE
Business Studies Department
St Peter's Community School
Passage West
Co. Cork

For my parents, who showed me the path that I follow;
for my wife, with whom I follow it;
and for my children, whose paths await them.

SECTION A: PEOPLE IN BUSINESS

Unit 1: Introduction to People in Business

Business is primarily concerned with people and their relationships. This section introduces the main parties in business and their roles, and it examines how they work successfully together. It also looks at areas where their interests may not coincide and how they may resolve such situations of conflict.

Objective: To enable pupils to understand the form and the dynamic nature of the relationship between the principal parties in business.

1. People and their relationships in business

People in business

Business is primarily concerned with people and their relationships. There are many different parties in business, including:

- entrepreneur
- investor
- producer
- supplier
- service provider
- employer
- employee
- interest group

ENTREPRENEURS

— have the ability to spot and evaluate business opportunities
— use initiative and enterprise to gather resources necessary to take advantage of these opportunities
— are action-oriented and highly motivated people who take calculated risks to achieve their goals
— are innovators who combine resources such as land, labour, capital and enterprise in a successful business venture.

INVESTORS

— provide finance to entrepreneurs to start up and develop business. Investors may be
(*a*) shareholders buying shares in a company—share capital
(*b*) a bank or building society investing in the form of loan-debenture finance.

PRODUCERS
— combine the use of machinery, labour and finance to transform raw material into a finished product to sell to consumers.

SUPPLIERS
— supply the raw materials and machinery required for production to producers
— supply consumers with finished goods.

SERVICE PROVIDERS
— provide a wide range of services for the efficient operation of business, including telecommunications, distribution, financial and professional services.

EMPLOYERS
— hire employees to produce goods or supply services. They reward employees with wages/salaries for their work.

EMPLOYEES
— work for employers in the production of goods and services, in return for a fee called wages/salaries.

INTEREST GROUPS
— wish to influence the political and decision-making process but are not part of the accepted political structure of the country. Examples include:

(1) *Business associations—speaking on behalf of business:*

Irish Business and Employers' Confederation (IBEC)
— represents employers; lobbies the Government to introduce policies of benefit to business.

Irish Management Institute (IMI)
— promotes high standards of management.

Institute of Public Administration (IPA)
— promotes high standards of management in the public sector.

chambers of commerce
— promote the development of business in a locality.

Irish Congress of Trade Unions (ICTU)
— lobbies the Government on behalf of workers and tries to influence the Government on wage levels and taxes.

(2) *Trade associations—representing business in a particular trade. Examples include:*
Society of the Irish Motor Industry (SIMI)
Irish Travel Agents' Association (ITAA)

RELATIONSHIP BETWEEN PARTIES IN BUSINESS

DYNAMIC RELATIONSHIP
The relationship between parties in business is constantly changing and is said to be ***dynamic***. Sometimes this relationship is co-operative: they help one another; at other times it is competitive, which may cause conflict.

CHANGING ROLE OF PEOPLE IN BUSINESS

At any time a person can have many roles—for example employee, consumer, investor—but over time a person can change from being an employee to being an entrepreneur or employer, etc.

RELATIONSHIP BETWEEN ENTREPRENEUR AND INVESTOR

Entrepreneurs are risk-takers: they exercise initiative and take a risk in starting up a business, with the hope of making profit.

Investors invest finance in an enterprise. An investor can be a bank, which grants a loan, or an equity investor, who buys shares with the hope of receiving dividends.

RELATIONSHIP BETWEEN PRODUCERS AND INTEREST GROUPS

Producers and suppliers

— manufacture goods or supply services that satisfy consumers' needs
— want high prices and profit.

Interest groups

Interest groups may affect these producer interests. Interest groups

— are groups that wish to influence the political and decision-making process but are not part of the accepted political structure
— put pressure on the Government or the European Union to accept their position on issues
— can cause bad publicity for a business; the image of the business may be damaged
— can increase costs of advertising to counter bad publicity.

RELATIONSHIP BETWEEN CONSUMERS AND BUSINESS

Consumers buy goods and services from a **business**. Consumers want good-quality goods and services at reasonable prices.

The relationship is good when consumers are happy with the quality of product or service provided. From the business point of view, a good relationship is necessary for sales, profit, or expansion.

If the relationship between consumers and business deteriorates, consumers may stop buying the product, with serious consequences for the business.

RELATIONSHIP BETWEEN EMPLOYER AND EMPLOYEES

Employers are interested in the management and planning of a business with a view to future success. Their aim is:

(*a*) to maximise output and keep production costs low, so that the firm remains competitive
(*b*) to increase profits, so that retained earnings can be built up and give good return on invested capital for the owners.

Employers want to maintain a good relationship with employees.

Employees

— want reasonable wages, good working conditions, and a good standard of living
— want job security and promotion.

RELATIONSHIP BETWEEN CONSUMERS AND PRODUCERS

Producers are interested in making a profit, but can only do so if they satisfy **consumers**' needs. They must consistently monitor consumers' behaviour and change in response to consumers' needs.

Producers want high prices and profit, while consumers want low prices and quality goods or services.

Co-operative and competitive relationships

People in business can either co-operate with each other and help one another or can compete with each other.

CO-OPERATIVE AND COMPETITIVE RELATIONSHIP BETWEEN INVESTORS AND ENTREPRENEURS

CO-OPERATIVE

There is a strong relationship when an entrepreneur seeks finance for a new project. The relationship will remain co-operative as long as the entrepreneur presents a strong business plan with projected cash flow forecast, profit and loss account, and balance sheet.

The investor wants to see plans for the repayment of funds to minimise risks.

COMPETITIVE

A competitive relationship will arise if an investor refuses to advance the funds required to establish a new business, or if the entrepreneur, having received finance, is not living up to the commitments entered into and is defaulting on repayments.

CO-OPERATIVE AND COMPETITIVE RELATIONSHIP BETWEEN TWO PRODUCERS IN SAME LINE OF BUSINESS

CO-OPERATIVE

Producers will have a co-operative relationship when undertaking activities for their mutual benefit, such as lobbying the Government for a change in legislation or a reduction in VAT, or agreeing a common scale of discounts for customers. They will also co-operate and help each other out in times of difficulty, such as when there is a fire in a premises.

COMPETITIVE

Producers will generally have a competitive relationship when they
— try to launch new products
— monitor each other's activities
— outsell each other's products
— attract customers to their own goods and services.

CO-OPERATIVE AND COMPETITIVE RELATIONSHIP BETWEEN EMPLOYER AND EMPLOYEE

CO-OPERATIVE

Employers and employees will co-operate when
— working out wages and conditions of work
— workers receive fair wages in return for productive work
— planning social occasions, such as an annual staff outing.

COMPETITIVE
When wages and working conditions are not satisfactory.

CO-OPERATIVE AND COMPETITIVE RELATIONSHIP BETWEEN CONSUMER AND PRODUCER

CO-OPERATIVE
Producers co-operate with consumers
— when they provide the products and services demanded
— when products are of top quality and reasonably priced.

COMPETITIVE
When poor-quality goods are supplied, the customer may go to other producers.

Law of contract

Because of the co-operative and competitive nature of the relationship that exists between parties in business, there will occasionally be some conflict. The law of contract has been developed over the years from decisions of judges to regulate how business should be done. It helps reduce conflict and ensures that business transactions are organised in a formal manner.

A CONTRACT IS AN AGREEMENT BETWEEN TWO OR MORE PARTIES THAT, IF IT CONTAINS THE ELEMENTS OF A VALID LEGAL CONTRACT, IS ENFORCEABLE BY LAW.

EXAMPLE OF A CONTRACT
Buying goods or services of any kind, for example a house, an insurance policy, supermarket shopping.

ELEMENTS OF A LEGALLY BINDING AGREEMENT
(1) agreement
(2) consideration
(3) intention to contract
(4) capacity to contract
(5) legality of form
(6) consent to contract
(7) legal purpose.

AGREEMENT
Agreement arises as a result of offer and acceptance.

OFFER
The formation of a contract involves one party making an offer to another party. An offer can be made orally, in writing, by conduct, or by post. It must be clear, complete, and unconditional, and it must be communicated to the person to whom the offer is being made.

Invitation to treat
An invitation to a person to make an offer—for example a television set displayed in a shop window for €99—invites people to enter the shop and make an offer for the television, which may lead to a contract. This offer can be accepted or rejected.

Terminating an offer

An offer may be terminated in a number of ways.

(1) *Revocation of offer*

The offeror may withdraw the offer at any time before acceptance. To be effective, revocation must be communicated to the person to whom the offer was made (offeree) before they have accepted the offer.

(2) *Rejection of offer*

This is when the offeree rejects the offer. They may express their rejection orally or in writing.

(3) *Lapse of time*

If a time for acceptance has been stipulated, the offer terminates when that time has expired.

ACCEPTANCE

Acceptance of the terms of an offer can be made orally, in writing, by conduct, or by post. When an offer is accepted it is binding on all parties. The offer must be accepted with all its conditions.

Conditional acceptance

Sometimes an offer may be accepted subject to conditions. This is called *conditional acceptance* and is classed as a counter-offer.

CONSIDERATION

This is something of value offered by a party to a contract in exchange for something of value received. Consideration usually takes the form of monetary payment in exchange for goods and services received.

INTENTION TO CONTRACT

It must be the intention of the parties to create a legally binding agreement before a contract can validly exist.

Social and personal agreements are not legally binding. If there is an agreement by two people to go to the cinema and one person does not turn up, the other person cannot sue, because there was no intention to create a legal agreement.

CAPACITY TO CONTRACT

In order for an agreement to be a valid contract the parties must have the legal capacity to make a contract.

There is no capacity to contract under the following circumstances:

(1) *Infants:* those under the age of eighteen cannot contract except for necessaries, i.e. items that are in keeping with the style of life to which they have become accustomed.

(2) *Drunkenness:* a person under the influence of alcohol has no capacity to contract.

(3) *Mental illness:* a person of unsound mind has no capacity to contract.

(4) *Diplomatic status:* diplomats are in a privileged position; if they break a contract they cannot be sued or prosecuted, that is, they can claim diplomatic immunity, unless they choose to submit to the jurisdiction of the Irish courts.

(5) *Ultra vires:* a company's powers are limited by its objectives in the memorandum of association. Directors who enter into agreements outside these powers have no capacity to contract.

LEGALITY OF FORM

A contract must be drawn up in the correct legal form. Contracts can be oral, but certain contracts must be written—for example hire purchase agreements and insurance policies—while other contracts can be implied by conduct.

CONSENT TO CONTRACT

The parties must be entering the contract voluntarily: no pressure or duress should be exerted.

ILLEGAL CONTRACTS

A court will not enforce a contract for an illegal purpose or for a purpose that offends public policy. These include

- contracts to commit a crime
- contracts that impede the administration of justice
- contracts to defraud the Revenue Commissioners

TERMINATION OF CONTRACT

A contract can be terminated by *performance, breach, agreement,* or *frustration.*

(1) *Performance*

The parties to the contract have carried out their side of the contract as agreed.

(2) *Breach*

One party to a contract has failed to perform their obligations in the contract. Breach of a **condition** (a clause that is fundamentally important and goes to the heart of a contract) entitles the injured party to rescind the contract and sue for damages.

Breach of a **warranty** (a less important clause) allows the injured party only to sue for damages.

(3) *Agreement*

The parties to the contract agree to end the contract.

(4) *Frustration*

If an unforeseen event occurs that makes the performance of a contract impossible, the contract is terminated: for example, a contract to sell an aircraft could be frustrated if it crashed before the contract was due to be implemented. Contracts are also frustrated by death, bankruptcy, or lapse of time: contracts entered into for a specific time are discharged when that period has elapsed.

REMEDIES FOR BREACH OF CONTRACT

When there is breach of contract, the following remedies are available:

(1) *Damages*

The injured party can sue for ***damages*** (monetary compensation) to put them in the same financial position they would have been in if the contract had been performed according to its terms.

(2) *Specific performance*
An order of the court containing an instruction to a party to a contract to perform the obligations as originally agreed.

(3) *Rescinding the contract*
The contract is cancelled, and each of the parties is put back into the position they were in before the contract was made. If either party incurs loss or damage, they may sue for compensation.

2. CONFLICTING INTERESTS AND HOW THEY ARE RESOLVED

Conflict in business

Conflict is a disagreement or divergence of interest, which may result in one party taking action against another. People working together sometimes have conflicting interests: they disagree over issues. Disagreement can develop into serious conflict between the parties involved if it is not controlled and managed.

Because of the competitive nature of relationships between parties, conflict is almost certain to arise.

REASONS FOR CONFLICT

1. The parties behave differently and have different attitudes and beliefs.
2. Parties in business have different objectives: for example, employers want to keep costs low and to increase the profit and capital of investors; employees want good wages and working conditions, fair treatment, and job security.
3. A poor communication system in business can lead to misunderstandings.
4. Poor conflict management:
   - no control of conflict within the firm
   - no procedures for dealing with disagreements.
5. Poor relationships between people in business, for example between the management and the shop steward.

EXAMPLES OF CONFLICT IN BUSINESS

CONFLICT BETWEEN INVESTOR AND ENTREPRENEUR

- Refusal of a loan
- Terms of loans
- Defaults in repayment of loans
- Investor not getting adequate return on investment

CONFLICT BETWEEN EMPLOYER AND EMPLOYEE

- Poor motivation, poor productivity, absenteeism
- Employer wanting to minimise costs, employees seeking wage increase or better working conditions
- Dismissals, promotions
- Health and safety at work

CONFLICT BETWEEN PRODUCER OR MANUFACTURER AND THEIR SUPPLIER

- Quality of raw materials supplied
- Late delivery of raw materials

CONFLICT BETWEEN RETAILER AND CUSTOMER

- Quality of product or service sold
- Late payment by customer for goods bought on credit
- Poor after-sales service

METHODS OF RESOLVING CONFLICT

If a business is to succeed, conflict must be resolved. There are two methods: *non-legislative* and *legislative.*

(1) NON-LEGISLATIVE METHODS

The parties come together and talk, or use a third party and negotiate a settlement acceptable to all. There is no involvement of legislation or an organisation set up under law to assist in resolving their conflict.

(2) LEGISLATIVE METHODS

Using relevant legislation to solve the conflict, or using an office or organisation set up as a consequence of a law to help in finding a resolution to conflict.

Conflict resolution—Non-legislative methods

(1) SIT DOWN, TALK, NEGOTIATE

This involves the parties sitting down and explaining their positions and, through a process of negotiations and discussion, reaching a mutually acceptable solution. Negotiations do not always provide a solution, so the involvement of a third party may be necessary to resolve the conflict.

(2) USING A THIRD PARTY TO SOLVE CONFLICT BETWEEN CONSUMER AND RETAILER

Third parties that may be involved in negotiations include the following:

CONSUMERS' ASSOCIATION OF IRELAND

The Consumers' Association works to protect and promote the interests of consumers. If a consumer experiences conflict with a retailer over damaged or defective products or poor after-sales service they may consult the Consumers' Association for help to resolve the conflict.

The association provides the consumer with the personal service method of resolving disputes.

TRADE ASSOCIATIONS

A trade association—for example SIMI or ITAA—may be consulted if the conflict involves one of its members.

OMBUDSMAN

The Ombudsman may be able to help if a member of the public is dissatisfied with the service received from any of the following bodies and has been unsuccessful in efforts to sort out the problem with the body concerned:

- Government departments (for example Department of Social Welfare, Department of Agriculture, Department of Education)
- local authorities
- health boards
- An Post
- Eircom.

The Ombudsman's office examines complaints from people who feel they have been unfairly treated in their dealings with these bodies. The Ombudsman can examine the complaint and, if he feels it is justified, recommend a solution. The Ombudsman cannot investigate a complaint against the President, the judiciary, the Garda Síochána, or the Defence Forces.

FINANCIAL SERVICES OMBUDSMAN

The office of the Financial Services Ombudsman is a statutory body funded by levies from the financial services providers and became operational on 1 April 2005.

The existing voluntary ombudsman schemes for both the credit institutions and the insurance sector were subsumed into it and the number of financial service providers covered by its remit was expanded considerably.

The Financial Services Ombudsman deals independently with unresolved complaints from consumers about their individual dealings with all financial services providers.

The Ombudsman is therefore the arbitrator of unresolved disputes and is impartial. This is a free service to the complainant.

The following financial service providers may be subject to investigation by the Ombudsman:

- banks
- building societies
- insurance companies
- credit unions
- mortgage, insurance and other credit intermediaries
- stockbrokers
- pawnbrokers
- moneylenders
- bureaux de change
- hire purchase providers
- health insurance companies

USING THIRD PARTIES TO SOLVE CONFLICTS BETWEEN EMPLOYER AND EMPLOYEES

1. CONCILIATION

- This is where a third party assists the parties in dispute in resolving their differences.
- The role of the conciliator is to encourage the parties to settle the dispute themselves through continued negotiation.
- The conciliator helps the parties clarify their differences and find a formula to settle the dispute. However, responsibility for the settlement rests jointly with the parties to the dispute. If there is still no resolution, both parties may agree to an arbitrator.

2. ARBITRATION

This is where a dispute is sent before an arbitrator or an independent arbitration board for resolution.

- The parties to the dispute agree in advance to the arbitration process; the arbitration decision may or may not be binding on them.
- The main types of dispute dealt with by arbitration are ones concerning employees, trade unions, and employers.

Conflict resolution—Legislative methods for solving conflict between consumer and retailer

If the consumer and retailer cannot come to a satisfactory agreement, the consumer can insist on their legal rights, as set out in the Sale of Goods and Supply of Services Act (1980) and the Consumer Information Act (1978).

Consumer legislation

SALE OF GOODS AND SUPPLY OF SERVICES ACT (1980)

RIGHTS OF THE BUYER OR CONSUMER IN RELATION TO GOODS SOLD OR HIRED

1. Goods must be of ***merchantable quality***—that is, the product or service must be of a reasonable standard and of a quality that would normally be acceptable for purchase and sale and as durable as it is reasonable to expect, having regard to any description applied to them and to the price.
2. Goods must be reasonably ***fit for the particular purpose*** indicated by the buyer: for example, glue for wood should glue wood.
3. Goods must be ***as described*** in written and oral statements by the seller, as in advertisements and brochures or as stated by a salesperson.
4. Goods must ***conform to sample***—for example wallpaper, curtains, paint.
5. The buyer is entitled to 'quiet possession' and the right of ownership: that is, the seller has a right to sell the goods, and the buyer can use them as they wish.

RIGHTS OF BUYER OR CONSUMER IN RELATION TO SERVICES

1. That the seller has the necessary skill to provide the service.
2. That the service will be provided with due skill and diligence.
3. That any materials used will be sound and fit for their purpose.
4. That any goods supplied as part of the service will be of merchantable quality.

ROLE OF SELLER OR RETAILER

1. The seller—not the manufacturer—is responsible for putting things right.
2. The seller cannot limit their responsibility by statements or signs such as

No money refunded

Goods will not be exchanged

Credit notes only

No liability accepted for faulty goods

3. The seller cannot limit their responsibility by way of a guarantee. A guarantee is an *addition* to your normal legal rights. If a consumer has a valid claim, it may be easier to claim under guarantee.

Guarantees must state clearly:
- the specific goods covered
- who is offering the guarantee
- the period of guarantee
- the procedure for making claims
- the remedies available.

4. Third parties, such as hire purchase companies, can be 'jointly and severally sued.' In hire purchase, the consumer can claim against either the retailer who sold the goods or the HP company that advanced the finance.

REDRESS FOR THE CONSUMER

1. ***Redress*** is a remedy or a method used for putting things right. The amount and nature of redress depend on how serious the fault is, when it occurred, and how soon the consumer complained about it.

   Redress can be by way of
   (*a*) full refund of the money paid,
   (*b*) replacement, or
   (*c*) compensation for loss.
2. If a consumer's complaint is valid, a credit note need not be accepted: the consumer can insist on a cash refund.
3. A consumer's complaints are not justified when faults are caused by misuse or abuse of the goods, or if the fault was brought to the consumer's attention before buying.

UNSOLICITED GOODS

This means sending goods to someone who has not ordered them and then seeking payment. It is an offence to demand payment for unsolicited goods.

ENFORCEMENT OF THE ACT

The Director of Consumer Affairs monitors the working of the act. He can prosecute traders who use signs, statements or notices limiting consumers' rights. He can also investigate various practices relating to the terms on which goods or services were supplied.

CONSUMER INFORMATION ACT (1978)

PURPOSE

To protect consumers against false or misleading claims about goods, services, and prices. The act makes it an offence to make false or misleading claims about goods, services or prices in the course of a business, trade, or profession. It does not give the consumer any *rights* but gives *protection.*

GOODS—WHAT FALSE CLAIMS ARE PROHIBITED?

The act covers most of the usual claims made about goods. False or misleading statements about the weight of the goods, how they were made, where they were made, how they work, their performance or what they are made of may be against the law. Examples include written claims, such as *Made in Ireland, Pure new wool,* and oral claims, such as *One previous owner.*

SERVICES

The act prohibits false or misleading claims about aspects of services. An offence is committed only if the trader knows the claim is false or misleading or if the claim is made without good grounds for believing it to be true, for example *One-hour cleaning, Delivery to all areas, Only two minutes from the sea.*

Prices

The act prohibits false or misleading indications of the price, the previous price or the recommended price of goods, services, or facilities.

Sales

Under the act, it is wrong to give a false or misleading indication of a previous price. If one price is crossed out and another put in, the previous price must be accurate and the goods must have been for sale in the same place at the previous price for at least 28 consecutive days in the previous three months.

Advertisements

It is forbidden to publish any advertisement that is false or misleading or that is likely to cause loss, damage or injury to a member of the public. If an advertisement for goods makes certain claims (known as ***trade descriptions***), the advertiser cannot say that the claim applies only to some of the goods advertised.

ENFORCEMENT OF THE ACT

The act set up the office of Director of Consumer Affairs.

FUNCTIONS OF THE OFFICE OF DIRECTOR OF CONSUMER AFFAIRS

(1) Receiving and investigating complaints.
(2) Prosecuting offences under the Consumer Information Act (1978) and the Sale of Goods and Supply of Services Act (1980).
(3) Encouraging higher standards in advertising by promoting codes of standards and ensuring that advertising complies with the law.
(4) Requesting that misleading advertising be withdrawn or amended; if necessary, applying for a court order to prevent such advertising.
(5) Publicising consumer protection legislation in various ways.
(6) Discharging a general responsibility to keep an eye on the truthfulness of advertising and descriptions of goods and services and ensuring that such descriptions are not false or misleading.

SMALL CLAIMS COURT

Disputes between retailers and customers are usually resolved by negotiation, but for specific enforcement a customer can bring the seller to the Small Claims Court for cases involving sums of up to €2,000.

A fee of €15 is paid, and a form is completed describing the complaint and sent to the Small Claims Registrar of the District Court.

The problem can be solved cheaply with the help of the Registrar and without the use of solicitors. If a case is not resolved it will go to the District Court for a full hearing.

Legislative methods for solving conflict between employers and employees

Employers and employees have different aims; therefore a conflict may arise in business over many issues.

CIRCUMSTANCES LEADING TO DISPUTES

(1) *Pay disputes:* involving wages, overtime, or holiday pay.
(2) *Working conditions:* hours of work, hygiene, safety standards, heating, canteen facilities.
(3) *Unfair dismissal.*
(4) *Discrimination:* employees treated differently because of their gender, marital status, family status, sexual orientation, religious belief, age, disability, race, or membership of the traveller community.
(5) *Promotion procedures.*
(6) *Redundancies:* threatened job losses.
(7) *Introduction of new technology.*
(8) *Poor industrial relations:* management not recognising workers' rights.

TYPES OF DISPUTES

If a conflict does not get resolved, workers may take industrial action by means of:

(1) OFFICIAL DISPUTE

This is where a union seeks approval through a secret ballot and then has the dispute confirmed by the ICTU. A minimum of one week's notice must be given to the employer before industrial action can be taken.

(2) UNOFFICIAL DISPUTE

Workers take industrial action without a ballot and without the approval of their union or the ICTU.

PROCEDURE FOR SOLVING DISPUTES

1. An employee reports a grievance to a supervisor.
2. If there is no resolution, the grievance is referred to a shop steward.
3. The human resources manager and the union become involved.
4. If there is no resolution, a third party may be asked to intervene, such as an industrial relations officer of the Labour Relations Commission (LRC).
5. The state provides the Labour Relations Commission with the services of rights commissioners, equality officers, industrial relations officers, and the Employment Appeals Tribunal.
6. If the Labour Relations Commission cannot resolve the dispute it may be referred to the Labour Court as a last resort.

INDUSTRIAL RELATIONS

This is the term used to describe relations between the management of a company and its employees.

If industrial relations are good, workers will be well motivated and morale and productivity will be high, which will benefit the firm and its customers. If industrial relations are poor, employees are discontented, resulting in poor motivation, absenteeism, high labour turnover, low productivity, and a marked tendency to take industrial action.

If employees are having difficulty in negotiations with the management they may join a trade union to strengthen their bargaining power.

TRADE UNIONS

A trade union is a body representing employees' views and their claims in negotiations with their employers. Union members elect a shop steward to represent them in negotiations with the employer.

REASONS FOR JOINING A TRADE UNION

(1) Increased bargaining power—one voice representing all workers.
(2) The benefit of having skilled negotiators on behalf of employees.
(3) Greater job security if the union is powerful.
(4) Higher standard of living for members.

LEGISLATION IN THE INDUSTRIAL RELATIONS AREA

(1) Industrial Relations Act (1990)
(2) Employment Equality Act (1998)
(3) Unfair Dismissals Acts (1977–1993)
(4) Data Protection Act (1988)

INDUSTRIAL RELATIONS ACT (1990)

The main provisions of the act are:

- peaceful picketing
- rules on balloting
- establishment of the Labour Relations Commission
- the reformed role of the Labour Court.

PICKETING

Peaceful picketing is legal. This involves employees gathering outside a work-place in which there is a trade dispute. Striking workers form a picket line, where they attempt to dissuade other workers, delivery lorries and customers from entering. Picketing an employer's home is illegal.

Primary picketing

Picketing the business premises of the employer involved in the dispute.

Secondary picketing

Picketing a second employer not involved in the dispute. Secondary picketing is legal only if picketers believe that the second employer directly assisted the first in order to frustrate industrial action, for example by delivering goods to the strikebound firm.

BALLOTING

A secret ballot of members must be held before industrial action can take place. One week's notice of action must be given to the employer involved in the dispute.

If a secret ballot takes place and if workers engage in industrial action they are legally protected from being sued by their employer for any loss arising from their action.

LABOUR RELATIONS COMMISSION

The Labour Relations Commission was established *to assist in settling disputes and to promote good industrial relations.*

Services provided by Labour Relations Commission

Conciliation service

The Labour Relations Commission provides an industrial relations officer (IRO), who brings both parties together to talk. He or she listens to both sides' arguments and then recommends a settlement.

Codes of practice

This is a collection of generally accepted rules, practices and procedures to be followed when dealing with conflict. They are used to improve the way industrial relations business is conducted.

The Labour Relations Commission offers guidance to firms drawing up a code of practice, and it will prepare codes of practice in consultation with unions and employers' organisations.

Equality services

The Labour Relations Commission provides equality officers for investigating industrial disputes under the Employment Equality Act (1998) on issues of equality and discrimination in the work-place.

The equality officer will hold informal and private hearings and issue a recommendation. When investigating, they can enter premises and seek records and any information they need.

An appeal against a recommendation goes to the Labour Court, whose decision is binding.

Rights commissioner service

The rights commissioner investigates disputes involving individual workers or small groups of workers concerning unfair dismissal or maternity leave but not concerning pay, hours of work, or holidays.

Recommendations of the rights commissioner are not binding on the parties. An appeal goes to the Labour Court, whose decision is final.

Assisting joint labour committees and joint industrial councils

The Labour Relations Commission assists JLCs and JICs in carrying out their functions.

A joint labour committee is a body set up by the Labour Court to investigate rates of pay and conditions of employment in industries where workers have no union. It recommends minimum rates of pay and conditions, which, if approved by the Labour Court, become Employment Regulations Orders (EROs), which are enforceable in law.

A joint industrial council is a voluntary body set up to solve disputes that may arise in a particular industry.

Industrial relations advisory service

The Labour Relations Commission offers advice to employers and unions on industrial relations matters and helps firms to identify underlying problems that cause disputes.

THE LABOUR COURT

The Industrial Relations Act (1990) reformed the role of the Labour Court. It is a court of last resort in industrial disputes.

Functions of the Labour Court

The Labour Court investigates disputes when

(*a*) the Labour Relations Commission states that it cannot resolve the dispute,
(*b*) the Labour Relations Commission waives its conciliation function in the dispute,
(*c*) the Minister for Enterprise and Employment refers a dispute to it, or
(*d*) exceptional circumstances exist that warrant investigation by the Labour Court.

Court of appeal

The Labour Court hears appeals against recommendations of equality officers under the Employment Equality Act (1998). Its recommendations are binding. It also hears appeals against recommendations of rights commissioners. These recommendations are also binding.

Joint labour committees and Employment Regulation Orders

The Labour Court establishes JLCs and registers employment regulation orders following the recommendations of the JLC.

Enforcement

Inspectors of the Department of Enterprise, Trade and Employment may begin proceedings on behalf of employees against employers for non-compliance with the terms of Employment Regulations Orders.

Investigating breaches of codes of practice

The Labour Court investigates breaches of codes of practice, provided the Labour Relations Commission has first considered the complaint.

Registering employment agreements

Agreements negotiated between employers and employees can be registered with the Labour Court. These agreements, once registered, become legally binding.

Inspectors of the Department of Enterprise, Trade and Employment may investigate whether registered employment agreements are being enforced. Employers must keep, and retain for three years, records showing compliance with agreements.

Enforcement

Labour Court recommendations are not binding, except in certain limited circumstances:

(1) When workers or their trade union refer a dispute to the Labour Court without the agreement of the employer concerned. Recommendations in this case are binding on the workers only.
(2) If all parties to a dispute ask for intervention by the Labour Court and all agree to be bound by it.

EMPLOYMENT EQUALITY ACT (1998)

1. Grounds of discrimination

- The act describes discrimination as the treatment of one person in a less favourable way than that in which another person is, has been or would be treated.
- Discrimination is outlawed on nine distinct grounds: gender, marital status, family status, sexual orientation, religious belief, age, disability, race, and membership of the traveller community.

2. Scope of the act

The act covers employees in both the public and private sector, as well as applicants for employment and training.

It outlaws discrimination by:

- Employers: with regard to access to employment, conditions of employment, training and promotion.
- In collective agreements: with regard to access to and conditions of employment and equal pay for like work.
- Advertising: advertising that might indicate an intention to discriminate.
- Employment agencies: against any person seeking employment or other services of the agency.
- Vocational training: any instruction needed to carry on an occupational activity.
- Certain bodies: trade unions, professional and trade associations with regard to membership and other benefits.

3. Equality between women and men

The act deals with the requirements of EU Equal Pay and Equal Treatment directives which apply in relation to the gender discrimination ground. Equal pay for work of equal value is made a term of every employment contract.

4. Sexual harassment

The act defines sexual harassment for the first time in Irish law. It outlaws sexual harassment in the work-place and in the course of employment, whether by an employer, another employee, or clients, customers or business contacts of an employer.

It places an obligation on employers to take all reasonable steps to ensure an environment free of sexual harassment.

5. Positive measures to promote equal opportunities

The act allows an employer to take positive measures to promote equal opportunities, particularly those geared to existing inequalities that affect women's opportunities in access to employment, vocational training, and promotion.

6. Defence Forces

The act extends protection to the Defence Forces for the first time in Irish Law.

7. New grounds of discrimination

The act deals in detail with new grounds of discrimination. An entitlement to equal pay for work of equal value is established from the coming into force of the legislation (18 October 1999). In addition, an equality clause is inserted into every contract of employment, and discrimination both direct and indirect is outlawed.

8. Positive action: non gender

The act allows positive action specifically geared towards the integration into employment of:

(a) people over the age of fifty,
(b) people with disabilities, and
(c) members of the traveller community.

There is also provision for giving positive action status to certain state training and work experience schemes.

The act also sets out the main exemptions that apply generally on age and family grounds and on disability grounds.

9. Equality Authority

The Equality Authority replaces the Employment Equality Agency. The authority has the following general functions:

- To work towards the elimination of discrimination in employment.
- To promote equality of opportunity in employment on the nine grounds covered by the act.
- To provide information to the public on, and to keep under review, the working of the act.

Codes of practice

New powers to develop codes of practice are assigned to the authority, with the following aims:

(a) the elimination of discrimination in employment
(b) the promotion of equality opportunity in employment.

The new codes of practice will be admissible in evidence and taken into account in determining any relevant case.

10. Remedies and enforcement

A new office of Director of Equality Investigations is to be established in the Department of Justice, Equality and Law Reform. The director, together with the equality officers and equality mediation officers, will operate as the main instrument of redress under the act.

The investigatory powers of the director extend to entering premises in pursuit of information, interviewing people with relevant information, and securing documentary evidence.

Right to information: a person who considers that he or she may be the subject of discrimination will have the right to approach the person who may have discriminated (for example the employer) for information. In response, the employer is obliged to give sufficient information to allow the person seeking the information to formulate and present a case in an effective manner.

11. Redress

All cases other than those involving dismissal and discrimination, on grounds of sex must be referred in the first instance to the Director of Equality Investigations.

The director will investigate each case submitted to him or her and will issue a decision. The decision is binding and enforceable through the Circuit Court. All decisions may be appealed to the Labour Court within forty-two days of issue.

Where the director finds that there has been discrimination, he or she may order:

- in an equal pay case: equal pay and arrears in respect of a period not exceeding three years preceding the referral of the case;
- in other cases: equal treatment and compensation up to a maximum of two years' pay.

Mediation

The director may, subject to the agreement of the parties to the claim, refer a case for mediation to an equality mediation officer if it appears possible to resolve it in that way. If a claim is sent for mediation and not resolved, the complainant may lodge the claim again with the director.

UNFAIR DISMISSALS ACTS (1977–1993)

PURPOSE OF THE ACT

To protect all employees, full-time or part-time, from being unfairly dismissed from their employment.

APPLICATION

The act applies to everyone aged between 16 and 66 who has been in continuous employment for at least one year and who is working at least eight hours per week.

BURDEN OF PROOF

The act operates on the principle that a dismissal is deemed to be unfair until proved otherwise. The burden of proof is on the employer, who must show that there were substantial grounds justifying a dismissal.

UNFAIR DISMISSAL

A dismissal is unfair if it was on the grounds of

- pregnancy
- race
- membership of the travelling community
- belonging to a trade union or being involved in a strike
- sexual orientation
- political or religious beliefs.

JUSTIFIABLE REASONS FOR DISMISSAL

1. The worker is incompetent.
2. The worker is incapable of doing the job.
3. The worker is being made redundant to make the firm more competitive.
4. The worker's qualifications are considered unsuitable for the job.

PROPER PROCEDURES IN A DISMISSAL CASE

1. The employee has a right to know the reason for the dismissal.
2. The employee has a right to reply to those reasons and to have their responses listened to before a dismissal takes place.

3. The employee has a right to an impartial hearing and the right to representation at a hearing into the dismissal.

Enforcement of the Act

A worker who feels that he or she has been unfairly dismissed can take the case to a rights commissioner. Alternatively, they can bypass the rights commissioner and take their case directly to the Employment Appeals Tribunal, whose decision is binding.

Redress available to workers unfairly dismissed

(1) Reinstatement without financial loss.
(2) Financial compensation, up to a maximum of two years' pay.

DATA PROTECTION ACT (1988)

The Data Protection Act was passed to deal with privacy issues arising from personal information about people kept on a computer, as distinct from manual files.

The act gives rights to individuals and puts responsibilities on those who keep personal information on computers.

Terms used in the act

data: information in a form in which it can be processed automatically.
data subject: a person who is the subject of personal data, for example an employee.
data controller: a person, firm or organisation that controls the content and use of personal data, for example a company.
data processor: a person or organisation that processes personal data on behalf of a data controller, for example a computer bureau.

Rights of data subjects

(1) *Right of access.* A person has a right to be given a copy of data kept about him or her on computer within forty days of making a written request.
(2) *Corrections of errors.* A person has a right to have errors corrected or inaccurate information corrected or deleted.
(3) *Compensation for mistakes.* Compensation is available if a person suffers as a result of incorrect information, for example the refusal of a loan.
(4) *Complaints to Data Protection Commissioner.* A person has a right to complain to the Data Protection Commissioner if it is evident that some data controllers are not complying with the act.

Obligations of data controllers

Data controllers have certain responsibilities in relation to information they keep on a computer. They must

(1) obtain and process information fairly;
(2) keep it only for one or more specified and lawful purposes;
(3) use and disclose it only in ways compatible with these purposes;
(4) keep it safe and secure;
(5) keep it accurate and up to date;
(6) ensure that it is adequate, relevant, and not excessive;
(7) retain it no longer than is necessary for the purpose;
(8) give a copy of his or her personal data to a person on request.

These provisions are binding on every data controller. Any failure to observe them would be a breach of the act.

ENFORCEMENT OF THE ACT

The Data Protection Act established the office of Data Protection Commissioner. The Commissioner's role is to ensure that those who keep personal information on computer comply with provisions of the act.

FUNCTION OF THE DATA PROTECTION COMMISSIONER

(1) Keeping a register of data controllers.
(2) Encouraging data controllers to develop a code of practice in relation to data protection.
(3) Issuing enforcement notices to compel data controllers to correct, erase or add to personal data.
(4) Issuing 'prohibition notices', which prohibit the transfer of personal data outside the country.
(5) Issuing 'information notices', which compel data controllers to provide information when requested.
(6) Investigating complaints made by members of the public.
(7) Prosecuting any data controller found guilty of offences under the act.

BARGAINING

COLLECTIVE BARGAINING

This is the process whereby employers and employees in a firm negotiate wages and other conditions of employment. When an agreement is reached it is called a ***collective agreement***. These agreements are voluntary and are not legally binding on parties.

NATIONAL AGREEMENTS

National agreements are negotiated every three years between the 'social partners'. These consist of the Government; employers, represented by IBEC; employees, represented by the ICTU; farmers, represented by the IFA; and community and voluntary organisations.

When an agreement is reached it is voted on by the social partners, and if it is accepted it then becomes a national agreement.

KEY TERMS

These are some of the more important terms introduced in unit 1:

agreement	entrepreneurs
arbitration	human relations
capacity to contract	industrial relations
conciliation	investors
consideration	negotiation
co-operation	producers
consumer	service industry

LEGISLATION

These are the more important laws described in unit 1:

- Employment Equality Act (1998)
- Unfair Dismissals Acts (1977–1993)
- Sale of Goods and Supply of Services Act (1980)
- Industrial Relations Act (1990)
- Consumer Information Act (1978)
- Data Protection Act (1988)

ON COMPLETION OF UNIT 1 YOU SHOULD BE ABLE TO

(1) list the main parties and people involved in business;
(2) describe the relationships between people as workers, trade union members, managers, entrepreneurs, investors, and customers;
(3) outline non-legislative ways of resolving conflict;
(4) outline how a major piece of legislation and the elements of contract law help in dealing with conflict;
(5) analyse the relationships between people in business **(HL)**;
(6) illustrate how legislation affects these business relationships **(HL)**;
(7) describe a possible business conflict, and show how the law could be used to solve it **(HL)**.

Examination-style questions and solution

People in business

(**A**) Contrast the aims of employers and employees in a company. **(10 marks)**

(**B**) Evaluate the competitive and co-operative relationships between the following parties in business:
  (i) investors and entrepreneurs;
  (ii) two producers in the same line of business. **(30 marks)**

(**C**) Describe a non-legislative and a legislative method of solving a business conflict. Illustrate your answer with an example of each. **(20 marks)**

Suggested solution

(A) *The following are the aims of employers:*

- *To keep production costs low so that the firm will remain competitive.*
- *To increase profits so that retained earnings can be built up and that there is good return on invested capital for the owners.*

The following are the aims of employees:

- *To obtain reasonable wages so as to be able to live comfortably.*
- *To have job security and be reasonably sure that redundancy will not happen.*

(B) *Investors and entrepreneurs are likely to have a strong relationship when the entrepreneur seeks finance for a new project. This relationship will remain co-operative as long as the entrepreneur presents a strong business plan with projected cash flow* *forecast, profit and loss account, and balance sheet. Investors will also want to see the plans for the repayment of the funds, to minimise the risks involved.*

The relationship between entrepreneurs and investors will be competitive if the investors refuse to advance the funds required to establish a new business, or if the entrepreneur, having received financial support, is not living up to the commitments entered into and is defaulting on repayments.

Producers will generally have a competitive relationship as they try to launch new products, monitor each other's activities, outsell each other's products, and attract customers to their own goods and services. The relationship between them becomes co-operative when they undertake activities for their mutual benefit, such as lobbying the Government for a change in legislation or for a reduction in VAT or agreeing to a common scale of discounts for their customers. They will also co-operate and help each other in times of difficulty, such as when there is a fire at a premises.

(C) *A non-legislative method of solving a business conflict means that the parties involved don't use a law, or an office or organisation set up under a law, to assist them in resolving their conflict.*

Example: *A shop has sold damaged goods to a customer. The customer, realising the problem, approaches the shop and asks for the problem to be rectified. The shop agrees to put matters right to the customer's satisfaction.*

A legislative method of resolving a business conflict is to use the wording of the law to solve the conflict, or to use an office or organisation set up as a consequence of a law to help in finding a resolution.

Example: *A man is promoted over a better-qualified woman. The woman tries unsuccessfully to resolve the conflict. She refers her case to the Director of Equality Investigations, who will investigate the case and issue a decision. This decision is binding and enforceable through the Circuit Court.*

Practice questions

Section 1

1. (*a*) Illustrate your understanding of the term 'interest group'.

____

____

____

____

(*b*) Give two examples of interest groups. ______________________________

____

2. What is the role of an equality officer?

____

____

____

____

3. The following notice appeared on the window of an electrical shop:

Dishwasher for sale: €99

Is this an offer? Yes/No. Circle the correct answer. Give a one-sentence explanation of your answer.

4. List three functions of the Labour Court.

5. Explain the term 'code of practice'.

Revision question

People in business

Business is primarily concerned with the relationships that exist between the people in it.

(**A**) Contrast the relationship that exists between entrepreneurs and investors in a business enterprise. **(20 marks)**

(**B**) Outline how the elements of contract law help contractual relationships in business. **(20 marks)**

(**C**) Evaluate the role of the Director of Consumer Affairs under the Consumer Information Act (1978). **(20 marks)**

[60 marks]

SECTION B: ENTERPRISE

Unit 2: Enterprise

Enterprise is the source of all business. Innovation is central to business development. This section looks at the nature of enterprise, characteristics of enterprising people and associated skills. Unit 2 also examines the application of enterprise in other areas of life.

Objective: To enable pupils to understand the importance of enterprise in business and the community.

3. Introduction and Definition of Enterprise

Enterprise

Enterprise is human activity that provides the initiative and carries the risk in setting up a business. It is the ability to spot opportunities in the market and to produce a product or service to fill a niche in the market.

It involves risk-taking: the risk of financial failure and personal failure. Enterprise is being creative, showing initiative, being flexible and dynamic, and accepting moderate risks.

ENTREPRENEUR

An entrepreneur is a person who provides the initiative and takes the risk in establishing a business. An entrepreneur is innovative and uses society's needs to create business opportunities and takes the initiative in setting up a business to avail of the opportunity and make a profit.

Well-known entrepreneurs include Richard Branson (Virgin Group), Pat McDonagh (Supermacs), Geoff Read (Ballygowan Spring Water), and Feargal Quinn (Superquinn).

ENTREPRENEURSHIP

This is the process of identifying a need and filling it.

INTRAPRENEUR

An intrapreneur is a person who is innovative and enterprising within a business and develops new ways of doing things, comes up with innovative ideas, and identifies new opportunities.

When 'enterprise' is mentioned, people automatically associate it with entrepreneurial activity and sometimes fail to see the importance of enterprise as a culture affecting all aspects of our lives.

Enterprise should be examined in its widest sense: personal enterprise, entrepreneurial enterprise, community enterprise, and public enterprise.

(1) PERSONAL ENTERPRISE

Personal enterprise plays a central role in our success at work, study, or leisure. It involves making decisions that affect our lives.

Examples of personal enterprise

- Choosing a career
- Renting a flat
- Buying a house
- Undertaking voluntary work abroad
- Taking night classes
- Taking a part-time job

(2) BUSINESS START-UP

Entrepreneurs should possess the following qualities: the ability to identify opportunities, and a willingness to take risks to capitalise on opportunity.

Examples of entrepreneurial enterprise

- Spotting a gap in the market for a product or service
- Developing new products
- Finding new markets
- Expanding business—acquisitions
- Diversification into other areas of activity
- Copying ideas from abroad
- Buying a franchise

(3) COMMUNITY ENTERPRISE

Local communities are full of people who show great enterprise in their lives. These may be local business people, community organisers, or members of sports clubs.

Examples of community enterprise

- Caring organisations
- Tidy towns groups
- Environmental project groups
- Establishing clubs and associations
- Restoration of unsightly derelict buildings

(4) PUBLIC ENTERPRISE

This incorporates a wide range of activities, including decisions made by the Government, TDs, the public service, teachers, etc. All can show enterprise in decisions made.

Examples of public enterprise

- Setting up the lotto—to give surplus money to community amenities and for sports facilities
- Introducing tax incentive schemes
- A TD visiting a factory in danger of closing
- A teacher bringing an LCVP class on a factory visit or inviting an entrepreneur into the classroom

4. ENTREPRENEURS AND ENTERPRISE SKILLS

Characteristics of entrepreneurs

The following are characteristics of entrepreneurs:

BEING SELF-CONFIDENT AND HAVING A POSITIVE SELF-IMAGE

Entrepreneurs have self-belief. They believe in the product or ideas they create and have the confidence to make the idea or business happen.

BEING FLEXIBLE

Entrepreneurs are adaptable and able to turn easily from one situation to another, especially if problems arise: priorities may change.

BEING REALISTIC

Entrepreneurs recognise their own limitations and seek advice when needed.

BEING A MODERATE RISK-TAKER

Entrepreneurs enjoy the challenge, unafraid of uncertainty and the unknown. They are prepared to take moderate risks; risks should be calculated to minimise the chance of failure. An entrepreneur is prepared to risk personal assets in order to set up a business venture.

BEING DECISIVE

Entrepreneurs collect all information, analyse information and situations, make quick and clear decisions.

BEING A GOOD LEADER

Entrepreneurs are able to get along well with others and are responsive to suggestions and criticism. They can get people to work together in teams and motivate people.

BEING A GOOD COMMUNICATOR

Entrepreneurs must communicate with all parties the business comes in contact with: customers, suppliers, and employees.

BEING ENERGETIC

Entrepreneurs are full of energy and eager to work. They are hard-working people who stick with the task until it is completed.

BEING INNOVATIVE OR CREATIVE

Entrepreneurs do something so far not done or do something differently. They are capable of coming up with new ways of making or doing things, using their imagination and applying ideas to new situations.

BEING INDEPENDENT

Entrepreneurs want to be in charge and dislike being controlled by others.

BEING OPPORTUNISTIC
Entrepreneurs are always on the look-out for opportunities, seeing a gap in the market and seizing the opportunity. Entrepreneurs are *proactive*, that is actively looking for opportunities and are always ready to initiate action; a person who is *reactive* will wait until someone else takes action and then act.

BEING HIGHLY MOTIVATED
Entrepreneurs have a need for achievement, seek personal satisfaction, are profit-oriented and ambitious.

Enterprise skills

A skill is an ability or expertise that people acquire through practice or experience and learning or training. Some people are born with a natural talent; skill is then said to be innate, while other skills can be learnt.

ENTERPRISE SKILLS INCLUDE:
INNER CONTROL
Taking control of your own situation, not wanting others to influence your life.

PLANNING AND GOAL-SETTING
Setting short-term and long-term goals and targets. Plans must be drawn up to achieve these goals. An entrepreneur must be able to work out their own **strengths**, **weaknesses**, **opportunities**, and **threats**; this is called a '**SWOT** analysis'. (See chapter 7.)

ASSESSING AND MANAGING RISK
Measuring, assessing and managing risk. Risk management means devising policies to eliminate or reduce the risk that the individual or business is exposed to.

INNOVATION
Applying ideas, new or borrowed, to situations where they have not been applied before.

DECISION-MAKING
Deciding between two or more courses of action. This skill can be learnt. An entrepreneur must be a good decision-maker: choices or alternatives must be considered, information must be analysed, and a decision made and implemented.

PRIORITISING
Ranking tasks in order of priority, the most important tasks getting the earliest consideration.

TIMING
Taking appropriate action at the appropriate time.

HUMAN RELATIONS MANAGEMENT
Managing people to achieve individual behaviour and performance that will enhance the effectiveness of the business.

COMMUNICATION
Using effective communication skills—essential in order to be able to relate to other people. Entrepreneurs must be able to recognise and overcome barriers to communication.

STRESS MANAGEMENT
Recognising the causes of stress and then coming up with some personal strategy for achieving a reduction, for example delegating tasks, time management, reducing work load, planning ahead, and avoiding situations that cause stress.

REALITY PERCEPTION
Seeing things as they really are and being aware of employees' and customers' needs.

NETWORKING
Working with other people and establishing contacts in the business community with people whose knowledge and expertise might prove useful.

Applications of enterprise skills to different situations

ENTERPRISE IN THE HOME
- Renovating or redecorating the house
- Planning a holiday
- Household budgeting
- Moving the family from city to country
- DIY jobs on the house

ENTERPRISE IN THE SCHOOL
- Unsupervised study
- Involvement in Young Scientist of the Year Exhibition
- Production of a school magazine
- Setting up clubs or societies
- Pupils organising a disco
- Mini-enterprises
- School tours
- Pupils preparing a profile on an entrepreneur
- Teacher introducing new teaching methods
- Principal introducing new courses, for example LCVP, SPHE, CSPE
- Fund-raising activities

ENTERPRISE AT WORK
Intrapreneurship can be shown by employees by
- devising new ways of dealing with customers' complaints
- new ways of improving administration and work methods
- new ways of supplying services to customers

ENTERPRISE IN THE COMMUNITY
- Establishing clubs, for example youth clubs, scout clubs
- Fund-raising for clubs

- Establishing local drama groups
- Becoming a member of the board of a credit union
- Organising 'meals on wheels'
- Helping old people or poor people
- Neighbourhood Watch and Community Alert schemes
- Taking mentally handicapped or physically handicapped people on holidays

ENTERPRISE AT LEISURE

- Taking courses to develop talents or new crafts, for example public speaking, drama, computers, ECDL

ENTERPRISE IN THE PUBLIC SERVICE

- Intrapreneurship: introducing cost-saving ideas
- Establishing suggestion boxes for employees

ENTERPRISE IN STARTING A BUSINESS

- Spotting a gap in the market for a product or service
- Financing a business
- Producing a product or service

ENTERPRISE IN AN EXISTING BUSINESS

- Increasing the range of products
- Finding new uses for existing products
- Finding new markets

THE IMPORTANCE OF ENTERPRISE IN BUSINESS AND IN THE COMMUNITY

1. Enterprise creates new business, with increased employment.
2. It brings about an increased standard of living for the community.
3. Local businesses will thrive, as workers have more money to spend.
4. Workers will come to live in the area.
5. Businesses will spend money in the area on services, raw materials, etc.
6. It may bring other enterprises to the area.
7. There is increased revenue for the Government from the success of enterprises.

KEY TERMS

These are some of the more important terms introduced in unit 2:

decision-making	innovation	SWOT (strengths, weaknesses, opportunities, threats)
enterprise	intrapreneurs	time management
entrepreneurs	networking	proactive
entrepreneurship	planning	reactive
goals	risk management	
human relations		

ON THE COMPLETION OF UNIT 2 YOU SHOULD BE ABLE TO

(1) define 'enterprise';
(2) identify the importance of enterprise skills in areas such as home, school, community, Government departments, and business start-up;
(3) explain the basic enterprise skills;

(4) identify the characteristics of enterprising people;
(5) analyse the importance of enterprise in business and the community **(HL)**;
(6) identify enterprise skills, opportunities, risks and rewards from information given **(HL)**.

Examination-style question and solution

Enterprise and identifying opportunities

(**A**) 'All successful people, in community life and in business, possess certain essential enterprising characteristics.' Do you agree with this statement? Support your opinion with reasons. **(20 marks)**
(**B**) Compare entrepreneurship and intrapreneurship in a business. **(15 marks)**
(**C**) Describe the skills needed for the successful development of new products or services. **(25 marks)**

Suggested solution

(A) *I agree with this statement. Successful people in community life and in business possess the following enterprising characteristics:*

(1) ***Being risk-takers***—*people who enjoy a challenge. They are not afraid of uncertainty and of the unknown; they like to take a chance or to gamble. An entrepreneur in business is willing to risk personal assets in order to set up their business venture.*

(2) ***Being opportunistic***—*people who see the need or gap in the market and seize on the opportunity. An entrepreneur may set up more than one business venture in their lifetime: once the business is established an entrepreneur may employ a manager to run it on their behalf and move on to developing their next idea.*

(3) ***Being innovative and creative***—*people who generate a new idea, having recognised the opportunity, doing something so far not done or doing something differently. Very often people in the community see the opportunity to set up and run a new club in their locality.*

(4) ***Being a leader and an agent of change***—*innovative people make things happen and show leadership by doing things for themselves. People in the community may take it on themselves to organise fund-raising for a local amenity that is badly needed.*

(B) ***Entrepreneurship*** *is described as the human activity that provides the initiative and carries the risk. It refers to the initiative, foresight and idea that are needed to develop, produce and provide goods or services for which there is a market. In a business, these are people who are innovative and show leadership.*

Intrapreneurship: *Generally, this refers to people working in an existing business or organisation who are encouraged to be enterprising and to generate new ideas that may develop new products or services or improve existing products or services. Intrapreneurs* *do not risk their own money. However, they can often place their position in the company at risk by risking its money in new ventures. People in business who are intrapreneurs often possess similar characteristics and skills to entrepreneurs, but they prefer to remain within the secure confines of their employment.*

(C) *Stages in the development of new products and services:*

1. *The first stage in developing new products or services is the* ***generation of ideas****, by recognising a gap in the market or anticipating consumers' needs. The skills that are needed here include innovative skills and the ability to apply ideas to situations where they have not been applied before.*
2. *The second stage is* ***screening*** *the ideas that are generated. This involves selecting, reviewing and testing the product or service that has the greatest potential. The skills needed at this stage include decision-making skills: this is the ability to make effective decisions quickly, but not rashly.*
3. *The third stage involves carrying out a* ***feasibility study*** *in order to determine the potential contribution of the product or service to sales, costs, and profits. Planning and setting goals are the skills required here, as a business plan will need to be prepared.*
4. *The fourth stage is the* ***development of a prototype.*** *It is often a lengthy, risky and expensive phase for a business. It is vital that risk be assessed and managed, which enables action to be taken in order to reduce the risk. This stage in the development process can be stressful for those involved, and the skill of stress management is very applicable here.*
5. *The next stage is* ***test marketing****, to determine the reaction of potential buyers. 'Reality perception' is an important skill at this stage, as it involves seeing people and situations for what they are. Reality perception is the skill of being aware of the needs of customers. If this skill is lacking, businesses would be test marketing products or services that customers do not want.*

Practice questions—Section 1

1. Distinguish between an entrepreneur and an intrapreneur.

____

____

____

____

2. Describe two enterprise skills.

(i) ____

____

(ii) ____

____

Unit 3: Managing 1

This section introduces the concept of management. It examines management as a planning and control process. As management is largely implemented through people, there is an emphasis on the management skills of communication, organisation, and motivation.

Objective: To enable pupils to understand the importance of management in business and the community.

5. Introduction and Definition of Management

Management is the process of setting objectives and the ability to achieve results through people. An objective is a goal or target to be achieved. There are many definitions of management, but they all centre around the following: '**A process involving the achievement of goals by working with and through people**.'

Management skills: leading, motivating, communicating
Management activities: planning, organising, controlling

The application of management to different areas

MANAGEMENT ACTIVITIES

Planning

Establishing goals or objectives and deciding on a course of action to achieve these objectives.

Home: Planning the replacement of electrical appliances; planning future spending; planning household budget; planning holidays.

School: Planning open days; parent-teacher meetings, curriculum; teacher planning programme of work for the year; school budget.

Business: Setting goals; how to achieve goals; implementing plans; delegating tasks.

Public life: Planning how to implement Government policy.

Local community: Planning activities; budgeting; fund-raising; distributing funds.

Organising

Allocating resources to achieve tasks and ensuring that objectives can be achieved. This includes co-ordinating employees.

Home: Organising social life and household, study timetables, shopping, cooking, cleaning.

School: Organising timetables for teachers, classes and examinations; allocating rooms; supervising rotas.

Business: Organising finance, labour and machinery etc.

Public life: Delegating tasks to civil servants to provide a satisfactory and effective service.

Local community: Leaders organising committees; meetings; fund-raising events.

CONTROLLING

Monitoring progress; comparing performance with targets set and correcting any deviations.

Home: Controlling expenditure.

School: Controlling school finances and expenditure in each department; controlling staff.

Business: Controlling cash; staff; quality of product or service; costs; credit given; monitoring performance.

Public life: Controlling staff; controlling each department's budget; controlling work to eliminate wasteful expenditure and duplication of services.

Local community: controlling cash; costs.

MANAGEMENT SKILLS

LEADING

Influencing or directing people to achieve goals.

Home: Parents influencing or directing children.

School: Principal leading staff; teachers directing pupils.

Business: Leadership skills in business start-up; manager directing staff.

Public life: Taoiseach leading Dáil.

Local community: Community leaders directing or leading members.

MOTIVATING

The drives, influences and forces that cause a person to want to achieve certain aims.

Home: Parents motivating children to study and to behave.

School: Principal motivating staff; teachers motivating pupils to achieve results; captain motivating a school team.

Business: Entrepreneur showing self-motivation to keep the business going; manager motivating employees.

Public life: Motivation of civil servants to be efficient and effective.

Local community: Leaders motivating committees or volunteers to work.

COMMUNICATING

The process of exchanging information.

Home: Communication with banks, insurance companies, tax office and service providers.

School: Communication with parents, teachers, and pupils; boards of management; teachers communicating with pupils.

Business: Communication with customers, suppliers, banks, Revenue Commissioners, insurance companies, and the public.

Public life: Communicating Government decisions to the country; communicating within and between Government departments.

Local community: Leaders communicating with members and the public.

6. MANAGERS AND MANAGEMENT SKILLS

Characteristics of managers

(1) ACTIVE LEADERSHIP

An effective manager must be an effective leader, very much involved in the organisation, always at hand to impart their knowledge of the business to employees.

(2) INTERPERSONAL SKILLS

Managers spend a lot of time dealing with people and must develop the art of motivating and communicating with people.

(3) EFFECTIVE PLANNER

Managers must be good planners. Effective managers must establish aims and objectives and must choose a course of action to achieve these objectives.

(4) GOOD ORGANISER

A manager must have the ability to organise people and finance and to run the business in an efficient manner.

(5) MOTIVATOR

A manager must have the ability to motivate employees.

(6) GOOD TIME MANAGER

A manager must have the ability to arrange their work, ensuring that tasks are completed on time and avoiding bottlenecks and time-wasting. It involves the best use of the time available.

(7) Decisiveness
A manager must have the ability to make quick and effective decisions.

(8) Hard-working
A manager must be willing to put in long hours and continuous effort until the job is complete.

(9) Controller
A manager must have the ability to control the business, ensuring that goals and objectives are achieved.

(10) Communicator
A manager must have the ability to communicate to those in the firm and to act as spokesperson when dealing with outside organisations.

(11) Charismatic
A manager must have personal appeal or the power of inspiring others to respect them.

(12) Self-confidence, self-belief
This is a firm belief in oneself and one's abilities.

(13) Desire to achieve
This is a strong desire to achieve goals and to make the business successful.

(14) Flexible, adaptable
A manager must respond to changing business situations.

The difference between enterprise and management

Enterprise

1. Initiative is shown in finding and generating ideas, finding new ways of tackling problems, spotting gaps in the market, and setting up a business.
2. Enterprise includes risk-taking. Entrepreneurs may risk their own money in setting up a new business and are ultimately responsible for its success or failure. There is also the risk of personal failure.
3. Enterprise can operate in the household, in the community, or in business, that is, in taking responsibility for creating opportunities: for example, an enterprising person may set up a club.

Management
1. Management is concerned with the day-to-day operation of a business.
2. It is concerned with planning and organising finance and people and helps control the various elements involved in running the business.
3. Management consists of implementing ideas, managing people, motivating employees, controlling resources, and undertaking the day-to-day running of the

business. Managers must ensure that this is done well, so that the aims and objectives are achieved.

4. Management also involves setting short-term targets and long-term goals, checking to see if they are reached, and making changes when necessary.

   In general, entrepreneurs show more initiative, are more innovative and take greater risks than managers.

Management skills

Management skills are **leading**, **motivating**, and **communicating**.

Leading

1. This is the ability to achieve results through people by influencing and directing them to achieve a goal.
2. It involves organising employees into groups or teams, motivating and directing, resolving conflict, and providing the resources for running the business.
3. Good leadership involves a person having certain traits: intelligence, initiative, self-assurance, maturity, vision.

STYLES OF LEADERSHIP

There are three main styles of leadership: **authoritarian, democratic** and laissez-faire.

Authoritarian leadership

- The manager makes decisions without discussion; the views of others are ignored. Orders are given and are expected to be followed without question.
- There is little delegation of responsibility, as the manager has little trust in the ability of employees to perform their tasks.
- Objectives may be achieved by fear or intimidation or the use of authority to get agreement.
- The result is usually poorly motivated employees and a lack of co-operation.

Democratic leadership

- Employees are involved in discussion, and the views of the majority are taken into account in decision-making.
- Tasks are delegated, as the manager trusts employees to do the work.
- The result is highly motivated and co-operative employees. Effective managers must direct their employees and delegate authority and responsibility.

Laissez-faire (free-rein) leadership

- Manager sets objectives for employees to achieve. Employees must decide how to achieve the objectives.
- Manager delegates responsibility and authority to make decisions to employees. There is little interference from the manager.
- The result is a relaxed atmosphere; there are few guidelines and directions resulting in poor productivity and lack of motivation as employees have little incentive to work hard.
- This style of leadership would be suitable where staff are self-motivated and can work on their own initiative, e.g. researchers.

DIRECTION
Employees are guided on the right course to achieve the objectives of the business. It involves getting employees to carry out tasks given to them; each person's work contributes to achieving the general objective of the firm.

DELEGATION
Delegation means passing on authority or power and the responsibility for certain tasks to people lower down in the organisation. As managers cannot do all the jobs, there needs to be some delegation of work and authority.

The person delegating authority still has to keep general responsibility for decisions and must ensure that the subordinate person is capable of carrying out the task.

The person who has been given tasks to perform is accountable for the performance of those tasks and answerable for the results.

Motivating
Motivation consists of all drives, forces and influences that cause people to want to achieve certain goals. It is the willingness of people to work without being pushed.

People are motivated by pay, working conditions, status and recognition, responsibility, promotion, a sense of achievement, and the opportunity to be involved. Motivation increases the desire to succeed and the urge to achieve, gives a sense of participation and job satisfaction, generates enthusiasm, raises morale, and increases confidence and sustained effort in the work-place.

MOTIVATION THEORIES
Many theories have been developed over the years to help the management identify how best to motivate people.

MASLOW'S HIERARCHY OF NEEDS
Abraham Maslow, an American psychologist, developed a theory to explain how people are motivated. He stated that each person has a hierarchy of needs, and as each lower need is satisfied the next-higher need becomes a motivating factor.

This model is known as the 'hierarchy of needs' and is shaped like a pyramid. Once a need is satisfied it no longer motivates, and people look towards the next-higher need. The first needs are physical needs—food, drink, and shelter—and once these are satisfied the next need, that of safety and security, becomes increasingly important, and so on.

MCGREGOR'S THEORY X AND THEORY Y
(See table on page 41)

The American psychologist Douglas McGregor devised two contrasting sets of ideas about what motivates people in organisations, called theory X and theory Y. McGregor suggested that autocratic managers were likely to subscribe to theory X and saw them organising production, directing people, controlling, supervising, setting targets, measuring work, and persuading workers to get things done. Employees may resent this approach, become unco-operative and poorly motivated, and do as little as possible.

McGregor also suggested that democratic managers were likely to work with the assumptions of theory Y and saw them delegating work, giving workers extra

Maslow's hierarchy of needs

Needs		How business can satisfy needs
Self-fulfilment: desire to become what you are capable of becoming. Sense of achievement and responsibility. Personal growth.	Self-actualisation Self-fulfilment needs	Offer a challenging job. Opportunities for promotion. Allow employees to participate in training to develop personal and technical skills.
Desire for self-esteem and self-confidence. Need to be congratulated. Need to be successful. Need for recognition and status.	Ego and esteem needs	Involving employees in decision-making. Give employees job title and visible rewards. Delegation of tasks and responsibility; recognition for work and effort.
Desire for love and affection. Being part of a group. Sense of belonging and friendship. Acceptance by others.	Social and acceptance needs	Good relationship with fellow-workers. Social outings etc.; social clubs. Staff interaction.
A house, family, safety and security. Predictable surroundings.	Security and safety needs	Secure job. Safe work-place. Opportunity to join a trade union.
Warmth, shelter, clothing. Food and drink.	Physiological and physical needs	Wages, bonus, commission. Good working conditions.

McGREGOR'S THEORY X AND THEORY Y

Theory X	Theory Y
1. Employees are inherently lazy, dislike work, and will avoid it if they can.	1. Employees wish to be interested in their work and want to undertake challenging jobs and, given the right conditions, will enjoy work.
2. Employees lack ambition, dislike responsibility, prefer to be directed, and want security.	2. Employees have the capacity to accept and seek responsibility and accept the rules of the organisation, imposing discipline in their work, given accepted targets.
3. Employees are self-centred, resistant to change, and not interested in the organisation.	3. The majority of workers are imaginative and creative and exercise ingenuity in solving problems.
4. Because they are motivated by money they require coercion, correction, direction and tight control to make them function adequately.	4. Motivated by their need for respect, esteem and wish to achieve and to have their achievements recognised, most employees will work to the best of their capabilities without coercion or control.

responsibility and encouragement in their work, and allowing them a say in decision-making. Employees are likely to be more co-operative and highly motivated.

McGregor maintained that in the majority of cases theory Y assumptions most accurately reflect employees' attitudes towards work.

Communication

Communication is the exchange of information in an organisation. It involves sending messages through a channel or medium of communication to a target person or group and then receiving some feedback from the recipient that the message has been understood and acted on.

THE IMPORTANCE OF COMMUNICATION IN MANAGEMENT

1. It facilitates good industrial relations.
2. It helps the management make decisions and pass them on to employees.
3. It resolves conflict in the work-place.
4. Communication skills are necessary for negotiating wages and conditions with employees.
5. Managers exercising leadership when communicating the firm's goals must be heard, understood and accepted and must get action taken.

TYPES OF COMMUNICATION

(1) INTERNAL COMMUNICATION

This is communication between people inside the company. There are many communication channels through which information flows between people in an organisation.

Downward communication

Orders, instructions or messages sent from a manager to a subordinate, for example the managing director communicating with the marketing director.

Upward communication

A subordinate communicating back to their manager, for example the marketing manager reporting back to the managing director.

Horizontal or lateral communication

Communication between people with the same level of authority in organisation, for example the production manager communicating with the marketing manager.

(2) EXTERNAL COMMUNICATION

Communication between a business and other parties (people, agencies, and organisations), including customers, suppliers, banks, Revenue Commissioners, Government agencies, insurance companies, accountants, service providers, and interest groups.

COMMUNICATION SKILLS

These include the ability to

- speak in a style of language appropriate to the listener
- write clearly and use visuals to clarify information
- listen to and interpret messages and obtain feedback
- read and understand written information
- understand body language
- be aware of what the listener needs to know.

CHOOSING METHODS OF COMMUNICATION

The following factors should be considered when choosing a method of communication:

(1) **COST**: how expensive is the method, telephone call, letter, fax, e-mail.
(2) **SPEED**: how fast can the information be transferred?
(3) **SAFETY**: will the item reach its destination safely?
(4) **WRITTEN RECORD**: it is important to keep a written record for future reference.
(5) **SECRECY**: if the information is confidential it is important to choose a secret form of communication, for example a face-to-face meeting.
(6) **DESTINATION**: over what distance is the communication? national or international?
(7) **ACCURACY**: will the method chosen transfer the information exactly? Telephone conversations can lead to misunderstandings.
(8) **NATURE OF MESSAGE**: this will dictate the method to be used.

BARRIERS TO EFFECTIVE COMMUNICATION

Barriers prevent a message from being communicated effectively.

(1) LANGUAGE: use of inappropriate language. If too much jargon is used, the recipient may not understand the message.
(2) TIMING: make sure the correct time is chosen for communicating.
(3) LISTENING: if the receiver is not listening or concentrating on the communication, the message may be lost.
(4) RELATIONSHIPS: if the relationship between sender and recipient is poor, communication may be ineffective.
(5) LACK OF PLANNING: the message and the reasons for sending the message were not planned in advance.
(6) WRONG MEDIUM used: for example, using the phone when a letter would be more appropriate.
(7) NO FEEDBACK: not getting confirmation that the message was received and understood.

METHODS OF COMMUNICATION

INTERNAL COMMUNICATIONS	EXTERNAL COMMUNICATIONS
Oral • face-to-face conversation • internal telephone system • internal meeting • intercom	*Oral* • face-to-face conversation • radio • telephone • exhibition • external meeting or seminar • public meeting • mobile phone • conference • paging • answering-machine, voice mail
Written • internal magazine or newsletter • memorandum • report • notice-board • internal computer network • suggestion scheme	*Written* • newspaper • post • external computer network • press statement • business documents
Visual (1) Visual aids • flip-chart • overhead projector • slides • multimedia projector • video (2) Diagrams • line graph • pie chart • bar chart • pictogram • histogram • break-even chart	*Electronic* (1) Electronic data interchange (EDI) (2) ISDN applications • file transfer • fax • teleworking • videoconferencing (3) Internet • electronic mail (e-mail) • worldwide web (WWW)

ORAL COMMUNICATION

Verbal communication includes face-to-face conversation, meetings, and telephone conversations.

Features of oral communication

- Speed
- Instant feedback
- Questions can be asked and answered
- Difficulties can be explained
- No record for future reference

THE APPLICATION OF ORAL COMMUNICATIONS IN BUSINESS

MEETINGS

A meeting is a gathering of a group of people to exchange ideas and make suggestions, enabling collective decision-making. It is a very useful means of communication for a business or organisation.

TYPES OF MEETING

Board meeting

The regular meeting of the board of directors of a company, usually held monthly, to review progress and to plan ahead.

Ad hoc meeting

A one-off meeting to discuss and solve an immediate problem that has arisen.

Annual general meeting (AGM)

The meeting of directors and shareholders of a company or of the members of an organisation held once a year.

Extraordinary general meeting (EGM)

A meeting of shareholders to discuss an important matter that cannot wait until the next AGM.

REASONS FOR HOLDING MEETINGS

(1) *To give information* about progress, decisions made, or plans for the future.
(2) *To receive information*—people's opinions, different viewpoints.
(3) *To make decisions.*
(4) *To co-ordinate* different departments through progress reports.
(5) *To discuss new ideas* and put forward proposals.

CHAIRPERSON

The chairperson is responsible for the running of a meeting.

Duties of the chairperson

(1) Planning the meeting—date, time, and place—in consultation with the secretary.
(2) Drawing up an agenda, in consultation with the secretary.
(3) Running the meeting: opening the meeting, welcoming those attending, calling the meeting to order, ensuring that a quorum is present and that the agenda is followed, maintaining order at the meeting.
(4) Ensuring that the minutes of the previous meeting are read, adopted by those present, and signed.

(5) Allowing discussion only of matters on the agenda.
(6) Allowing all present time to express their views and encouraging full participation.
(7) Putting motions to a vote, having a casting vote in the event of a tie, and announcing the result.
(8) Summarising the decisions made, reminding members of work to be completed before the next meeting, and declaring the meeting closed.

Secretary

The secretary has responsibility for all administration work in an organisation.

Duties of the secretary

(1) Drawing up the agenda, in consultation with the chairperson.
(2) Sending out notice and agenda of the meeting to all members entitled to attend.
(3) Checking the venue, ensuring that all necessary facilities are provided, such as adequate seating, tables, refreshments, overhead projector, etc.
(4) Reading the minutes of the previous meeting.
(5) Dealing with correspondence received by the organisation, and keeping records of all important documents for future reference.
(6) Taking notes of decisions taken at meeting and writing the minutes of the meeting.
(7) Arranging the next meeting, in consultation with the chairperson.

Notice and agenda of a meeting

Notice

The notice gives the date and time of the meeting and the venue.

Agenda

The agenda is the programme for the meeting, that is, the list of matters to be discussed and the order in which they will be taken.

SAMPLE NOTICE AND AGENDA FOR THE AGM OF BUSINESS INNOVATIONS LTD

Notice is hereby give that the second annual general meeting of Business Innovations Ltd will be held at the company's offices in Bridge Street, Dublin 4, on 5 February 2014, beginning at 1:30 p.m., for the following purposes.

(1) Minutes of the 2013 AGM
(2) Matters arising from the minutes
(3) Chairperson's report
(4) Auditor's report
(5) Dividends
(6) Election of directors
(7) Appointment of auditor for coming year
(8) Auditor's remuneration
(9) Any other business

By order of the board
John McGrath
Company secretary
5 January 2014

MINUTES OF A MEETING

The minutes are a brief and accurate record of the business transacted at a meeting. They should contain details of proposals and decisions made.

Minutes of the second annual general meeting of Business Innovation Ltd

The second annual general meeting of Business Innovations Ltd was held in the company's offices at Bridge Street, Dublin 4, on 5 February 2014.

1. The meeting was opened at 1:40 p.m. by the chairperson, Martin Ryan. The attendance consisted of all the directors, fifty shareholders, and the auditor.
2. The minutes of the previous meeting were read, adopted, and signed by the chairperson.
3. There were no matters arising from the minutes.
4. The chairperson then addressed the meeting, stating that the company had had a very successful year, with a reported profit increase of 30 per cent.
5. The auditor, Roy Kenny, then presented his report, and the accounts were adopted without query.
6. A dividend of 4 per cent was declared.
7. John O'Leary and Patrick O'Mahony were elected to the board of directors.
8. The auditing firm of Cole and Yorke was reappointed for the coming year.
9. The auditor's remuneration was agreed, with an 8 per cent increase on the previous year.
10. As there was no other business, the meeting closed at 4:15 p.m.

Martin Ryan
Chairperson
7 February 2014

TREASURER

Voluntary organisations elect a treasurer, who is responsible for the organisation's financial affairs.

Role of the treasurer

(1) Collecting subscriptions from members.
(2) Making payments on behalf of the organisation.
(3) Keeping financial records and proper books of account.
(4) Dealing with banks and other financial institutions on behalf of the organisation.
(5) Reporting on the state of the finances at ordinary meetings and presenting an annual report to the AGM.

TERMS USED

These are some of the more important terms used in connection with meetings:

agenda: a list of matters to be discussed at the meeting
minutes: a written record of the business transacted at the meeting
quorum: the minimum number of people who must be present before a meeting can begin
standing orders: the rules for running a meeting

WRITTEN COMMUNICATION

This means sending messages in written form, such as memos, letters, or reports.

Features of written communication

- There is a permanent record for future reference.
- Technology speeds up written communication.
- Messages can be re-read to help in understanding any difficulties.
- Response is slow: it takes time to get a response in writing to know whether the message was understood. E-mail is an obvious exception, as is fax.
- It is suitable if the subject matter is detailed.

APPLICATIONS OF WRITTEN COMMUNICATION IN BUSINESS

Memos (memorandums)

Memos are used for internal communication. They are an important mode of written communication, providing a written record of a message and proof that the message has been passed on. They are used for giving information, reminding people of events, describing progress on some developments, giving instructions, and putting forward proposals.

There is usually only one topic, and they may be typed or handwritten on printed memo forms.

MEMORANDUM

To: All staff
From: Brendan Parkinson
Date: 1/5/2014
Subject: Staff in-service training

A staff in-service day will take place on Friday 10 May 2014 at the Shelbourne Hotel.
Agenda to follow later.

Brendan Parkinson
Principal

Business letters

Letters are an important means of communication with customers, suppliers, banks, Revenue Commissioners, etc. They are used for making enquiries, requesting payment, disciplining employees, making complaints, responding to complaints, replying to letters of application for jobs, etc. A permanent record is created.

SAMPLE BUSINESS LETTER

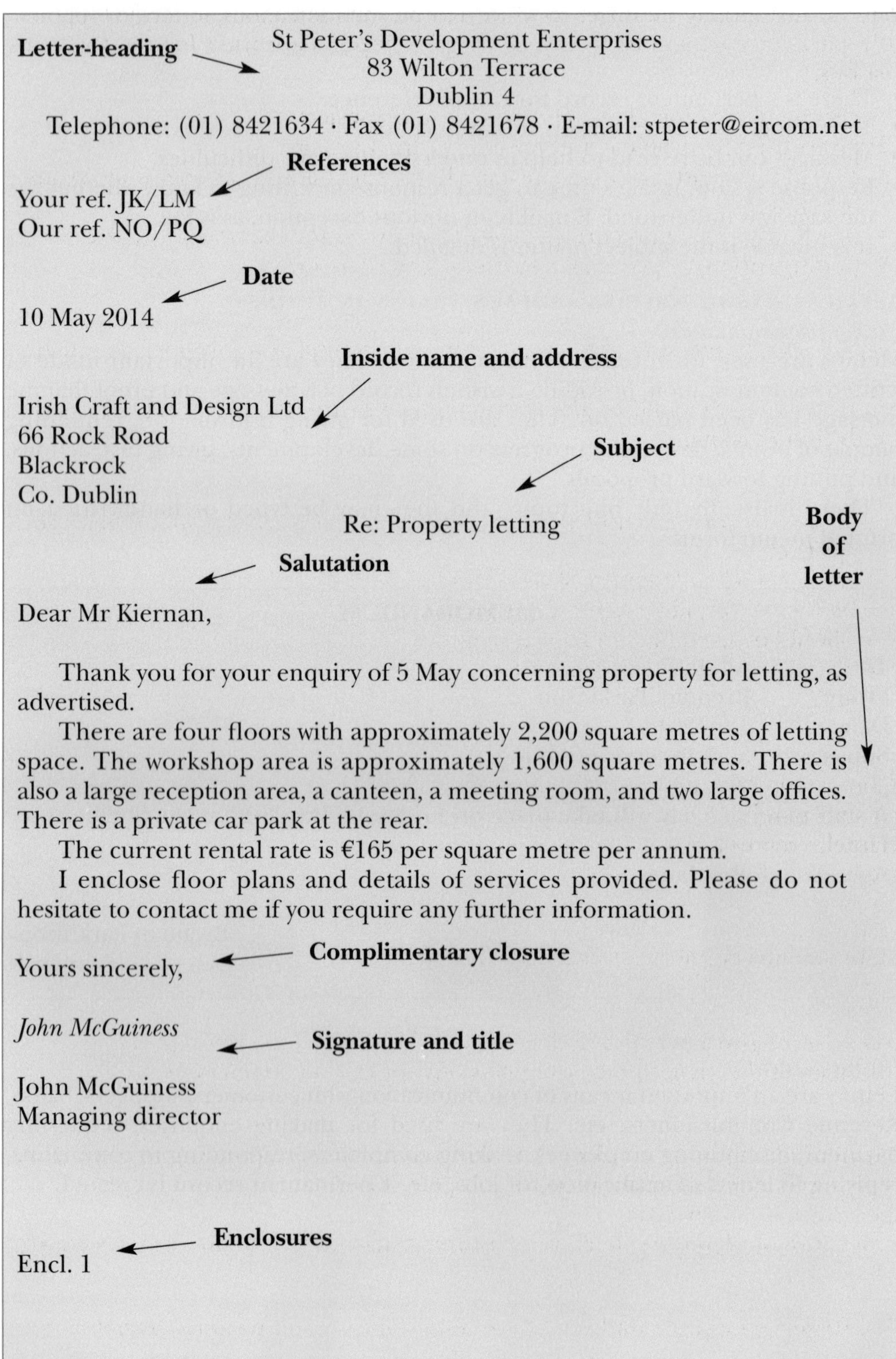

St Peter's Development Enterprises
83 Wilton Terrace
Dublin 4
Telephone: (01) 8421634 · Fax (01) 8421678 · E-mail: stpeter@eircom.net

Your ref. JK/LM
Our ref. NO/PQ

10 May 2014

Irish Craft and Design Ltd
66 Rock Road
Blackrock
Co. Dublin

Re: Property letting

Dear Mr Kiernan,

Thank you for your enquiry of 5 May concerning property for letting, as advertised.

There are four floors with approximately 2,200 square metres of letting space. The workshop area is approximately 1,600 square metres. There is also a large reception area, a canteen, a meeting room, and two large offices. There is a private car park at the rear.

The current rental rate is €165 per square metre per annum.

I enclose floor plans and details of services provided. Please do not hesitate to contact me if you require any further information.

Yours sincerely,

John McGuiness

John McGuiness
Managing director

Encl. 1

REPORT-WRITING

A report is a formal presentation of written information about a specific topic sent to a particular person or group of people. Reports are used for the following reasons:

(1) giving information about progress on some project;
(2) investigating a problem and presenting the findings;
(3) evaluating a study, for example a feasibility study, and recommending a course of action;
(4) providing a written record of a particular event, for example an accident;
(5) putting forward a proposal and arguing the case for it.

TYPES OF REPORTS

Routine reports—made at regular intervals, for example sales report, production report.
Special reports—prepared on the instructions of a superior, requiring information for decision-making.

RULES FOR REPORT-WRITING

- The purpose of the report must be clear, so that the report team will have clear objectives.
- Simple and clear language should be used.
- The report should be as brief as possible.
- It should be presented in logical sequence.
- It should be well researched and accurate.

STRUCTURE OF A REPORT

1. *Title page*

Title—stating the subject of the report.
Writer's name.
Who the report is for.
Date.

2. *Table of contents*

Main sections of the report and page numbers.

3. *Executive summary*

Intended to give a person who has not got time to read the full report a summary of the main findings, conclusions, and recommendations.

4. *Introduction*

Terms of reference—the reasons why the report is written. Instructions given to the report-writer and the matters that the report covers.
Background information
Procedure used in the collection of information—questionnaires, interviews, etc.

5. *Findings*

The writer sets out the findings of the report in a clear and logical sequence.

6. *Conclusions*
The writer assesses the evidence and identifies problem.

7. *Recommendations*
Specific course of action to be taken to solve the problem.

8. *Appendixes*
Copy of questionnaires.
List of tables, diagrams, or maps.
Transcript of interviews.
Bibliography—a list of the publications and other sources of information used by the writer.

STAGES IN REPORT-WRITING

- Preparation—setting out the objectives and scope of the investigation.
- Researching and assembling information.
- Analysis of information—checking for accuracy and reliability.
- Writing of first draft.
- Revision of draft, making any changes necessary.
- Presentation of report to appropriate person or organisation.

FORMAL REPORT

REPORT ON REASONS FOR BUSINESS FAILURE IN FIRST YEAR OF TRADING

Report writer: Brian Kavanagh
To: Mr Seán Perrott, Director, Small Firms Association
Date: 25 April 2014

Table of contents

Executive summary
The main reasons for business failure in the first year of trading are: overtrading; poor research; poor management; inadequate capital; no industrial experience in the area of activity.

Introduction
Terms of reference
The purpose of the report is
(1) to investigate the reasons for business failure in the first year of trading and
(2) to make whatever recommendations are appropriate to reduce the number of failures.

→

Procedure
A survey of fifty businesses that failed in the first year of trading was undertaken. Interviews were conducted with managing directors, and information was gathered from other personnel involved by way of questionnaires.

Findings
The most common problems faced by businesses in the first year of trading were:
(1) *Overtrading:* the business was trying to expand too quickly and found itself short of cash.
(2) *Poor research:* many entrepreneurs failed to carry out proper research on their business proposal.
(3) *Poor management:* a lack of finance at the outset often leads to an inability to employ senior management.
(4) *Inadequate capital structure:* high loan repayments at the outset and borrowing to pay wages and buy stock.
(5) Starting a business with little or no industrial experience in an area of activity.

Conclusions
The main reasons for early business failure are:
(1) a lack of commitment by the owners
(2) inadequate business planning at the outset
(3) lack of expertise by the owners
(4) unforeseen financial problems.

Recommendations
The following course of action should be taken by an entrepreneur to ensure the success of a business:

1. Start a business in a familiar area. This reduces the risk.
2. The entrepreneur must be customer-oriented and market-oriented.
3. Build up a strong team with competent people in areas such as finance, production, and marketing.
4. The entrepreneur must be fully committed and be prepared to work long hours to ensure the success of the business.

Appendixes
Copy of questionnaires with personnel involved.
Transcript of interviews with managing directors.
Tables and charts on business failures.

Brian Kavanagh
25 April 2014

VISUAL COMMUNICATION

Visual communication allows complex information to be understood more easily. It is usually used together with oral or written communication to reinforce the message.

FEATURES OF VISUAL COMMUNICATION

- It is good for emphasising the main point of the topic and summarising at the end.
- Messages are easily understood and remembered.
- It is easier to spot trends and comparisons.
- It improves presentation by clarifying information.

THE APPLICATION OF VISUAL COMMUNICATION IN BUSINESS

Graph

A graph (or 'line graph') illustrates a trend over time.

1998	1999	2000	2001	2002	2003	2004	2005
34	32	39	26	27	24	11	15

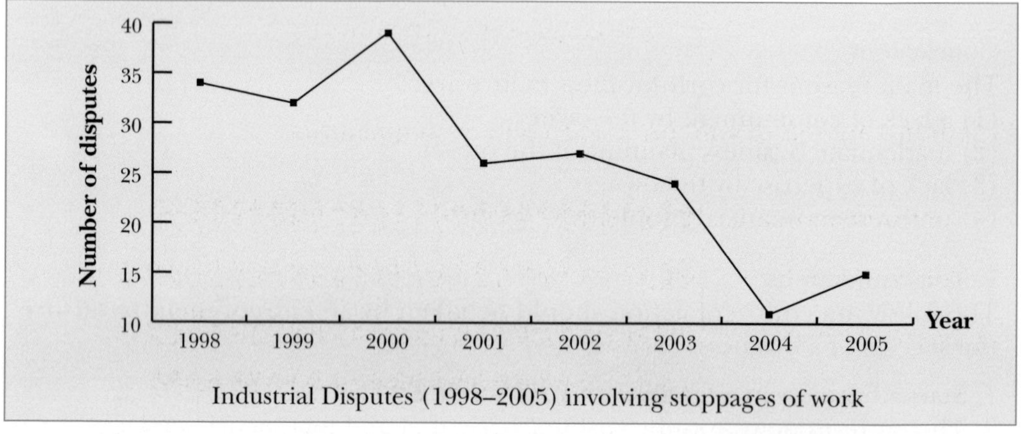

Industrial Disputes (1998–2005) involving stoppages of work

Pie chart

A pie chart is a circle divided into sectors. Each sector shows a figure as a percentage of the total. Pie charts are useful for showing comparisons.

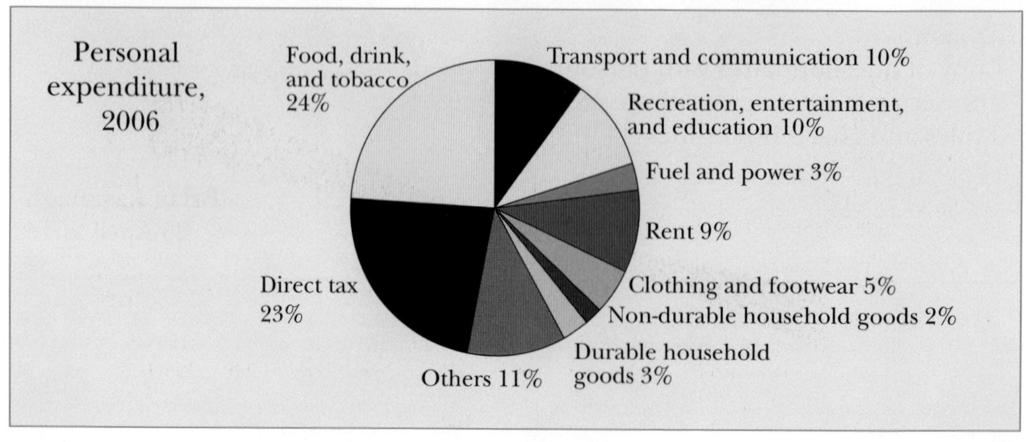

Bar chart

A bar chart displays information in a series of bars. Each bar is the same width: the length of the bars shows the quantity. Bars can be drawn vertically or horizontally. This is an effective method of presenting information when it is necessary to emphasise different quantities.

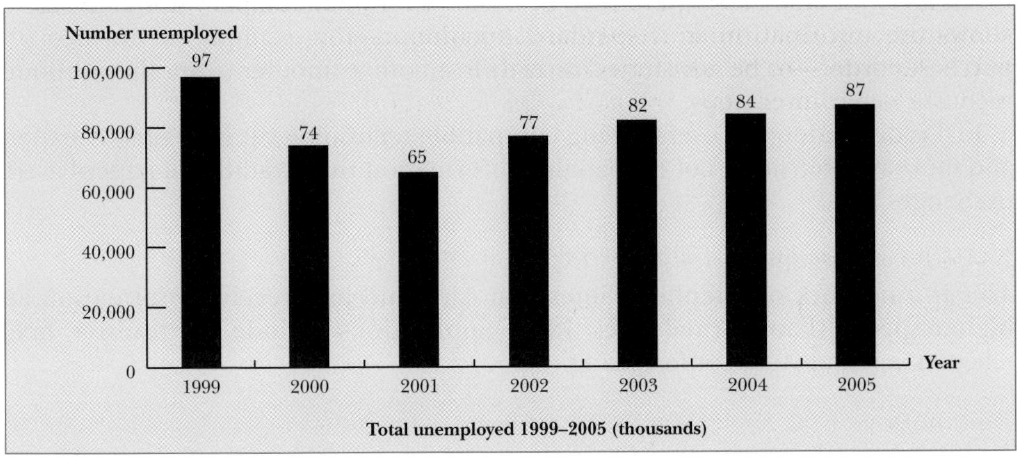

Pictogram

Pictograms are sets of symbols used to represent quantities.

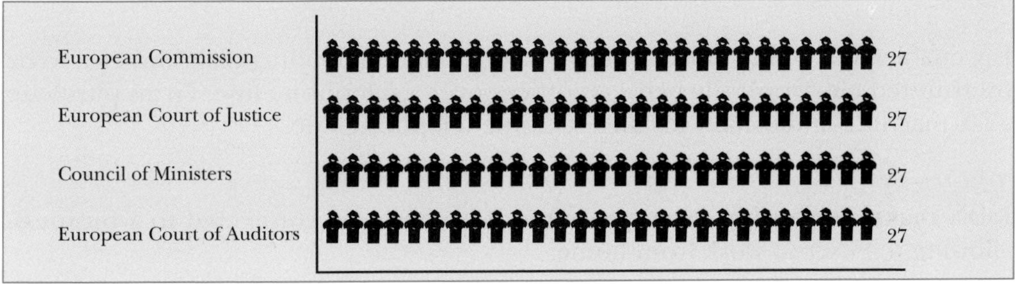

Break-even chart

A break-even chart shows the level of sales or output required to break even, that is, where total income is going to cover total costs. The break-even point is where total revenue (TR) equals total costs (TC).

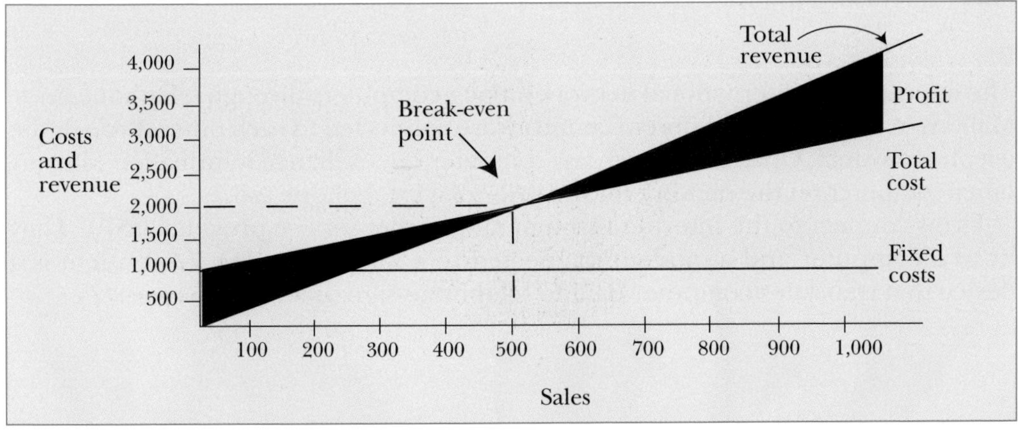

ELECTRONIC COMMUNICATION

Business today operates in a global market, and the ability to communicate is greatly increased by using modern information technology.

Electronic data interchange (EDI)

EDI is an electronic data system used by business for inter-company transactions. It allows the information in a standard document—for example an invoice or purchases order—to be transferred directly from one computer to another without recourse to a printed copy.

EDI is dependent on users having compatible technology. It is a faster, cheaper and more reliable means of exchanging information than traditional paper-based exchanges.

Integrated services digital network (ISDN)

This is a network of telephone lines that can send and receive information at higher speeds than normal lines. ISDN applications include file transfer, fax, teleworking, and videoconferencing.

File transfer

An ISDN line allows computer files to be transferred quickly and efficiently. This is very useful in the printing and publishing industries, where people are working in different places on the same project.

Fax

Fax enables a facsimile or exact copy of a document, including diagrams etc., to be transmitted electronically between offices over a telephone line. Firms purchase a fax machine and usually install a separate telephone line.

Teleworking

ISDN makes it possible for a computer at home to be connected to a business, allowing the user to work from home.

Videoconferencing

This is a meeting held between people who are in different places. Visual and sound signals are transmitted over a telephone line, and all participants can see and hear each other. It eliminates the cost of travelling to meetings. A telephone line, camera and monitor are needed.

The internet

The internet is an international network linking computers through telephone lines. Millions of computers in different countries are connected to each other through the telephone system. Once connected, any computer can exchange information with any other computer on the network for the price of a local phone call.

Firms connect to the internet through an internet service provider (ISP). They need a computer and a modem connected to a telephone line. (A modem is a device that translates computer data to telephone signals and vice versa.)

Companies throughout the world are rapidly discovering that the internet is a valuable tool for business, giving them the chance to see and be seen on the world stage. For any business, the internet has three important benefits:

- *speed*: the internet is fast: it takes just minutes to send an e-mail message or to log on to a web site; potential customers are just a short step away;
- *cost-efficiency*: customers can interact with a business directly, and an efficient business can respond accordingly, customers can be impressed by a well-designed web site and efficient interaction;
- *effective marketing*: the internet allows access to global markets at minimal cost and allows a business to react quickly to market changes, which is pivotal to success in a competitive environment.

Broadband

Broadband is currently the fastest means of internet access. Broadband offers:

- *Permanent 'always on' internet access:* no dial-up or waiting for connection.
- *High speed internet access:* fifteen times faster than dial-up allowing downloading and other on-line transactions to be completed more efficiently.

Internet services

Electronic mail (e-mail)

- This is a way of sending a typed message and computer files directly from one computer to another over the internet. It is the most popular use of the internet.
- It is a fast, efficient, convenient and cheap way of sending messages.
- Each user has a unique e-mail address.
- You can send a copy of your message to any number of people at the same time.
- Files containing spreadsheets and graphics can be attached to e-mail messages.
- Messages are held in a 'mailbox', access to which can be controlled by your own password.

E-commerce

E-commerce or e-business is a method by which goods and services are bought and sold on the internet. There are two basic types of interaction.

(1) Business-to-consumer

Selling products or services directly to customers

(2) Business-to-business

Selling products or services to another business, or using electronic methods for greater efficiency in the supply chain.

Worldwide web

- This is a vast collection of linked documents available over the internet. It is the world's biggest information gateway.
- A special program, called a browser (such as Netscape Navigator or Internet Explorer), is needed to give you access to the web.
- Many businesses have their own web sites, on which they display information about the firm and its products.

7. MANAGEMENT ACTIVITIES

Management activities are **planning**, **organising**, and **controlling**.

Planning

This means establishing goals, objectives or targets and deciding on a course of action to achieve these objectives.

PRINCIPLES OF PLANNING ('SMART')

1. The objectives must be clear and **specific**.
2. It should be possible to **measure** whether the plan was successful.
3. The plan must be **agreed** on by all concerned.
4. The plan must be **realistic** and possible to achieve.
5. The plan must be achievable within a reasonable **time**.

OBJECTIVES

These are the particular goals that a business is trying to achieve.

GENERAL OBJECTIVES

These apply to the whole company—for example, to achieve a return on capital employed of 20 per cent by the end of the financial year.

SPECIFIC OBJECTIVES

These are targets for one functional department—for example, to increase sales by 50 per cent in the first six months of the trading year.

POLICIES

Policies are the means used to achieve objectives. They are usually written statements that direct the management in decision-making when trying to achieve objectives.

Policy documents describe procedures to be followed, recommend work practices, and dictate a course of action to be followed. Examples include marketing policy, dividend policy, promotion policy.

SWOT ANALYSIS

Before drawing up any plans, a business should assess its internal **strengths** and **weaknesses** and external **opportunities** and **threats**. This is called a 'SWOT analysis'.

STRENGTHS

A business must analyse its strengths and see how it can build on them.

- Quality of the product
- Skills of the employees
- Production technique
- Distribution system
- Adequate cash flow
- Sales techniques

WEAKNESSES

A business must examine its weaknesses and determine how they can be overcome.

- Staff problems
- Cash flow problems

- Areas where the business could do with improvement—for example already extended production line, poor servicing facilities
- Lack of sales and marketing skills

OPPORTUNITIES

A business must investigate opportunities that can be exploited in the future.

- New markets or products
- Export opportunities
- Consumer demand
- Vulnerability of a competitor

THREATS

A business must look at threats facing it and see how best they can be confronted or eliminated.

- New competition
- New competitors' products
- Diversification by a competitor
- Forthcoming legislation

MISSION STATEMENT

This is a statement setting out the general purpose and objectives of a company. The mission or purpose is the reason for the existence of the firm. The mission statement communicates this purpose to shareholders and to employees.

The mission statement of a post-primary school might be:

- To educate pupils in a safe and caring environment.
- To recognise the value of each individual.
- To contribute to the life of the community.

TYPES OF PLANNING

There are two main types of planning: **strategic** planning and **tactical** planning.

STRATEGIC PLANNING

Strategic planning is long-term master planning covering a period of more than five years. Plans are normally drawn up by senior managers and are based on the company's main mission or purpose.

TACTICAL PLANNING

Tactical planning is short-term planning covering a period of one or two years. Plans are drawn up by the middle management and relate to a particular function of the business, for example a plan to launch a new advertising campaign.

CO-ORDINATION

The process of synchronising the work of different people and different departments to achieve the desired goals of the organisation.

Organising

This involves arranging available resources (people, equipment, and finances) into the most suitable form to achieve the objectives.

A business must have a framework for organising employees, called the organisation structure. This structure

- establishes a line of authority
- improves the efficiency and quality of work
- improves communication—sets down channels of communication.

STRUCTURES OF ORGANISATIONS

FORMAL STRUCTURE

- This identifies different levels of authority in a business and sets out a definite chain of command (who is responsible to whom). People on the same level have no authority over each other and should co-operate.
- An organisation chart is used to show the management structure, different levels of management, chain of command, and span of control. Authority is delegated down a line from senior management to middle management to supervisors and then to employees on the factory floor.

A formal structure :

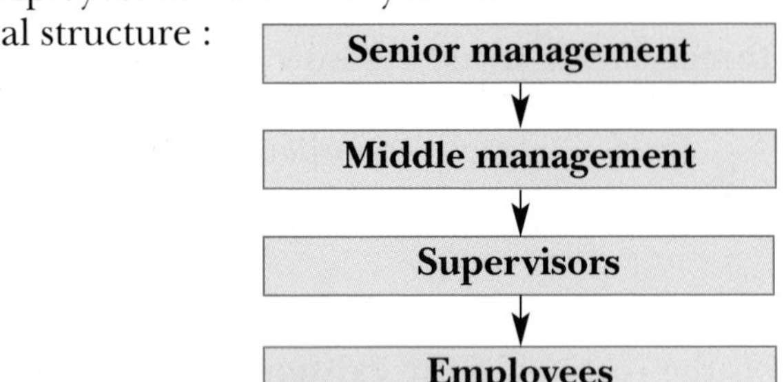

TYPES OF ORGANISATION STRUCTURE

Different types of organisation structure include functional structure, product structure, geographical structure, and matrix structure.

FUNCTIONAL STRUCTURE

This divides a company according to the main functions performed, such as finance, production, sales and marketing, purchasing, human resources. There is one person in charge of each department, and all are answerable to the managing director.

A functional structure: line organisation

This structure is called a line organisation, as each person in the line is answerable to the person above. There is usually a span of control in this type of structure.

Span of control

Span of control is the number of subordinates who are delegated authority and report directly to the manager or supervisor above them. It can be wide if the manager has many direct subordinates, or narrow if there are few.

Span of control depends on:

- the ability of managers
- the ability of workers
- the nature of the work
- the cost involved.

The span of control in the illustration above consists of the five departmental heads who are answerable to the managing director.

Line and staff organisation

Specialists are added to line organisation to help managers carry out their functions and to increase the efficiency of the company: for example, the financial controller would advise and assist all other managers on budgeting etc.

Specialists are appointed in an advisory role because of their expertise in helping managers run their departments more efficiently.

PRODUCT STRUCTURE

The firm is structured according to the products produced. Each product line has its own production, marketing, finance and human resources manager.

Product structure

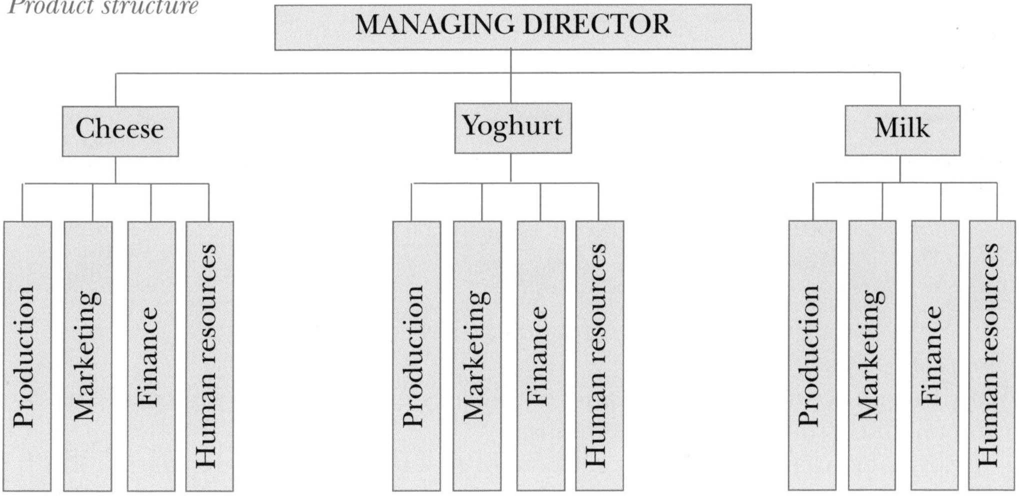

GEOGRAPHICAL STRUCTURE

The company is structured according to the geographical areas in which it operates. This structure might be used if a company is selling in many different countries where customers' needs and markets are different. Marketing efforts are specialised and carried out by geographical area.

A geographical structure

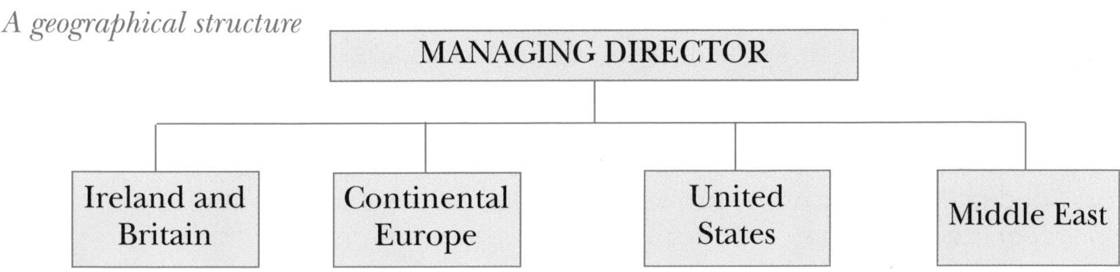

MATRIX STRUCTURE

This is a combination of functional and product structure. It is used when a company is involved in large or complex projects and when experts from different areas of the business are required to ensure the completion of the project.

Members of the project team are drawn from various departments and, for the duration of the project, are responsible to the team leader. The project leader is responsible for co-ordinating their efforts and ensuring that the project is completed successfully.

Once the project is finished, the team members and leader return to their own departments.

Employees are members of both a functional department and a project team. They have two supervisors: the department manager in the course of their normal duties and, when they are involved in specific project work, the project leader.

Matrix structure

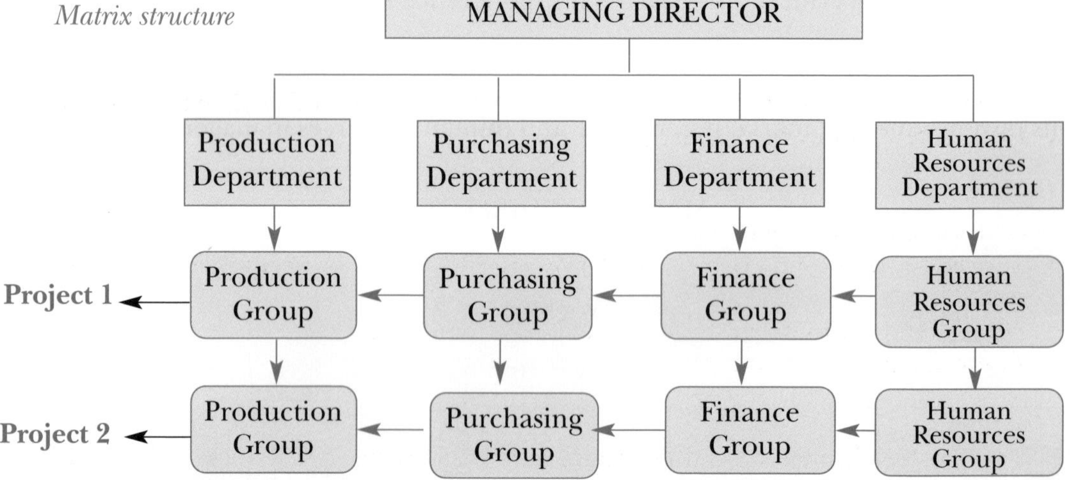

INFORMAL STRUCTURE

With this structure, managers and employees communicate informally in the canteen, in corridors, or at sports clubs.

Informal contact can be of great benefit to a company, as information can be collected and people's ideas and opinions sought to help in decision-making.

STAFFING

This involves the recruitment and training of effective and efficient employees to ensure that the goals of the company are achieved. Staffing is a function of the human resources manager.

PROJECT TEAMS

These are teams of specialists from the areas of marketing, finance, human relations, and production. Each member of the team is an expert in one of the areas and competent in all other areas.

The team is given a set objective to achieve. The project manager is appointed to co-ordinate the activity of the project. Examples include the designing of a tunnel.

Controlling

This means measuring performance to check whether it is in line with the targets set out in plans. Corrective action must be taken if there are deviations from planned performance. Control is concerned with making sure that objectives are achieved.

PRINCIPLES OF CONTROL

(1) Setting standards of performance
(2) Measuring the performance of the business and comparing it with the standard set.
(3) Taking action if there are significant deviations: correcting deviations or revising standards.
(4) Applying the lessons learnt in setting future standards, making sure that mistakes are not repeated.

TYPES OF CONTROL

STOCK CONTROL

A system for ensuring that the firm has the correct amount of stock at all times to satisfy demand—never too much, never too little.

Holding too much stock

- Cash is tied up in stock.
- There are increased costs for warehousing, transport, handling charges, and security.
- Stock deteriorates or goes out of date.
- There are higher insurance costs.

Holding too little stock

- There is possible disruption to production if stocks run out.
- There may be a loss of customers.
- There may be a loss of discount available for bulk buying.

Just-in-time (JIT) system

This is a manufacturing system in which material, components and products are delivered to the next stage of production at the exact time when they are needed. It is designed to minimise the cost of holding stocks of raw materials, components, work in progress and finished goods by carefully planned scheduling and flow of resources through the production process.

JIT requires very efficient ordering and delivery reliability. It is widely used in Japan by car manufacturers as a means of cutting costs.

CREDIT CONTROL

This is the system that monitors the amount of goods sold on credit to ensure that outstanding debts are paid within a reasonable time, to minimise the risk of bad debts. It involves devising a credit policy that establishes:

- credit limits—how much customers can purchase on credit
- the length of credit given
- procedures for collecting outstanding debts.

QUALITY CONTROL

This is a check on the efficiency of production, a technique used to make sure the product will meet the standards expected by customers. Systematic inspections are carried out during the production process to ensure that high standards of quality are achieved.

A good quality control system can lead to significant cost savings on rejected products, reduced warranty and servicing costs, and fewer complaints from customers. Quality control is also concerned with finding and eliminating the causes of quality problems.

Quality standards

Firms strive to obtain recognised quality standards, such as the Q mark and ISO 9000. These prove to customers that the firm has obtained a recognised standard of quality.

The quality mark (Q mark)

This indicates that a product has achieved the desired quality standard. Approval is obtained from the Irish Quality Association and is one of the most valuable brand marks on the Irish market.

ISO 9000

This is certification in accordance with an international standard. Approval opens up overseas markets to a company.

The standard requires a company to implement a quality management system in all its activities. Inspection is carried out by the National Standards Authority of Ireland (NSAI). On approval, the firm is awarded the ISO 9000 mark, which can be used on advertising and stationery. Continuous inspections ensure that standards are maintained.

BUDGETARY CONTROL

This is the process by which financial control is exercised within a company by the use of budgets.

A budget is a plan showing expected income for a period matched against estimated expenditure. Projections in budgets are compared with performance to establish variances (differences between figures). The cause of these variances should be investigated.

Budgets are prepared for most functions of a business in advance of the accounting period in areas such as purchasing, production, marketing, capital expenditure, and cash.

KEY TERMS

These are some of the more important terms introduced in unit 3:

agenda	information technology	objectives
chairperson	internal and external communication	organisation structure
control	internet	planning
co-ordination	leading	quality control
credit control	management	secretary
delegation	minutes	span of control
EDI (electronic data interchange)	modem	stock control
electronic mail	motivation	terms of reference

LEGISLATION DISCUSSED IN UNIT 3
Data Protection Act (1988)

ON COMPLETION OF UNIT 3 YOU SHOULD BE ABLE TO
(1) define 'management';
(2) identify the importance of management skills in areas such as home, school, local community, Government departments, and business start-up;
(3) list the characteristics of managers;
(4) explain the basic management skills;
(5) explain the central role of communications in business and management;
(6) identify and explain the main barriers to effective communication;
(7) demonstrate business information in the form of memos, reports, and business letters; draft a visual presentation from given data;
(8) identify the duties of a chairperson and secretary and draft an agenda and minutes of a meeting;
(9) distinguish between the methods of communication;
(10) discuss the importance of general communication skills **(HL)**;
(11) differentiate between enterprise and management **(HL)**;
(12) explain the contribution of both managers and entrepreneurs to business **(HL)**;
(13) discuss the nature of management activities and their linkages **(HL)**.

Examination-style questions and solution

Managing

(**A**) Distinguish between 'managing' and 'being enterprising' in the context of either a business or a community activity. **(15 marks)**
(**B**) Illustrate the five levels in Maslow's hierarchy of needs. Explain, using examples from a business, how these needs can be met. **(25 marks)**
(**C**) Analyse how new technology has changed the way management operates. **(20 marks)**

Suggested solution

(A) *'Managing' a business means managing people, resources, products or services, machines and time from day to day. Managing must ensure that this is done well, so that the aims and objectives of the company are achieved. Managing also involves setting short-term targets and long-term goals, checking to see whether they are reached, and making changes where necessary.*

'Being enterprising' is the business activity that provides the initiative and carries the risk involved in setting up an enterprise and in producing a product or providing a service. Being enterprising involves taking all the risk for the ultimate success or failure of the product or service.

(B) *Maslow's hierarchy of needs:*

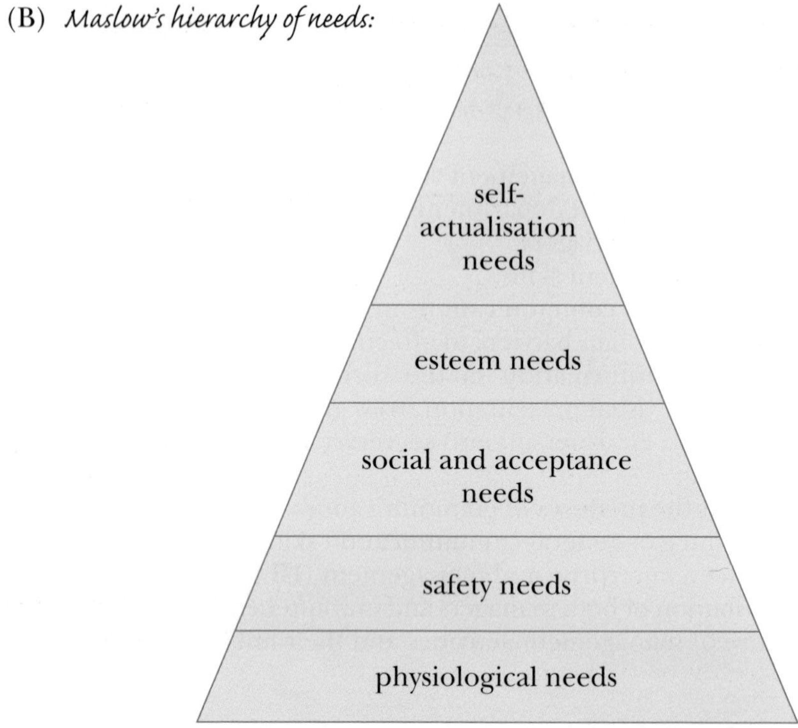

Maslow stated that each person has a hierarchy of needs, and that he or she will seek to satisfy a higher need only when the lower one has been satisfied.

Businesses can meet the five needs illustrated above in the following manner:

Physiological needs: *Pay employees adequate wages, so that they can afford to feed, clothe and provide shelter for themselves and their dependants.*

Safety needs: *Businesses can satisfy this need by ensuring that employees feel secure in the environment in which they work, for example security of tenure (a low risk that they may lose their jobs) and high standards of safety in the work-place.*

Social and acceptance needs: *These needs could be met by providing employees with the time and opportunity for social interaction with each other. This could be achieved both during and outside working hours, for example during break or lunch times, with social clubs and company outings, etc.*

Esteem needs: *Businesses can meet these needs by ensuring that the management treat employees with respect and that good work done is rewarded with acknowledgment and genuine praise. Other practices that could be adopted by the management include delegating tasks, sharing responsibility, and involving employees in the decision-making process.*

Self-actualisation needs: *A business can provide a working environment in which employees are encouraged to participate in training and in developing their personal and technical skills, so that they can achieve promotion in their careers and realise their potential.*

(C) *Technology has changed the way management operates in the following ways:*

(1) ***Communications and information technology***

Management use computers and e-mail instead of phone and faxes to communicate with people.

Electronic data interchange: Management use computers to exchange business documents in a highly efficient way.

Videoconferencing: People do not have to be in the same place to be able to communicate face to face. This enables people in businesses throughout the world to communicate person-to-person.

(2) ***Decision-making***

Management uses computers in financial forecasting and planning for the future. Changes may be made to budgets at the press of a button, enabling quicker decision-making on the part of the management.

(3) ***Production***

Advances in production technologies have resulted in high levels of automation, for example robots instead of people working on assembly lines, computer-aided design (CAD), and computer-aided manufacturing (CAM).

(4) ***Motivation***

The management and even some employees may work from home, by linking their home computers with computers in the firm. Productivity may increase, because employees are free to work at home at their own pace.

Practice questions—Section 1

1. Name one type of organisation structure.

___

Draw a chart of that structure.

2. Delegation requires:

___

___

___

___

3. What is the difference between enterprise and management?

4. Complete the pie chart below from the following information on the age of a firm's work force:

Age	Under 20	21–40	41–55	56+
Percentage of work force	12.5%	37.5%	25%	25%

Revision question

Managing

(A) Draft a memo from the management to all staff in an enterprise outlining to them a recently agreed method of staff reward. **(15 marks)**

(B) Differentiate between enterprise and management. Illustrate your answer. **(15 marks)**

(C) 'Controlling is the most important management activity.'
Do you agree with this statement? Support your opinion with reasons and examples. **(30 marks)**

[60 marks]

Unit 4: Managing 2

The applications of management are the theme of this unit. It looks at those functions that are common to the management of a household and of a business. It examines organisational applications, including human resource management, and the changing role of management.

Objective: To enable pupils to understand management as it applies to a household and a business.

8. Household and Business Manager

Finance

Households and businesses have similar sources of income and incur similar expenditure.

CASH FLOW FORECAST

Cash flow

The flow of money in and out of a household or business. Careful attention must be given to cash flow: if bills cannot be paid, finance has to be arranged. A business may cease trading, irrespective of the level of profitability, if it has cash flow problems.

Purpose of cash flow forecast

To identify when a household or a business might find itself facing a cash flow problem.

Ways of overcoming cash flow problems

Household

Reducing expenditure; raising additional finance; increasing earnings.

Business

Increasing sales; reducing costs; delaying payment to creditors; arranging additional finance; collecting money from debtors; selling a fixed asset; issuing shares.

Household cash flow forecast or household budget

The cash flow forecast for a household shows sources of finance and the uses of finance over a certain period.

Income	*Expenditure*
• wages/salaries • overtime, bonus, commission • interest on savings or investments • child benefit • unemployment benefit • tax rebate • loans	Regular • mortgage or rent • car loan, tax, insurance • house insurance Irregular • telephone • ESB • groceries • clothes • school books and uniforms • coal, gas, or oil • car service, petrol or diesel Discretionary • holidays • entertainment • cinema and theatre • newspapers and magazines

CASH FLOW FORECAST—HOUSEHOLD

	January	February	March	Total
Income	€	€	€	€
Wages, John Ryan	1,000	1,000	1,000	3,000
Wages, Jean Ryan	800	800	800	2,400
Bonus	100	—	—	100
Interest	—	—	10	10
Child benefit	80	80	80	240
(A) Total income	1,980	1,880	1,890	5,750
Payments				
Regular				
Mortgage	300	300	300	900
Car loan	220	220	220	660
Car tax	320	—	—	320
House insurance	—	—	380	380
	840	520	900	2,260
Irregular				
Telephone	270	—	190	460
ESB	—	320	—	320
Groceries	400	400	400	1,200
Clothes	180	—	—	180
Oil	200	—	—	200
Coal and gas	50	50	50	150
Household appliance	—	—	300	300
Car service	—	—	220	220
Car running costs	80	80	80	240
	1,180	850	1,240	3,270
Discretionary				
Birthdays	80	—	—	80
Entertainment	150	20	70	240
	230	20	70	320
(B) Total payments	2,250	1,390	2,210	5,850
(C) Net cash (A – B)	(270)	490	(320)	(100)
(D) Opening cash (D)	50	(220)	270	50
Closing cash (C + D)	(220)	270	(50)	(50)

QUESTIONS AND SOLUTIONS ON CASH FLOW FORECAST

1. *Did the household live within its means for the three months?*
—No. There was negative cash flow, with €100 more predicted expenditure than income.

2. *Identify the causes of the deficits in January and March.*
—January: Car tax payment for the year
High expenditure on clothes (January sales)
Purchase of oil
Large expenditure on birthdays and entertainment
—March: House insurance
Car service
Household appliance

3. *What action can the household take to avoid this problem?*
—January: Pay car tax for three months
Defer payment of the oil bill to February
Reduce discretionary expenditure
—March: Pay house insurance by monthly instalments
Buy household appliance on hire purchase or pay it off over a year

4. *What sources of finance can the Ryan family use to cover these deficits?*
—January: Bank overdraft
Accrued expense (defer payment of the oil bill)
—March: Bank overdraft
Hire purchase or term loan (house appliance)

BUSINESS CASH FLOW FORECAST

The cash flow forecast for a business shows sources of income (inflows) and payments (outflows) over a period.

Income (inflows)	*Payments (outflows)*
(1) Cash sales, goods and services (2) Debtors (3) Deposit interest (4) Investment income (5) Government grants and subsidies (6) Loans (7) Share capital (8) Sale of assets (9) VAT refunds	(1) Purchase of assets (capital expenditure) (2) Cash purchases of goods and raw materials (3) Payments to creditors (4) Tax (VAT, PAYE) (5) Repayment of loans (6) Business expenses (current expenditure) (7) Dividends

IMPORTANCE OF A CASH FLOW FORECAST FOR A BUSINESS

- A cash flow forecast predicts the movement of cash into and out of the business.
- It shows future cash inflows and outflows and their sources and timing; this assists the business in decision-making.

- It draws attention to possible shortages in the future. Negotiations on meeting the cash needs of the business can begin in good time.
- Comparing budgeted figures against actual figures over a period helps control the cash of the business.

CASH FLOW FORECAST—BUSINESS

	October	November	December	Total
Receipts	€	€	€	€
Cash sales	20,000	25,000	40,000	85,000
Debtors	10,000	20,000	25,000	55,000
Deposit interest	—	—	1,000	1,000
Loan	—	80,000	—	80,000
Share capital	—	50,000	—	50,000
(A) Total income	30,000	175,000	66,000	271,000
Payments				
Buildings	—	130,000	—	130,000
Cash purchases	15,000	18,000	20,000	53,000
Creditors	5,000	15,000	18,000	38,000
Taxation	—	—	12,000	12,000
Expenses	12,000	16,000	25,000	53,000
(B) Payments	32,000	179,000	75,000	286,000
(C) Net cash (A – B)	(2,000)	(4,000)	(9,000)	(15,000)
(D) Opening cash	5,000	3,000	(1,000)	5,000
Closing cash (C + D)	3,000	(1,000)	(10,000)	(10,000)

QUESTIONS AND SOLUTIONS

1. *Give reasons why a business prepares a cash flow forecast.*

—To ensure that it has enough cash inflows to meet cash outflows; to find out when it is going to have surpluses or deficits so that it can deal with them.

2. *Will this business live within its means for three months?*

— No. It has a negative cash flow in each of three months totalling €15,000.

3. *What sources of finance could the business use to cover these deficits?*

— Bank overdraft, creditors, or accrued expenses.

SOURCES OF FINANCE

Household	Business
Short-term sources (0–1 year) Bank overdraft Creditors Accrued expenses (unpaid bills) Credit card	*Short-term sources (0–1 year)* Bank overdraft Creditors Accrued expenses (unpaid bills) Taxes
Medium-term sources (1–5 years) Hire purchase Leasing Personal loan	*Medium-term sources (1–5 years)* Hire purchase Leasing Term loan
Long-term sources (over 5 years) Long-term loan; mortgage Savings	*Long-term sources (over 5 years)* Long-term loans or debentures Share capital (equity) Retained earnings

SHORT-TERM SOURCES OF FINANCE (0–1 YEAR)

Bank overdraft

The holder of a current account is granted permission by the bank to withdraw more than the amount of money in their account, up to a certain specified limit (the *overdraft limit*).

Interest is calculated daily on the overdrawn balance and charged to the account at the end of every three months.

Households use overdrafts to cover temporary shortages, for example Christmas or back-to-school time.

Businesses use an overdraft accommodation to pay for supplies or wages or whenever there is a cash shortage.

Creditors

Credit purchases in a household are mainly for things such as milk, newspapers, bread, coal or oil deliveries, and purchases from a local retailer or co-operative, where payment is made at the end of a week or a month.

In business, suppliers give retailers credit for an agreed period. The retailer sells the goods and has the use of the money until the invoice has to be paid. No interest is charged, and no security is required. If invoices are not paid by the due date, discounts may be lost, and the credit rating of the customer may be affected.

Accrued expenses (unpaid bills)

Services such as Eircom, the ESB and An Bord Gáis give customers a number of days to pay bills. During this time the money can be used for other purposes. No cost is involved, and, provided the bill is paid by the due date, the service will not be affected.

Tax

Tax in a business is also paid in arrears: for example, VAT is collected in the normal course of business, and PAYE is deducted from employees' wages and remitted to the Revenue Commissioners later.

MEDIUM-TERM SOURCES (1–5 YEARS)

Hire purchase

This is a method of buying assets whereby an initial instalment is paid and the balance of the hire purchase price is paid in an agreed number of instalments.

The customer gets immediate possession and use of the asset but does not become the legal owner until the last instalment is paid.

It is an expensive source of finance, as the rate of interest is high; interest is charged on the initial sum borrowed for the full duration of the agreement.

The hire purchase company has the right to repossess the asset if the hirer defaults on payment, subject to certain conditions.

Leasing

This is a method of acquiring fixed assets without incurring a large capital outlay.

The finance company buys the asset and leases it to the business or individual for a fixed period in return for agreed instalments.

The lessee (hirer) never obtains title (ownership) to the asset.

Assets such as motor vehicles, office equipment, computers, plant and machinery are assets commonly leased by companies, as they quickly become obsolete.

At the end of the lease period the asset is returned to the finance company, but arrangements may be made to buy the asset.

The cost of leasing can be offset against tax in the profit and loss account.

Personal loan or term loan

A term loan is repaid in fixed instalments over an agreed period, arranged to suit the customer's ability to repay.

It is negotiated with the bank manager after completing a loan application and is granted for a stated reason, such as buying vehicles, computer equipment, or home improvements.

A term loan for a household or an individual is called a personal loan.

Banks may demand security, that is, something valuable the bank can sell if the loan is not repaid, for example the title deeds of premises, shares, or life policies.

Interest on a business term loan can be offset against tax in the profit and loss account.

LONG-TERM SOURCES (OVER 5 YEARS)

Long-term loans, mortgages, and debenture loans

Long-term loans for a household are available from banks and building societies; they are usually advanced to buy a residence or other property. These are called *mortgages* and are secured on the asset purchased. This means that the title deeds are given to the lender, and if the borrower defaults before the mortgage is paid in full, the financial institution can sell the asset to recoup the balance of the loan.

A *debenture loan* is a long-term loan to a company, usually for expansion. It usually carries a fixed rate of interest and a specific repayment date. Security is normally required, which may be some specified asset or a charge on all the assets of the business. Interest payments on debenture loans are an allowable expense against tax in the profit and loss account.

Savings

Savings are an important source of finance for the household, individual, or business. Money saved may be used to buy assets, which reduces the amount of borrowings.

Share capital (equity)

This is provided by the owner or shareholders, who buy shares in a company. The capital remains in the company as long as it exists and is repaid only on winding up. Shareholders are rewarded by dividends out of profits at the end of the year.

Ordinary shareholders have voting rights at the AGM, giving them a say in the running of the business and some control over the company's affairs.

Retained earnings

This is profit after tax that the directors of a business decide not to distribute to their shareholders but to keep in the business.

It increases the capital and reserves of the business and may be used to expand the business through the purchase of assets. Retained profit will be re-invested in the business in the form of increased assets. It is an important source of finance for business expansion.

COST OF FINANCE

Households and businesses must try to obtain the cheapest source of finance, that is, the lowest rate of interest.

CURRENT ACCOUNT

This is an active account in a financial institution. Money is lodged personally or by credit transfer, and withdrawals are made by cheque, ATM, Laser card, or smart card. Wages can be paid directly into a current account through Paypath.

The financial institution supplies regular statements listing all transactions and the current balance.

If the customer wishes to withdraw more money than is in the account, an *overdraft* is created, on which interest is paid, calculated daily on the overdrawn amount.

COMPARISON OF AN APPLICATION FOR A CURRENT ACCOUNT FOR A HOUSEHOLD AND A BUSINESS

Household	*Business*
(1) Name and address of applicant (2) Occupation (3) Name of employer (4) Income	(1) Name and address of business (2) Names of directors (3) Nature of business (4) Memorandum and articles of association (5) Income—final accounts

WHAT THE BANK WILL REQUIRE ON A LOAN APPLICATION

	Household	Business
1. Reasons	Car or television	Machinery or vehicles
2. Ability to repay	Income	Final accounts
3. Record	Account-holder	Account-holder
4. Security	House deeds or shares	Deeds of premises
5. Own investment	Trade-in	Share capital

THE IMPORTANCE OF FINANCE FOR BUSINESS

- The business must use the cheapest sources of finance.
- Finance is required to cover costs and expenditure.
- Finance is required for business expansion.

Insurance

This is a contract whereby a person (the *insured*) pays a fee (*premium*) to an insurance company (the *insurer*), which in return promises to compensate the person for any financial loss suffered.

BASIC PRINCIPLES OF INSURANCE

(1) INSURABLE INTEREST

The insured must have a financial interest in the item to be insured, that is, must benefit from its existence and must suffer from its loss. Anyone may insure their own property, as they would incur a loss if it was damaged or destroyed; but you cannot insure your next-door neighbour's property. Without an insurable interest a person is unable to enforce an insurance contract.

(2) UTMOST GOOD FAITH

The person seeking insurance must provide all the information the insurer needs and must disclose all material facts to enable the insurer to calculate the correct premium for the risk involved, or to reject the risk.

Nothing must be withheld from the insurer, even if they do not ask for the information on the proposal form.

If an insured person is found to have withheld a material fact or given false information, the insurer can treat the policy as void, and any claim by the insured can be refused.

Examples of material facts not disclosed would be having a serious medical condition when seeking life assurance, or not disclosing a previous accident when seeking motor insurance.

(3) INDEMNITY

The aim of insurance is to put the policy-holder in the same financial position as they were before the loss occurred. There must be no element of profit to the policy-holder, nor any element of loss. For example, if a three-year-old car that cost

€20,000 is written off in a crash, the amount of compensation will be the value of a three-year-old car, not of a new one.

Most insurance policies are *indemnity contracts*, with the exception of personal accident and life assurance, as it is impossible to calculate the value of a lost life or limb.

(4) Subrogation

Having paid compensation, the insurer is entitled to sue the third party who was responsible for the loss. For example, if a neighbour is responsible for breaking a person's window and compensation has been paid, the insurer can take over the policy-holder's legal right to claim the cost of the repair from the neighbour.

Having paid compensation on damaged stock or property, the insurance company is entitled to claim the ownership of any goods remaining or to take over what remains of the property.

(5) Contribution

If the same item is insured with more than one insurer, the insurers will share the compensation in proportion to the amount of risk covered.

As the insured is not entitled to claim more than the full value of the item, each insurer pays a share of the compensation.

(6) Average clause

The principle of the average clause applies if a partial loss occurs and a person is under-insured: for example, if you are only half-insured you will get compensation only for half the loss suffered.

Example

A house is valued at €180,000 and is insured for €90,000. It is damaged by fire to a cost of €20,000.

Formula:

$$\frac{\text{value insured} \times \text{amount of loss}}{\text{value of property}}$$

$$\frac{€90{,}000 \times €20{,}000}{€180{,}000} = €10{,}000$$

RISKS AND COSTS

Risk is the possibility of suffering some loss or damage. Risks that can be covered by insurance include fire, theft, burglary, motor accidents, personal accidents, sickness, and death.

The greater the risk, the higher the premium. There is a higher risk of accidents among young drivers: therefore a young person's car insurance will be high. There is a higher risk of burglary and car theft in towns than in the country. Premiums will therefore be higher in high-risk areas.

A smoker would be charged a higher premium for life assurance than a non-smoker.

DIFFERENCE BETWEEN INSURANCE AND ASSURANCE

Insurance is protection against a risk that may happen, for example a fire or accident. Assurance provides for a risk that will happen, for example death.

TYPES OF HOUSEHOLD INSURANCE

(1) PROPERTY INSURANCE

This covers buildings and contents.
Buildings insurance covers the cost of repairing or replacing buildings should they be damaged or destroyed by fire or accident.
Contents insurance covers loss or damage to contents caused by fire, burglary, water damage, or accidents.

(2) MORTGAGE PROTECTION INSURANCE

If the mortgagee dies before the mortgage is fully paid, the policy will cover the balance due.

(3) MOTOR ACCIDENT INSURANCE

The various types of motor accident insurance policies are:

Third-party insurance

This is compulsory for all motor vehicles. The insurer and the policy-holder are the two parties to the insurance contract: any other person to whom there is a legal obligation is therefore a third party. A motorist must have third-party cover for any personal injuries or damage to vehicles or property suffered by someone as a result of an accident when the insured is at fault.

Third-party, fire and theft insurance

This covers third parties and loss or damage to the insured vehicle caused by fire or theft.

Comprehensive insurance

This covers everyone, including the insured, and all vehicles and property involved in an accident.

(4) PERSONAL ACCIDENT INSURANCE

This covers a person for personal injuries due to accidents. The amount of compensation paid will depend on the extent of the injury.

(5) HEALTH INSURANCE

This covers the cost of hospital care in the event of an accident or serious illness. Private health care insurance is provided by the VHI and BUPA.

(6) PERMANENT HEALTH INSURANCE

This covers a person's income if they are unable to work because of an accident or serious illness. Payments of up to 75 per cent of income may be made, depending on the premium paid.

(7) Critical illness insurance

This covers loss of income suffered because of a critical illness, such as cancer, stroke, or heart attack.

(8) Life assurance

Life assurance provides compensation on the death of the insured. Types of assurance include:

Whole-life assurance

The insured pays a premium for the rest of his or her life, and compensation is paid to dependants on the death of the insured.

Endowment life assurance

The insured pays the premium, and compensation is paid either on the insured reaching a certain age or on their death, whichever comes first.

Term assurance

This provides cover for a specific period. Compensation is paid only if death occurs within that period. A term assurance policy is often used to cover a loan if the borrower dies before the loan is repaid.

(9) Pay-related social insurance (PRSI)

Payments are deducted by the employer from each employee's wages. The employee can then claim social welfare benefits or entitlements.

TYPES OF BUSINESS INSURANCE

Property insurance

This covers buildings, equipment, stock and other assets against loss or damage as a result of a fire or accident.

Motor insurance

All vehicles owned by a business must be insured. The same types of policy and the same rules as household insurance apply.

Employer's liability insurance

This covers employers against claims made by employees as a result of accidents at work.

Public liability insurance

This covers employers against claims made by members of the public as a result of accidents while on the business's premises.

Fidelity guarantee insurance

This covers an employer against the dishonesty of employees.

Product liability insurance

This covers the business against claims made by members of the public for loss or damage suffered as a result of a defective product.

BURGLARY INSURANCE
This covers the business against loss or damage caused by a break-in.

KEY PERSON INSURANCE
This provides compensation for the loss of valuable employees through death, for example the managing director or a highly talented employee.

GOODS-IN-TRANSIT OR CASH-IN-TRANSIT INSURANCE
This covers stock in transit or cash in transit to or from the bank.

PAY-RELATED SOCIAL INSURANCE (PRSI)
Each employer must pay a portion of the total PRSI contribution for each employee.

CONSEQUENTIAL LOSS POLICY
This covers the business against loss of income or profit if the company is forced to close temporarily because of an accident or fire.

INSURANCE DOCUMENTS

PROPOSAL FORM
A person seeking insurance must complete an insurance proposal form, stating the type of insurance cover required and disclosing all material facts.

PREMIUM
The insurance company will calculate the premium or fee to be paid to cover the risk. The person who calculates the premium is called the actuary.

INSURANCE POLICY
This is the contract for insurance between the insurer and the insured. It sets out details of the risks covered, the period of cover, and other terms and conditions.

CLAIM FORM
If a claim is made, a claim form must be completed and submitted to the insurer, giving details of the loss suffered and the amount of compensation being sought.

An **assessor** is a person who assesses the amount of the loss suffered by the insured and calculates the amount of compensation to be paid.

THE IMPORTANCE OF INSURANCE FOR BUSINESS
- A business should have adequate insurance cover, otherwise the average clause will apply.
- The business will be protected against risks.
- The business can continue and survive despite unforeseen events.

Tax
Tax is a levy charged by the Government on individuals and companies to finance Government expenditure.

INCOME TAX
The main source of revenue is tax charged on people's wages. Income tax is deducted by the employer each time wages are paid and is remitted to the Revenue

Commissioners. This is called the pay-as-you-earn (PAYE) tax system. Pay-related social insurance (PRSI) and a health levy are also collected through the PAYE system. The Income Tax Year is 1st January to 31st December.

THE PAYE SYSTEM

The pay-as-you-earn (PAYE) system applies to anyone who has income from employment.

Tax credits

A tax credit reduces the amount of tax payable by the taxpayer.

Standard rate cut-off point

This is the proportion of the taxpayer's income on which they pay tax at the standard rate. Any income earned over the standard rate cut-off point is taxed at the higher rate of tax.

Form P12

This is the taxpayer's income tax return for the year. It is used to obtain tax credits and standard rate cut-off point for the new tax year. When an employee completes Form P12 and returns it to the Revenue Commissioners they issue the following:

1. To each taxpayer: Notice of determination of tax credits and standard rate cut-off point

The inspector of taxes sends a notice of tax credits to each taxpayer, setting out the credits to which the taxpayer is entitled and the standard rate cut-off point.

2. To each employer: Certificate of tax credits and standard rate cut-off point

A certificate of tax credits is also sent to each employer, informing them of employees' total credits and standard rate cut-off point. In the absence of a certificate of tax credits, *emergency tax* must be deducted.

Form P60

At the end of the tax year each employer gives every employee form P60, showing their gross pay for the year and tax and PRSI deductions made during the year. This is required if you are claiming repayment of tax.

Form P45

When an employee leaves a particular employment, the employer gives him or her form P45, showing their gross pay and tax and PRSI to the date of their leaving.

The same form is given by the employee to their new employer, so that tax and PRSI can be deducted at the correct rate. The employee may also need it if claiming social welfare benefits or claiming a refund of tax.

Form P21

This is a balancing statement. It is provided by the Revenue Commissioners on request from a taxpayer who feels that he or she has paid more tax than was due. A common reason for requesting a balancing statement is that there may be some additional credits or deductions not claimed during the year. They should be documented and sent with the annual return and form P60 to the inspector of taxes with the request for a balancing statement. A PAYE balancing statement, form P21, is then issued by the inspector of taxes. This compares tax paid with the amount that should have been paid. If tax was overpaid, a refund is made; if underpaid, a further tax demand will be made.

PERSONAL TAX

COMPUTATION PROCEDURE USING THE 'TAX CREDITS' SYSTEM

1. The employee is taxed on the full amount of their income, that is, income multiplied by the appropriate rate (or rates) of tax.
2. The employee's tax credits are deducted from their tax liability. This gives the net amount of income tax payable.
3. PRSI and the health contributions are added to give the total income tax, PRSI and health contributions.

INCOME TAX COMPUTATION QUESTION AND SOLUTION

The following information relates to Mark Ryan, a sales manager.

Gross salary	€60,000
Benefit in kind	€10,000
Tax credits	
Single person credit	€1,630
PAYE credit	€1,490
Tax rates	
20% of first	€32,000
42% of balance	
PRSI 4% up to €46,600	
2% health contribution on all income	

Calculate

(i) Net annual take-home pay
(ii) Net monthly take-home pay

Solution: Income tax computation for Mark Ryan

Gross salary			60,000
Benefit in kind			10,000
			70,000
Income Tax			
32,000 × 20%	6,400		
38,000 × 42%	15,960		
Gross income tax before tax credits		22,360	
***Less* tax credits**			
Single person tax credit	1,630		
PAYE tax credit	1,490	(3,120)	
Income tax payable		19,240	
PRSI and health contribution			
PRSI: 4% × 46,000	1,864		
Health contribution: 2% × 70,000	1,400	3,264	
Total income tax, PRSI and health contribution			22,504
Net annual income (60,000 – 22,504)			37,496
Net monthly take-home pay			3,124.66

SELF-ASSESSMENT — PAY AND FILE

Self-assessment applies to all self-employed people. During October the Collector-General sends each self-employed person a *notice of preliminary tax due.* The taxpayer can pay this amount or replace it with their own calculation or estimate of tax due. Preliminary tax must be paid before 31 October each year.

A full tax return for previous year must be made by 31 October, with the balance of tax due for previous year to be paid by 31 October. *A balancing statement* is issued, and if there is a balance due it must be remitted to the inspector of taxes; if tax was overpaid, a refund is made. Self-assessment tax returns are liable to random audits to ensure that the returns made and amount paid are honest and correct.

BUSINESS TAX

CORPORATION TAX

This is tax on company profits. The Government reached an agreement with the European Commission for the introduction of a 12 $\frac{1}{2}$ per cent corporate rate on trading income from 1 January 2003.

VALUE-ADDED TAX (VAT)

Value-added tax is a tax charged on the sale of goods and services. All businesses with sales of goods over €55,000 and suppliers of services with sales of over €27,500 must register for VAT.

When goods are sold from one trader to another, a VAT invoice is issued showing the price excluding VAT, the amount of VAT, and the total price including VAT.

The trading year is divided into six two-month tax periods: January–February, March–April, May–June, July–August, September–October, and November–December.

When goods are bought, VAT is paid. When goods are sold, VAT is charged and collected. If more VAT is collected than paid, the trader must submit the difference to the Revenue Commissioners, accompanied by a VAT return (form VAT 3) by the nineteenth of the month following the taxable period. If more VAT is paid than collected, the trader is entitled to claim a refund.

There are various rates of VAT, depending on the product or service sold.

CAPITAL TAXATION

CAPITAL GAINS TAX

This is tax on profit from the sale or disposal of assets such as property or shares. The rate of capital gains tax is 20 per cent, with an annual exemption of €1,270 for a single person and €2,540 for a married couple. Other exemptions include profit on the sale of the principal private residence, including up to one acre of land, and gains made on Government securities, prize bonds, lottery winnings, bonuses on Post Office or state savings schemes, and gains from life assurance policies.

CAPITAL ACQUISITIONS TAX

This is tax paid by the recipient of a gift (while the donor is alive) or an inheritance. The amount of tax paid depends on the relationship between the giver and receiver and the amount of the gift or inheritance. There is a single tax rate of 20 per cent.

Capital acquisitions tax no longer applies on the transfer of the family home, provided the following conditions are met:
(1) it is the principal private residence of the disponer or recipient;
(2) the recipient has been living in the home for three years before the transfer;
(3) the recipient has no interest in any other residential property.

Exemptions from capital acquisitions tax

(1) All gifts and inheritances between spouses.
(2) Small gifts up to €1,270 in a year.
(3) Charitable donations.
(4) Reasonable payments received from a family member and used for support.

IMPORTANT IMPLICATIONS OF TAX FOR BUSINESS

- A business must pay its taxes
- Tax is a significant administrative cost for a business
- Tax reduces profit

SIMILARITIES IN MANAGING A HOUSEHOLD AND A BUSINESS

(1) *Decision-making*
- Budgetary decisions: for example, when to trade in a car (household), when to expand (business).
- Which insurance policy to take out.

(2) *Completing documents*
- Income tax: form P12 (household), forms P60 and P35 (business).
- Current account applications.
- Loan applications.
- Vehicle tax form; driving licence.
- Proposal form for insurance.

(3) *Payment of taxes*
- PAYE.
- Capital gains tax.
- VAT and corporation tax (business).

(4) *Borrowing money*
- Applying for loans.
- Mortgage, car loan, household appliances (household).
- Buying assets or working capital (business).

(5) *Managing people*
- Family members (household), employees (business).

(6) *Managing finance and resources*
- Planning for and selecting suitable source of finance.
- Managing finance to make the best use of it.

(7) *Record-keeping*
- Keeping records of all financial affairs.
- Keeping accounts of income and expenditure, preparing budgets, comparing performance with targets set.
- Filing bank statements.

(8) *Communication*
- Between family members (household); between management, employees, customers, financial institutions, suppliers, etc. (business).

DIFFERENCES IN MANAGING A HOUSEHOLD AND A BUSINESS

(1) *Scale of activities*
- There are more people to manage in a business than in a household.
- More finance is involved in a business than in a household.
- More details must be supplied in completing forms.
- Business borrowings are much larger than a household's.
- A much greater risk is involved in a business.
- The amount of tax paid in business is much larger than in a household.

(2) *Motivating factors*
- Managing finance to improve the standard of living (household).
- Managing finance to earn a profit (business).

(3) *Legislation*
- Both organisations are subject to laws, but a business is subject to more legislation than a household, for example company law, keeping detailed financial accounts.

(4) *Market research*
- This is required by a business but not by a household.

9. HUMAN RESOURCE MANAGEMENT (HRM)

Human resource management is concerned with the management of people in a company: the process of evaluating the personnel needs of the company and finding suitable people to fill those needs.

The responsibility of the human resources manager is to ensure that good working relationships are established and maintained within the company.

Functions of human resource management

- Manpower planning
- Recruitment and selection
- Training and development
- Industrial relations: employer-employee relationships
- Performance appraisal
- Rewarding employees

Manpower planning

Identifying the type and number of human resources (employees) needed in the company and planning how these needs are to be met.

Objectives of human resource planning
- Ensuring that the company finds and keeps the human resources required.
- Ensuring that the company makes the best possible use of its human resources.

Human resources plan
- Analyse present manpower resources. Check on skills of the present work force.
- Estimate future manpower required.
- Identify those known to be leaving shortly.
- Develop a recruitment plan to ensure that the human resource needs of the company are met.

- Include recruitment, selection, training and development, promotion, redundancy, and early retirement.
- Ensure that the firm has the correct amount of human resources.

Recruitment and selection

Recruitment is the process of attracting a group of potential candidates with appropriate skills and abilities to apply for a specific vacancy that the company has available. ***Selection*** is choosing the most suitable candidate from the applicants attracted.

Stages in the recruitment and selection process:

(1) Job analysis
(2) Recruitment
(3) Selection

JOB ANALYSIS

This is specifying the job and defining what the job demands in employees' qualities and behaviour. Job analysis includes:

- job description
- person specification.

JOB DESCRIPTION

This describes the duties and responsibilities of the job, and includes:

- job title
- details of work
- place of work
- conditions of employment: pay, hours of work
- duties and responsibilities
- promotion prospects
- benefits of undertaking the job
- who to report to.

PERSON SPECIFICATION

This describes the qualities sought that best match the job description:

- age limits
- educational standard and academic qualification required
- skills, knowledge and experience required
- essential and desirable characteristics
- interests, attitudes, ambitions
- personality traits.

RECRUITMENT

Having designed a job description and person specification, the management's next task is to attract a group of suitable candidates. They must also decide whether recruitment will be internal or external.

INTERNAL SOURCES

- Transfers
- Promotions
- Demotions

EXTERNAL SOURCES

(1) *Universities, institutes of technology, job centres, FÁS*
Large employers visit universities and training centres to meet potential employees and to obtain recommendations on staffing from the college authorities.

(2) *Advertising in newspapers and magazines*
This is one of the most popular ways of recruiting employees; each week newspapers and magazines publish recruitment supplements that reach a wide audience. Every Friday the *Irish Examiner* publishes a 'Money and Jobs' supplement.

(3) *Headhunting from other companies*
This is identifying a good employee in another firm and encouraging him or her to change jobs.

(4) *Selection and human resource consultants, employment agencies*
These companies will advertise, select and interview candidates and put forward the most suitably qualified.

Whatever method of recruitment is used, the company must obtain details of the education, qualifications, abilities and aptitudes of all candidates. This will be found by asking the candidates either to submit a CV or to complete an application form.

ADVERTISING THE VACANCY

An advertisement is drawn up, using the job description and person specification. The advertisement should give details of the company and the business sector involved; details of the job, including responsibilities and who the person will be reporting to; the experience, qualifications and skills required; the pay offered; and the term of the contract.

Advertising and Promotions Executive

DUBLIN

Our client, a subsidiary of a major industrial enterprise, is a dynamic supply and distribution company in a fast-changing business sector. Effective marketing policies will form a key element of the company's strategy. MERCS Partners have been retained to recruit a marketing professional to develop such policies.

Reporting to a senior marketing executive, the person appointed will be responsible for devising and implementing marketing strategies for specific products and services and for leading and managing a team that will carry out advertising and promotional campaigns. Managing liaison with the company's advertising agency, corporate centre, regional marketing functions and other business units will also be a key task.

The successful candidate will be an experienced marketing professional with a marketing degree or relevant professional qualification. He or she will have a minimum of seven years' experience in brand management, advertising or allied areas gained in a blue-chip environment. Strong interpersonal and influencing skills, together with excellent communication ability, both written and oral, and an ability to think strategically, will be required.

An attractive payment package will apply to this appointment, which will initially be offered on a two-year fixed-term contract.

Please write, in strictest confidence, quoting the reference number 5408 and enclosing a CV, to:

MERCS Partners

128 Merrion Square
Dublin 2

SELECTION

1. Once the application forms are received, the selection process begins. Screening is carried out to allow the compiling of a short list. *Selection* means assessing this short list to try to find the most suitable person for the job.
2. The most common selection technique is the *interview.* It allows the employer to acquire information about the candidates and to assess their suitability for the job, and it enables candidates to obtain information about the job and the company.
3. A number of tests may be carried out to assist in the selection decision, such as intelligence tests, aptitude tests, and personality tests.
4. Checking of references is undertaken to confirm the information already obtained and to establish past performance.
5. Once the most suitable person is selected, an offer of the job is made in writing. A contract of employment is drawn up, signed by both parties, and given to the new employee.

Training and people development

TRAINING

Training supplies skills, knowledge and attitudes needed by employees to improve their ability to perform their job.

TYPES OF TRAINING

Induction

The initial training of new employees is called *induction.* This introduces employees to their colleagues, provides information about the firm's activities, rules, and practices, and describes health and safety rules, codes of conduct, and procedures for solving problems and disputes. Induction training aims to help new employees feel comfortable in their new jobs quickly.

On-the-job training

This is the training of employees through practical experience gained from working with and observing experienced employees performing their duties.

Off-the-job training

This is training outside the company, for example attending training courses or university courses.

DEVELOPMENT

Development prepares people for new and greater challenges that they will encounter in a more demanding job. It is a wider process than training, in that it provides employees with additional skills but also involves the general enhancement, growth and development of their skills to enable them to seek promotion and more challenging work in the company in the future.

EMPLOYER-EMPLOYEE RELATIONSHIPS (INDUSTRIAL RELATIONS)

There is one team in business, comprising two groups: the employer group and the employee group. These groups must co-operate and work together on matters such as pay and conditions to achieve good industrial relations.

If the relations between the management and the work force are good, the workers will be well motivated to work hard for the benefit of the company and its customers. If industrial relations are poor, management and workers will find the work-place a hostile environment, causing discontent, poor motivation, and a tendency to take industrial action.

Promoting good industrial relations is the responsibility of the human resource management and is essential if the firm is to get the best effort and performance from employees.

MERITS OF GOOD INDUSTRIAL RELATIONS

- Employees and employers work together and co-operate as a team.
- There is improved morale and motivation and higher productivity.
- Problems can be resolved quickly, as there are agreed procedures for solving disputes.
- Because of agreed procedures there is less risk of industrial action.
- There is reduced absenteeism and low labour turnover.

FEATURES OF POOR INDUSTRIAL RELATIONS

- Employees do not co-operate with the management, resulting in poor productivity and poor performance, lost sales, and dissatisfied customers.
- There is low morale and poor motivation of employees.
- There is a high risk of industrial conflict, as there are no agreed procedures for solving disputes.

HOW CAN HUMAN RESOURCE MANAGEMENT CREATE A GOOD INDUSTRIAL RELATIONS CLIMATE?

- Regularly communicating information to employees, encouraging better two-way communication and allowing workers to negotiate about how their jobs are done.
- Ensuring that procedures for handling disputes exist and are implemented.
- Consulting employees regularly on issues affecting them.
- Establishing agreed procedures on important issues where possible conflicts may arise, for example promotion, redundancy.
- Recognising the contribution of each employee to the general success of the company.
- Developing teams within the business—empowering workers by transferring responsibility to them.
- Drawing up agreements about work practices and always adhering to those agreements.
- Making available training and development opportunities for all employees.
- Rewarding employees fairly for effort and performance.
- Ensuring employees' job security.

TRADE UNIONS

A trade union is a body representing employees. Trade unions contribute enormously to good industrial relations by

(1) negotiating on behalf of employees on pay, working conditions, job security, and other issues;
(2) ensuring that agreements made on behalf of the workers are adhered to;
(3) representing employees who have grievances.

SHOP STEWARD

This is an elected representative of the union members in a work-place. He or she acts as a communication link between the management and the workers and also between members and their union.

REDUNDANCY

This is when an employee's contract of employment is ended because the job no longer exists or the employee is no longer required. Workers who are made redundant have a right to receive redundancy payments, in the form of a lump sum, which varies according to length of service.

Disputes about redundancy and redundancy payments can result in conflict between employees and the management. The human resources manager must ensure that employees and unions are consulted and that agreed procedures are followed.

JOB-SHARING
This is dividing the work of one full-time employee between two or more employees. Pay and benefits are shared in proportion to the hours worked.

Performance appraisal
This is the process of evaluating the performance, progress, contribution and effectiveness of an employee over a period and assessing their potential. Evaluating employees' performance and assessing their potential is an important function of human resource management.

OBJECTIVES
(1) To see whether employees are fulfilling the requirements of the job.
(2) To identify training and development needs.
(3) To identify people with promotion potential.
(4) To provide feedback to employees and the company on their performance.
(5) To identify problems and assess prospects.
(6) To improve communication between the management and employees, which strengthens commitment and motivation.
(7) To help decide on future pay levels.

Appraisal may be conducted by a manager or a supervisor who is responsible for the work of a subordinate.

APPRAISAL METHODS
(1) PERFORMANCE INDICATIONS OR JOB TARGETS
The manager or supervisor evaluates the degree to which specific objectives have been achieved.

(2) INTERVIEW
An interview between the employee and their immediate manager or supervisor is held, covering:
- review of goals set and performance achieved
- identification of problems encountered
- identification of resources needed to achieve goals, for example training.

(3) OBSERVATION
The manager or supervisor observes the incidence of good and bad performance and uses this to assess performance.

(4) REVIEWS
A report is written on each worker by the manager or supervisor.

The results of the appraisal may be used in deciding on employees' future pay, career prospects, and training and development requirements.

Reward

This is payment for work done; it can be a significant source of motivation. The pay package agreed between employer and employee is written in the contract of employment. The main determinants of pay are length of service, skills, qualifications, and ability.

FINANCIAL REWARDS

(1) Basic wage or salary

Employees receive an agreed rate of pay per week or per month. This is easy to administer and provides stability of earnings.

(2) Time rate

Employees are paid an amount per hour worked, irrespective of output. Overtime is paid at a higher rate.

(3) Piece rate

Employees are paid according to output, that is, according to how much they produce. There will be an incentive to increase productivity to increase pay; quality control must be monitored carefully.

(4) Bonus

Payment is made to employees who reach or exceed an agreed target. A bonus payment might also take the form of a fixed sum not tied to any output figure, for example a Christmas or end-of-year bonus. The bonus must be agreed in advance, and if it is to act as an incentive it should be achievable.

(5) Commission

This is payment according to the amount of sales made. Most salespersons receive a basic wage with commission as an additional incentive.

(6) Performance-related pay

This is a pay system where part of an employee's pay is based on their performance, on the principle that the opportunity to increase pay will act as an incentive to the employee to work harder and increase productivity.

OTHER REWARDS

Benefit in kind

Workers receive some of their pay in non-monetary form, such as a company car, beneficial loan, medical insurance, subsidised canteen, or shares in the company.

Profit-sharing

Employees are given a percentage of a profit they have helped to generate, in addition to normal wages; it is a type of bonus. It provides an incentive and rewards employees for their efforts in generating profit.

Share options

Employees are given an option to buy shares in the company, usually at a reduced price. They become shareholders and receive dividends on the company's profits.

Teamwork

A team is a group of people working together towards a common objective. Teamwork promotes participation and co-operation.

To function, a team must have a variety of personalities, with good communication skills. The team is responsible for achieving a clearly stated objective. They share responsibility for decisions and for the success or failure of the project.

TEAM-BUILDING

The stages in team-building are *forming, storming, norming,* and *performing.*

FORMING

- The team is brought together.
- The ideal team has a lot of expertise in the areas of marketing, production, finance, human relations, and information technology.
- Each member should be a specialist in one of the areas and competent in all other areas.
- The team should also possess personnel with good communication, problem-solving and decision-making skills.
- The team discusses the project or objective to be achieved. The members are at the stage of getting to know each other; the atmosphere is polite and courteous.

STORMING

- A leader is appointed, and key roles are established.
- Conflict may occur at this stage as different views are put forward and challenged and people compete for leadership positions.
- Arguments may occur as strong personalities emerge. People on the team are getting to know each other.

NORMING

- The team begins to work together.
- Members of the team begin to listen to and accept alternative views.
- The team leader must ensure that any conflict is resolved so that the team can work towards achieving its objective.

PERFORMING

- The group uses its strength to perform the task.
- Responsibilities are delegated to members.
- The team will work together and co-operate to achieve the objective.

BENEFITS OF TEAMS IN FIRMS

1. There is greater use of people's talents.
2. People working in teams are more likely to reach better decisions.

Career planning

A person makes decisions about his or her future career. A company must find out the career aspirations of its employees and try to match them with its needs and objectives. It must make sure its development policy is fully implemented to ensure that employees get training and promotion opportunities, so that their career plans are met without leaving the company.

10. THE CHANGING ROLE OF MANAGEMENT

Changes affecting management

Business managements today are having to cope with rapid change. Many factors are forcing the pace of change, including the following:

(1) CHANGING TASTES AND FASHIONS
A company must respond quickly and appropriately to whatever changes occur.

(2) THE ENVIRONMENT
Businesses must change as the environment changes.

(3) GLOBALISATION AND INCREASED COMPETITION
Irish companies have to change structures and organisation to compete globally.

(4) TECHNOLOGICAL DEVELOPMENTS
The internet, fax and videoconferencing have greatly facilitated information exchange and increased efficiency. They force companies to change and keep up to date. Companies must be aware of the opportunities and challenges of new technologies.

(5) STANDARDS OF EDUCATION
Employees are better educated, demand more opportunities, and are less willing to accept authority. They want more autonomy and a say in decision-making. Companies must respond to change and provide opportunities for employees.

These are the driving force behind the changing role of management and new relationships between management and employees.

Managing new relationships

In a changing business world, managements must change how they apply their skills and practise their activities, from being *controller* to *facilitator*.

CONTROLLER
In traditional organisational structures there is a clear line of authority from manager to subordinates. The manager gave orders to employees, and they were expected to carry them out without question. There was constant supervision and direction from the management. Employees had no say in decision-making: if they came up with new ideas, they had to be directed back to the management for consultation and approval.

Facilitator

In business today there are many different structures, with employees working in teams or in groups to achieve a goal. The management must facilitate this new relationship and take on the role of coach or trainer, resource-provider, and facilitator.

(A) Coach or trainer

The manager trains and develops employees' skills and fully uses their talents. He or she monitors improvements and develops them.

(B) Resource-provider

The manager provides all resources necessary to carry out the job, for example finance, training, equipment, new technology, extra staff.

(C) Facilitator

The manager supports people in their work, encouraging and stimulating the development of new ideas and tasks and building new relationships through the involvement and empowerment of employees.

NEW RELATIONSHIPS

Involvement of employees

1. The management shares knowledge, information, funds and power with employees.
2. Employees are involved in the affairs of the company through limited decision-making or through financial participation, that is, share ownership.
3. Involvement is usually at the immediate job level. Employees may be given an opportunity to consider, recommend and implement changes to the way tasks are performed.
4. The idea behind involvement is that employees have talents and knowledge about their jobs that can be used to improve performance and that involvement in decision-making encourages commitment.

Involvement of employees can be achieved through:

Job enlargement

Increasing the number of tasks and responsibilities involved in a job to provide more variety and overcome boredom among employees who have repetitive jobs. Examples are job rotation and job enrichment.

Job rotation

Widening the activities of workers by switching them between a number of work tasks, on the grounds that a greater variety will lead to greater job satisfaction.

Job enrichment

Motivating by giving employees work that allows them the opportunity to use their abilities in deciding how tasks should be performed. An enriched job should give employees more responsibility and more involvement in decision-making.

EMPOWERMENT

Empowerment is placing real power, responsibility, authority and decision-making in the hands of employees to achieve a specific goal. Responsibility and authority increase satisfaction and fulfilment and usually lead to greater rewards and enhanced prospects. They also enable potential talents to be identified and developed.

Empowerment requires that managers provide training and support and give authority and control to employees, leading to increased efficiency and a better-quality product or service for the consumer.

Empowerment is more than delegation, in that real power is given to employees. It implies a degree of self-regulation and freedom to decide what to do and how to do it. Employees are then responsible for the achievement of the goal set.

Managers spend less time supervising employees, allowing them more time to concentrate on other matters. In general it is a motivating strategy to achieve a specific goal set by the management.

Employees can influence decisions. They use their initiative. The work is more effective, and they have control over their own situation.

TOTAL QUALITY MANAGEMENT

TQM = customer-orientation + continuous improvement + empowerment + teamwork + quality assurance

Total quality management is a company's approach to achieving total quality products or services through total involvement, commitment, and a shared vision of the entire company, with the main emphasis being on satisfying customers' needs and expectations. It is a way of managing a company so that every job is carried out properly the first time and every time. It attempts to prevent mistakes and problems arising rather than having to find and correct them.

Total quality management involves:

Customer-orientation

This means finding out customers' requirements, designing and producing a product or service to meet or exceed customers' requirements.

Continuous improvement

This means designing the production process so that tasks are carried out correctly the first time and monitoring performance to ensure that continuous improvement takes place. The effort to improve quality must be continuous, leading to quality products or services.

Empowerment

Workers must be given responsibility, authority, and control. They must be allowed to make decisions and make changes where necessary.

Teamwork

There must be teamwork and co-operation to ensure quality improvement.

Quality assurance

Every employee should be trained in quality control and be responsible for producing goods or services to meet the quality standard. Quality assurance means the management ensuring that the product or service is of the highest quality and that quality standards are agreed and met throughout the company to ensure customers' satisfaction and doing everything possible to prevent quality problems.

QUALITY CIRCLES

Quality circles can be used to achieve TQM. Small groups of employees are brought together regularly to identify, discuss and solve problems relating to quality and efficiency. They put forward ideas for improving a process or a product. The aim is to develop teamwork, bring forward ideas and improve motivation as well as solving problems.

BENCHMARKING

This means identifying how well a firm's performance stands up against standards set by the best-performing manufacturers in the market. By adopting those standards it will improve further.

WORLD-CLASS MANUFACTURING

This is a term used to describe the world's leading businesses. They continuously produce top-quality goods and services to the highest standards.

HOW TO ACHIEVE TQM

- Successful TQM requires the continuous commitment of the senior management. This commitment must be action-oriented and must be a whole-organisation approach.
- Quality must be the responsibility of all employees and all departments.
- The approach must be the prevention of quality defects rather than trying to identify mistakes after they have happened. The theme should be one of continuous improvement.
- Successful TQM can give rise to internationally recognised quality standards, such as ISO 9000 certification.

THE BENEFITS OF SUCCESSFUL IMPLEMENTATION OF TQM

- Improved quality through quality controls
- Increased customer satisfaction
- Increased job satisfaction
- Improved company image
- Greater productivity
- Reduction in costs: fewer mistakes, fewer delays, better use of time
- Improved competitive position—if it leads to lower prices and higher quality.

MANAGING CHANGE

Because of the changing nature of the business environment, the management of change has become increasingly important in business.

Change today is a continuous process: as soon as a company responds to one change it is faced with another.

Companies must adapt to meet change. Managers and employees must be willing to change and to anticipate future developments in the company. There must be constant negotiations and communications in the introduction of change.

STRATEGY FOR MANAGING CHANGE

Change management is a process of planning, preparing, implementing and evaluating changes in business strategies.

The essential element of change management is trust. Employees must have faith in the motives and the competence of managers, otherwise they may not help implement the desired change. A strategy for introducing and managing change must be developed to overcome resistance and remove people's fears and worries about the future.

THE SUCCESSFUL MANAGEMENT OF CHANGE REQUIRES

- establishing in advance a sense of *common purpose and trust* between employees and management
- *communication* between management and employees, explaining the need for change and the type of change being proposed, with an attempt at getting the reasons understood and accepted
- *negotiations* between management and employees on possible options for implementing change, ensuring that employees' views have a significant impact on the eventual strategy
- *financial resources* for investing in new products or methods and for the training and development of employees in new skills required as a result of the change
- *drawing up new agreements* to implement change
- setting a clear *timetable* for the entire process of change and monitoring progress to ensure that the change is progressing as agreed.

Managing new technology

Technology is the application of scientific principles and knowledge in the development and operation of industrial processes, systems, and products.

The technological environment is constantly changing. All companies must keep up to date with technological developments.

Technological developments mean that companies can increase efficiency with significant cost savings and improved quality output.

HOW TECHNOLOGY CHANGES THE ROLE OF MANAGEMENT

PRODUCTION TECHNOLOGY

Technology affects the production techniques used by companies. Computers are used extensively for product design and manufacturing.

Advances in production technologies have resulted in high levels of automation, with robots instead of people working on assembly lines.

Computer-aided design (CAD)

CAD is the use of computers in the design of new products or the redesign of existing products. Designs can be shown on a computer display and redrawn to produce different versions. CAD can eliminate the need for prototypes.

Computer-aided manufacture (CAM)

CAM uses computers to assist in the manufacture of goods. Computers are used to control such industrial processes as brewing, chemical manufacture, and oil-refining.

CAM imparts information to machines and robots employed in the production systems. It makes it possible for production scheduling to be completed efficiently and quickly.

INFORMATION TECHNOLOGY

Information technology is the gathering, storing, processing and distribution of information using computers and telecommunications.

Communications

Managements use technology to communicate; the more advanced the technology, the easier it is to communicate and to manage companies. Developments such as the internet, e-mail, EDI, fax, ISDN and videoconferencing have greatly facilitated information exchange. Distance is no longer a problem.

Productivity and motivation

Many companies are using computers, the internet and fax to enable employees and managers to work from home. Work can be arranged across different time zones.

Productivity and motivation may increase, because employees are free to work at home at their own pace.

Decision-making

Managements use computers in the area of financial forecasting and planning. Data can be acquired at the push of a button, calculations can be computed on data, and changes can be made to budgets, making possible quicker decision-making by the management.

Marketing

Many companies use a web site to provide information about goods and services, and they can carry out market research on the internet.

Giving information

Banks and other financial institutions can provide information on the internet, such as interest rates and mortgage rates.

Global business opportunities

Information technology creates global business opportunities. Managements must avail of these opportunities.

IMPACT OF TECHNOLOGY ON PERSONNEL

Global communication

This is made possible through advanced technology.

Teleworking

Managers and employees can work from home and can be linked to the office by telephone, fax, and modem.

Training

Computers are widely used in the training of employees.

Reduced work force
Fewer employees are required in offices and on production lines.

Advanced skills
These are required by companies for the operation of the new technologies.

More competent managers
Managers with skills and training in TQM and the empowerment of workers are required.

Increased business efficiency
Managers and salespersons can communicate instantly with the office through mobile phones, fax, and laptop computers.

Changes in occupations
There is a move from traditional labour-intensive industries to knowledge-based technological jobs, for example computer programmers, computer analysts.

IMPACT OF TECHNOLOGY ON BUSINESS COSTS

Investment in technology—the capital costs of introducing communication equipment and production equipment and installation and maintenance costs.

Better-quality goods—increased quality, less waste, fewer returns, and fewer complaints, all leading to cost savings.

Training costs—proper training of employees in the use of technology.

Reduction in cost of production—using CAM and CAD.

Delayering—changes in organisational structures with the removal of tiers in a company's hierarchy; middle managers are susceptible to redundancy, with increased redundancy payments but a lower wages bill.

Teleworking—can benefit a company by reducing the office space required and reducing administration costs.

Less travel—less commuting of managers to meetings with communication through videoconferencing.

IMPACT OF TECHNOLOGY ON BUSINESS OPPORTUNITIES

Business opportunities—in the manufacture of computer hardware, software, fax machines, videoconferencing equipment, mobile phones, etc.

New ways of conducting business—for example, insurance and pensions companies using laptop computers.

Teleworking—a home office linked to the business.

Videoconferencing—removing the need to travel to meetings.

Development of new services—mobile phone networks, ISDN network, internet service providers, EDI service.

Increased productivity—more sales, more profit.

New industries, new markets—the creation of new industries and new markets, for example the development of Playstation Portable (PSP) by Sony, portable DVD players, iPod Nano by Apple and Xbox 360.

Setting up web sites—giving every business equal opportunity, regardless of size.

11. MONITORING THE BUSINESS

Accounts and business information

Financial information is important to a business, as it tells the owners or shareholders and the management how the business is performing and allows them to make decisions. It also provides useful information to other interested parties.

FINAL ACCOUNTS

The financial statements used by a business are:

- trading account
- profit and loss account
- balance sheet.

TRADING ACCOUNT

This shows the gross profit or gross loss made by a business in the trading period.

Sales – cost of sales = gross profit or gross loss
Cost of sales = opening stock + purchases – closing stock

PROFIT AND LOSS ACCOUNT

This shows the net profit or net loss made by a business in the trading period, that is, profit after the deduction of all expenses, such as rent, insurance, telephone, etc. It also shows how profit is allocated, that is, either paid out as dividends or re-invested in the business.

BALANCE SHEET

This is a statement of the assets, liabilities and share capital of a business on a particular day.

assets: property a business owns
liabilities: debts a business owes
share capital: money invested in the company by its owners or shareholders (money owed to shareholders)

SAMPLE TRADING AND PROFIT AND LOSS ACCOUNT

Trading and profit and loss account for the year ending 31/12/2014

Value of all sales during the year →	Sales			200,000
	Less cost of sales			
	Opening stock		20,000	
	Purchases		130,000	
	Cost of goods available for sale		150,000	
	Less closing stock		(30,000)	
Cost of goods actually sold during the year →	Cost of sales			(120,000)
Profit made on buying and selling →	Gross profit			80,000
Running expenses →	<u>Less expenses</u>			
	Distribution, e.g. carriage out		15,000	
	Administration, e.g. insurance		10,000	
	Financial, e.g. audit fees		5,000	(30,000)
Profit after deducting expenses →	Net profit			50,000
Profit left over from the previous year →	Add opening balance			10,000
				60,000
Amount of net profit distributed to shareholders →	Less dividends			(20,000)
Profit retained and re-invested in the company →	Retained earnings			40,000

Sample balance sheet

Balance sheet on 31/12/2014

Permanent assets in the business	Fixed assets			
	Land			180,000
	Buildings			100,000
	Machinery			50,000
	Total fixed assets			330,000
Assets continuously changing from one form to another and easily turned into cash	Current assets			
	Closing stock	30,000		
	Debtors	50,000		
	Bank	20,000		
	Cash	10,000	110,000	
Debts that have to be repaid within one year	Less liabilities falling due within one year			
	Creditors	30,000		
	Dividends due	20,000	50,000	
Finance available for the day-to-day running of the business (CA – CL)	Working capital			60,000
	Total net assets			390,000
Where the capital comes from to finance assets	Financed by		Authorised	Issued
Maximum amount of capital the company can raise through selling shares / *Actual amount of shares sold to shareholders*	300.000 Ordinary shares		300,000	200,000
Amount retained by the company for future use	Reserves			
	Retained earnings			40,000
Debts that will be repaid in the long term, usually between five and twenty years	Liabilities falling due after one year			
	Term loan secured			150,000
	Capital employed			390,000

Where the money comes from to finance assets: ordinary share capital + reserves + long-term liabilities

Ratio analysis

Accounts must be interpreted or made clear for the benefit of interested parties. Ratios are used to show the relationship between figures; these figures are then compared with

(*a*) the previous year's figures,
(*b*) those of other firms in the same industry, and
(*c*) industry norms.

INTERPRETATION OF ACCOUNTS USING RATIOS

A company can be assessed in the following areas:

- profitability—the effectiveness of the management in using business resources
- liquidity—the ability of the business to pay its short-term debts
- debt-equity ratio—how the business is structured financially.

(1) PROFITABILITY RATIOS

Profitability ratios show how successful the management was in making profit in the company. The profitability ratios are:

Ratio	*Formula*	*Answer*	*Information given by ratio*
Return on investment	$\frac{\text{net profit} \times 100\%}{\text{capital employed}}$	Percentage %	Shows the return on the total amount of funds invested in the company; should be compared with the return from financial institutions and other firms in the same line of business.
Gross profit percentage/ margin	$\frac{\text{gross profit} \times 100\%}{\text{sales}}$	Percentage %	This is gross profit as a percentage of sales. It tells us how much gross profit was made on each €1 of sales; compare with last year or with other firms in the same line of business.
Net profit percentage/ margin	$\frac{\text{net profit} \times 100\%}{\text{sales}}$	Percentage %	This is net profit as a percentage of sales. It tells us how much net profit was made on each €1 of sales; should be compared with last year or with other firms in the same line of business

(2) LIQUIDITY RATIOS

Liquidity is the ability of a company to pay its short-term debts as they fall due. It measures whether the business can survive in the future. Liquidity is measured by subtracting current liabilities from current assets.

Working capital is the day-to-day finance available for running a business, that is, assets that can be converted into cash and is available to pay debts.

Formula: current assets – current liabilities = working capital.

If working capital is positive, the firm is said to be *liquid*. If working capital is negative, the firm is said to be *overtrading* (that is, it cannot pay its debts as they arise).

THE LIQUIDITY RATIOS ARE:

Ratio	*Formula*	*Information given by ratio*
Current ratio (working capital ratio)	current assets: current liabilities	Tells us whether the company has enough current assets to pay its current liabilities. The recommended current ratio is 2:1, that is, current assets should be double current liabilities.
Acid test ratio (quick asset ratio)	current assets – closing stock: current liabilities	Stock is omitted from current assets as it may not be quickly turned into cash; it is a better measure of the liquidity of firm. The recommended ratio is 1:1, that is, a healthy firm should be able to pay current liabilites out of liquid assets.

(3) DEBT-EQUITY RATIO

This shows the financial structure of the company.

The debt-equity ratio (gearing) shows the relationship between debt capital and equity capital in the company.

debt capital = long-term debt + preference share capital

equity capital = ordinary share capital + reserves

Formula: debt capital: equity capital

If debt is less than equity, the company has low gearing (low risk). If debt is greater than equity, the company has high gearing (high risk). If debt is equal to equity, the company is neutrally geared.

ADVANTAGES OF LOW DEBT-EQUITY RATIO (LOW GEARING)

Owners' capital

The greater part of the capital of the company is provided by the owners.

Profit available for dividends

There are no major interest commitments; a large proportion of the profit is available to pay dividends or to re-invest in the company.

Future borrowings

This allows a business the choice of more borrowing in future, as interest payment on future loans could be easily paid.

Easy to sell additional ordinary shares

It will be easy to sell additional ordinary shares in the future because of good dividends.

CONSEQUENCES OF HIGH DEBT-EQUITY RATIO (HIGH GEARING)

High interest

High interest payments on borrowings must be met before the company can pay dividends to shareholders or re-invest profits in the company.

Difficulty of raising finance in future

It may be difficult to raise further finance, as assets may already be tied up as security on existing borrowings.

Low dividends, low share price

If profits fall, interest on borrowings must still be paid. There may be little profit left to pay dividends to ordinary shareholders; shareholders may become dissatisfied with their investment and may sell their shares, resulting in a fall in share price.

Management pressure

There is great pressure on the management to produce profits to pay interest and to have profit available to pay ordinary share dividends.

Difficult to sell additional shares

It may be difficult to sell additional ordinary shares in the future because of poor outlook on dividends.

IMPORTANCE OF ACCOUNTS AND BUSINESS INFORMATION IN MONITORING PERFORMANCE

Performance

They indicate how efficient the management was in generating profit and in general performance.

Financial position

They determine the real financial position and show trends over time.

Planning

Financial information is important for future planning and decision-making.

Plans and objectives

They show whether plans and objectives are being achieved.

Liquidity

They show details of liquidity and cash flow and the ability of the business to survive in the future.

Financial structure
They show how the company is structured financially—whether by the owners (equity) or outside debt.

Unprofitable areas
They draw attention to unprofitable areas of the business or unprofitable products.

Comparisons
They enable the firm to compare itself with other firms in the industry and with industry norms.

Assess risk
They enable financial institutions and investors to assess the risk involved in providing finance in the future.

USERS OF ACCOUNTS AND BUSINESS INFORMATION

OWNERS (SHAREHOLDERS)

The owners will want to know
- how successful the management was in running the business and using the company's resources to generate profit
- how much profit the business has made
- how much they can expect in dividends
- the risk attached to their investment
- the security of their investment.

MANAGEMENT

The management will want to know
- how the business is performing; accounts information is vital to the management in assessing the performance of the business in achieving its objectives; it is also used in planning, decision-making, and controlling.

FINANCIAL INSTITUTIONS

Financial institutions will want to know
- the ability of the business to repay existing loans, overdrafts and interest when due
- whether to advance finance to the business in future.

TRADE CREDITORS AND SUPPLIERS

Creditors and suppliers will want to know
- whether the business can pay for goods supplied on credit
- whether it is advisable to grant credit in future.

POTENTIAL INVESTORS

Investors will want to know
- whether the company is a good investment
- how to compare different companies to find the top performers in profit and return.

GOVERNMENT

State agencies will want to know
- how grants were spent
- whether the company is adhering to legal requirements.

REVENUE COMMISSIONERS

The Revenue Commissioners will want to know
- how much profit the company is making to assess it for tax purposes.

CUSTOMERS

Customers will want to assess
- the firm's reliability as a supplier
- the future viability of the company.

EMPLOYEES

Employees will want to assess
- security of employment and the prospects of promotion
- the future prospects of the company
- its ability to meet wage demands in the future
- its ability to expand its work force in future.

COMPETITORS

Competitors will want to assess
- how the business is performing
- its strengths and weaknesses
- its future potential.

GENERAL PUBLIC

The public will be interested in
- the amount of finance invested in the community
- an assessment of the employment potential in the area
- the effects of the business on the local environment
- range of activities and development plans.

PERFORMANCE OF A BUSINESS OVER TIME

Sample question and solution

Trading and profit and loss account of Thompson Ltd for the years ending

31/12/2014	€	31/12/2015	€
Sales	280,000	Sales	540,000
Less cost of sales	168,000	Less cost of sales	216,000
Gross profit	112,000	Gross profit	324,000
Less expenses	89,200	Less expenses	267,000
Net profit	22,800	Net profit	57,000
Add opening balance	6,600	Add opening balance	25,000
	29,400		82,000
Less dividends	4,400	Less dividends	22,000
Retained earnings	25,000	Retained earnings	60,000

Balance sheet of Thompson Ltd on 31/12/2014 and 31/12/2015

			€			€
Fixed assets						
Land			100,000			122,000
Buildings			70,000			70,000
Machinery			40,000			40,000
Total fixed assets			210,000			232,000
Current assets						
Closing stock	20,000			25,000		
Debtors	10,000			20,000		
Bank	5,000			10,000		
Cash	5,000	40,000		5,000	60,000	
Less liabilities falling due within one year						
Creditors	55,600			8,000		
Dividends due	4,400	60,000		22,000	30,000	
Working capital			(20,000)			30,000
Total net assets			190,000			262,000
Financed by		*Authorised*	*Issued*		*Authorised*	*Issued*
300,000 ordinary shares		300,000	145,000		300,000	170,000
Reserves						
Retained earnings			25,000			60,000
Liabilities falling due after one year						
Term loan—secured			20,000			32,000
Capital employed			190,000			262,000

Assume that you are a financial consultant, Thomas Ryan, of 20 Beech Road, Wexford. Study the final accounts and balance sheets. Prepare a report, using today's date, for the shareholders of Thompson Ltd

(*a*) comparing the performance of the company in the two years under the headings of profitability and liquidity (using suitable ratios),

(*b*) contrasting the sources of finance used,

(*c*) commenting on the importance of the debt-equity ratio in deciding on further sources of finance, and

(*d*) identifying suitable assets the business could use as security for a loan.

SUGGESTED SOLUTION

Report to the shareholders of Thompson Ltd

20 Beech Road
Wexford

15 June 2016

Comparison of performance of Thompson Ltd in years 2014 and 2015
Prepared by *Thomas Ryan, financial consultant*

INTRODUCTION

The following is a report on the financial affairs of Thompson Ltd, as requested, under the following headings:

Profitability and liquidity
Sources of finance
Debt equity
Suitable assets as security.

Relevant ratios are attached to the report.

FINDINGS

PROFITABILITY

The company is profitable. Profit in 2015 is bigger than in 2014.

	2014	2015
Gross margin	40%	60%
Net margin	8.14%	10.56%
Return on investment	12%	21.75%

Thompson Ltd is profitable, and its profitability is increasing. The gross margin has increased by 20% from 2014 to 2015. The net margin increased by 2.42%. Return on investment increased by 9.75%.

These rates are usually compared with the prevailing interest rates in financial institutions or the average return on investment in the particular industry at the present time.

→

Liquidity

The company had a negative working capital in 2014. It therefore has a liquidity problem. In 2015 working capital is positive.

	2014	2015
Working capital ratio	*0.66 : 1*	*2 : 1*
Acid test ratio	*0.33 : 1*	*1.16 : 1*

The liquidity position is improving, and in 2015 it is at the recommended levels of 2:1 (working capital) and 1:1 (acid test).

SOURCES OF FINANCE USED

Share capital

An extra €25,000 was raised through the issue of shares during 2015. Issued capital stands at €170,000 at the end of the year, but a further €130,000 can be raised through shares, as the authorised capital stands at €300,000. The cost of this source is a dividend payable out of profits.

Retained earnings

Reserves available to the business rose from €25,000 in 2014 to €60,000 in 2015, reflecting good profit performance in the year. This source is available out of profits. Shareholders have to forgo these reserves in cash if they are invested in the business.

Long-term loan secured

A new loan of €12,000 was raised during 2015, bringing total long-term loans to €32,000. This loan is secured on fixed assets, which stand in the balance sheet at €232,000 at the end of the year. There is adequate scope for using the remaining fixed assets to secure further debt should this be needed. Interest rates payable on the loan may vary over time and increase costs.

Debt-equity ratio

The debt-equity ratio is the ratio that exists between the long-term debt of a business and equity share capital, that is, ordinary shares plus reserves.

2014	2015
1 : 8.5	1 : 7.1

The debt-equity ratio is very low.

A small loan of €12,000 was raised in 2015. The total long-term debt stands at €32,000 at the end of the year. There is adequate scope for raising further capital from debt (loans) in the future. Financial institutions would view this business as a reasonable risk, because of the high proportion of capital being invested by the owners compared with the amount of debt capital.

There is adequate scope for using the title deeds of land or buildings as security for a loan. The amount of security available stands at €160,000, which is €192,000 less €32,000 already secured on the existing loan.

Conclusion

This business is in excellent financial condition, and the future can be planned for with confidence.

Thomas Ryan

Financial consultant

Appendix
Ratio analysis

Ratio	*Formula*	*Figures*		*Answers*	
		2014	**2015**	**2014**	**2015**
Gross margin	$\frac{\text{gross profit} \times 100\%}{\text{sales}}$	$\frac{112{,}000 \times 100\%}{280{,}000}$	$\frac{324{,}000 \times 100\%}{540{,}000}$	40%	60%
Net margin	$\frac{\text{net profit} \times 100\%}{\text{sales}}$	$\frac{22{,}800 \times 100\%}{280{,}000}$	$\frac{57{,}000 \times 100\%}{540{,}000}$	8.14%	10.56%
Return on investment	$\frac{\text{net profit} \times 100\%}{\text{capital employed}}$	$\frac{22{,}800 \times 100\%}{190{,}000}$	$\frac{57{,}000 \times 100\%}{262{,}000}$	12%	21.75%
Working capital ratio	CA : CL	40,000 : 60,000	60,000 : 30,000	0.66 : 1	2 : 1
Acid test ratio	CA – stock : CL	20,000 : 60,000	35,000 : 30,000	0.33 : 1	1.16 : 1
Debt-equity ratio	debt : equity	20,000 : 170,000	32,000 : 230,000	1 : 8.5	1 : 7.1

THE USE OF SPREADSHEETS IN PREPARING FINAL ACCOUNTS

A spreadsheet is a grid made up of rows and columns in which calculations are carried out. When a change is made to a cell that is connected by means of a formula to another cell, the number in that cell is changed automatically. A spreadsheet program on a computer is used to create spreadsheets for financial calculations, including accounts, budgets, stock records, payroll, business planning, and break-even analysis.

Spreadsheets are used in business for forecasting because they will recalculate the outcome for each set of values that is entered. They allow the user to ask 'what if' questions and immediately see a result: for example, if sales might rise by 10 per cent, the company could see at a glance what the implications were for income, costs, and profit. Final accounts can be stored, accessed, edited and printed quickly. Projections can be made based on budgeted figures.

KEY TERMS

These are some of the more important terms introduced in unit 4:

acid test ratio	net margin	shares
current and savings accounts	net pay	spreadsheet
dismissal	net profit	teamwork
empowerment	overtime	total quality management (TQM)
form 12	performance appraisal	training and development
gross margin	personnel	utmost good faith
gross pay	P45, P60, P21	working capital
gross profit	proposal form	working capital ratio (current ratio)
indemnity	recruitment	
insurable interest	retained earning	
job description	redundancy	
job sharing	return on investment (ROI)	
loan	selection	

LEGISLATION DISCUSSED IN UNIT 4

Industrial Relations Act (1990)

ON COMPLETION OF UNIT 4 YOU SHOULD BE ABLE TO

(1) outline the differences between managing a household and managing a business;
(2) explain the importance of finance, insurance and tax implications for business;
(3) identify activities common to managing a business and a household, including the completion of relevant forms;
(4) understand the similarities and the differences between these activities in a household and in a business;
(5) calculate and interpret the main profitability and liquidity ratios and debt-equity ratio;
(6) explain the main functions of human resource management;
(7) explain the changing role of a manager, from controller to facilitator;
(8) understand the importance of employee participation;
(9) understand how technology changes the role of management;
(10) understand the relationship between employers and employees and the role of trade unions;
(11) understand the central role of human resources in management **(HL)**;
(12) identify the strategies for managing change **(HL)**;
(13) discuss the importance of total quality management **(HL)**;
(14) understand the importance of accounts and business data in the monitoring of the business enterprise **(HL)**.

Examination-style question and solution

Household and business manager

(A) 'Managing a household is similar to managing a business enterprise, in the areas of finance, insurance and taxation.' In your opinion, is this statement valid? Explain the reasons for your answer. **(30 marks)**
(B) Illustrate the relationship between risk and the cost of insurance. **(10 marks)**
(C) Calculate the average net (take-home) pay per month for an employee from the following figures: **(20 marks)**

Annual gross pay:	€60,000
Total annual tax credits:	€3,120
The standard rate cut off point is	€32,000

PAYE is deducted at 20 per cent on the first €32,000 and on the balance at 42 per cent.
PRSI and health contributions are charged at 6.75 per cent.

Suggested solution

(A) Yes. This statement is valid, for the following reasons:

Finance
Households and businesses have to manage their finances carefully by
—keeping accounts of their actual income and expenditure;
—preparing budgets and comparing targets with the outcome;
—applying for loans at the appropriate time and appropriate rate of interest;
—planning for and selecting suitable sources of finance.

Insurance
Households and businesses have to
—take out appropriate and adequate insurance, that is, to insure their houses or premises and their contents or stocks;
—complete proposal forms;
—apply risk reduction measures in order to minimise premiums.

Tax
Households and businesses have to
—pay their taxes on time and at the appropriate rates, that is, taxes on income (PAYE and corporation profits tax) and on purchases (VAT);
—complete the relevant forms—P12, P60, and P35 (for business);
—apply tax reduction schemes to minimise the amount of tax due.

(B) The relationship between risk and cost of insurance is:

THE HIGHER THE RISK, THE HIGHER THE COST.

Example: Pat is twenty years old and is taking out his first insurance. He has a provisional driving licence. He will be a higher risk and will therefore pay a higher premium than Eileen, aged forty, who has been insured for a number of years and has a full licence.

(C)
MONTHLY NET PAY CALCULATION (TAX CREDIT SYSTEM)

Annual gross pay			60,000
Income tax: €32,000 at 20%	6,400		
€28,000 at 42%	11,760		
Gross income tax before tax credits		18,160	
Less tax credits		3,120	
Income tax payable		15,040	
Add PRSI: 6.75% of gross pay		4,050	
Total income tax and PRSI			19,090
Net Annual Income			€40,910
Monthly net pay			**€3,409.16**

Examination-style questions

Human resource management

(**A**) Describe three methods of recruiting new employees for work in a business enterprise. **(15 marks)**

(**B**) Explain the process of team development, and outline two benefits of teams in business organisations. **(30 marks)**

(**C**) 'Total quality management (TQM) is important to both customers and the business.' Discuss. **(15 marks)**

Suggested solution

(A) *The following are three methods of recruiting new employees for work in a business:*

(1) *Advertising in newspapers and magazines.*

This is one of the most popular ways of recruiting new employees, as each week the papers publish recruitment supplements, and magazines and newspapers reach a wide audience.

(2) *Headhunting from other businesses.*

This means identifying a good employee in another firm and encouraging him or her to change jobs.

(3) *Recruiting from universities and training centres.*

Large employers visit colleges to meet potential employees and to obtain recommendations from college personnel.

(B) *The process of team development might take place as follows:*

Objectives are set for the team, and people with the right skills are then selected. The team is ***formed*** *and begins to meet and discuss the project.*

Team members argue with each other until their various roles are clarified. This is called ***'storming'.***

The team then begins to work as an effective unit; in other words, ***'norming'*** *takes place. The team then begins to* ***perform*** *and achieve its goals.*

The following are two benefits of teams in business organisations:

1. *There is a greater use of people's talents in businesses.*
2. *People working in teams are likely to reach better decisions.*

(C) *Total quality management means that the policy of the business is to place the emphasis on the customer. It ensures that the processes and products are of the highest quality.*

Total quality management is important to customers because *under this system, employees are enabled to produce goods and services that meet customers' needs in quality and price.*

Total quality management is important to the business because *it enables the firm to control its processes, quality and costs, so that its output sells well, generates income, and adds to profit.*

Examination-style question

Monitoring the business
Incorporating report-writing

Trading and profit and loss account of Premier Ltd for the years 2015 and 2016:

	2016	2015
Net profit:	€30,000	€20,000

Balance sheet on:		31/12/2016		31/12/2015
		€		€
Total fixed assets		190,000		140,000
Current assets	21,000		12,000	
Less liabilities falling due within one year	17,000		10,000	
Working capital		4,000		2,000
Total net assets		194,000		142,000
Financed by	**Authorised**	**Issued**	**Authorised**	**Issued**
300,000 ordinary shares	300,000	140,000	300,000	126,000
Reserves				
Retained earnings		35,000		16,000
Liabilities falling due after one year				
Term loan secured		19,000		
Capital employed		194,000		142,000

(**A**) Assume you are Mary Mulligan, managing director of Premier Ltd, suppliers of business information. Study the final accounts and balance sheets. Prepare a **report** for the directors of the company, on today's date,

(*a*) comparing the return on investment for the two years,

(*b*) contrasting the sources of finance used in the two years, and

(*c*) commenting on the importance of the debt-equity ratio in deciding on further sources of finance. **(45 marks)**

(**B**) Explain the importance of a cash flow forecast in the preparation of a business plan. **(15 marks)**

Suggested solution

Report to the directors of Premier Ltd
Prepared by Mary Mulligan, managing director

Introduction
The following is a report on the financial affairs of Premier Ltd, as requested, under the following headings: Return on investment, Sources of finance, Debt-equity ratio.

Findings

(1) **Return on investment**

Return on investment in 2016 was 30,000/194,000 = 15.46%. In 2015 it was 20,000/142,000 = 14.08%.

The return on investment has increased by 1.38% from 2015 to 2016. This is a growth of nearly 10% in one year. (These rates are usefully compared with the prevailing interest rates in financial institutions.)

(2) **Share capital**

An extra €14,000 was raised through the issue of shares during 2016. The issued share capital stands at €140,000 at the end of the year, but a further €160,000 can be raised through shares, as the authorised capital stands at €300,000. The cost of this source is the dividend payable out of profit.

Retained earnings

Reserves available to the business rose from €16,000 in 2015 to €35,000 in 2016, reflecting the good profit performance in the year. The source is readily available out of profits. The shareholders have to forgo the benefit of the reserves in cash if they are invested in the business.

Long-term loan secured

A new loan of €19,000 was raised during 2016 and secured on the fixed assets, which stand in the balance sheet at €190,000 at the end of the year. There is adequate scope for using the remaining fixed assets to secure further debt should this be needed. The interest rates payable for the loan may vary over time and may indeed increase costs.

(3) The debt-equity ratio is the ratio between the long-term debt of a business and the equity share capital, that is, the ordinary share capital plus the reserves.

2016: 19,000 : 175,000 = 1 : 9.2
2015: 0 : 126,000

A small loan was raised during 2016, but there is adequate scope for raising further capital from debt (loans) in the future, as the debt-equity ratio is only 1:9 at present. Financial institutions would view this business as a reasonable risk, because of the high proportion of risk capital being invested by the owners compared with the amount of fixed-interest debt capital.

→

Conclusion
The business is in excellent financial condition, and the future can be planned for with confidence.

Mary Mulligan

Mary Mulligan
Managing director

(B) A cash flow forecast is a bookkeeping statement predicting the movement of money into and out of a business. It shows the future cash inflows and outflows of the business and their sources and timing. This assists with business decision-making, that is, it shows where cash will be spent.

It draws attention to possible shortages in the future. Negotiations on meeting the cash needs of the business can begin in good time.

The measurement of budgeted figures against actual figures over time helps to control the cash of the business.

Practice questions—Section 1

1. A house valued at €90,000 is insured for €60,000. A fire causes €24,000 worth of damage.
   (*a*) Calculate the amount of compensation to be paid.

   ____

   (*b*) Explain your answer.

   ____
   ____
   ____

Workings

2.

	2014	2013
Fixed assets	€100,000	€140,000
Current assets	€75,000	€60,000
Current liabilities	€35,000	€50,000

Workings
2014 2013

(a) Calculate the current ratios for each year. 2014.——:——, 2013——:——
(b) Comment on the trend.

____
____

3. TQM helps business because

4. Performance appraisal involves:

5. Which principle of insurance do you feel is the most important one?

Explain why.

6. Empowerment of workers means

7. Identify two contrasting activities in managing a household and managing a business.

Revision questions
Question 1

Managing / Business in action

Management activities are very relevant to the efficient running of both households and businesses.

(**A**) Compare the activities common to managing a business and managing a household. **(20 marks)**

(**B**) Contrast the contents of the cash flow forecast that would be prepared for a household and the one that would be prepared for a business. **(20 marks)**

(**C**) Discuss the importance of choosing the correct source of long-term finance for the expansion of a business. Refer to two long-term sources of finance in your answer **(20 marks)**

[60 marks]

Question 2

Managing

(**A**) Explain the importance of good financial information (for example financial ratios) to the management team of a business. Use examples to illustrate your answer. **(20 marks)**

(**B**) Examine the following figures from Savin Ltd.

	2015	2014
Current assets	€91,500	€80,450
Current liabilities	€62,400	€43,200
Closing stock	€49,000	€40,100
Equity share capital	€250,000	€250,000
Long-term debt	€253,000	€120,000
Retained earnings	€20,000	€18,000

(*a*) Calculate for 2015 and 2014
—the working capital ratios
—the acid test ratios
—the debt-equity ratios.

(*b*) Applying your knowledge, comment on two trends that you notice developing in the business. Suggest what you would do about them.

(40 marks)

[60 marks]

Unit 5: Business in Action

This unit views business as a living, dynamic activity. It examines a business start-up from the generation of the original idea to the development of the business plan. There is an emphasis on the relationship between the business and its customers and on how the business must develop in response to changes in the market.

Objective: To enable pupils to understand the stages involved in setting up a business enterprise.

12. Identifying Opportunities

Business ideas and opportunities come from a wide variety of sources. These include *internal sources* and *external sources.*

Internal sources of opportunity

(1) Hobbies and interests
Sporting or craft interests can be a source of new venture ideas, for example furniture, boatbuilding, sailboarding.

(2) Suggestion schemes
Ideas for new products or services can be collected from employees.

(3) Marketing manager
The marketing manager and his or her research staff may come up with ideas for a new product or service.

(4) Research and development
Some companies have an R&D department, staffed with engineers and scientists who are concerned with both invention (discovering new products) and innovation (bringing these inventions to the market).

(5) Sales personnel
Sales representatives may generate ideas for a new product or service.

(6) Brainstorming
This is a technique for generating ideas in which members of a group express ideas as they think of them. The objective is to compile a list of ideas that can later be considered and evaluated in greater depth.

(7) UNEXPECTED OUTCOME
While searching for a treatment for heart diseases, Pfizer Pharmaceutical Company discovered a treatment for impotence, Viagra, a multi-million-dollar product.

(8) RESEARCH
By undertaking market research, a company obtains feedback from customers, which may result in ideas for a new product or service.

(9) IMPORT SUBSTITUTION
This means producing a raw material or product that was being imported.

External sources of opportunity

(1) CUSTOMERS
Consumers can often suggest ideas for improvement in a product; or innovative ideas may come from customers' complaints or from customers' changing needs: for example, many consumers are demanding organically grown food and low-fat products. Observing customers' behaviour can often lead to ideas.

(2) POTENTIAL BUYERS
Potential customers may approach a business with ideas for products or services they would like to see on the market.

(3) COMPETITORS
Ideas may come by monitoring competitors, seeing what products they are developing and what customers they are neglecting.

(4) ADVERTISING AGENCIES AND BUSINESS CONSULTANTS
These agencies may come up with ideas for a product or service.

(5) PRIVATE RESEARCH
A business may carry out research or surveys to find out what product or service is not provided or is of poor quality.

(6) SPOTTING PRODUCTS ABROAD
Travel abroad makes it possible to see what products are available there but not in Ireland. These may—subject to patent rights—be adapted to suit the Irish market. Many ideas for new food and drink products come from abroad.

(7) ADAPTING AN EXISTING PRODUCT
A technique called *attribute-listing* is used. When thinking of adapting or developing an existing product or service, you take a particular product, list its attributes—for example its shape, size, design, material, colour, functions, or cost—and find as many alternatives as possible.

(8) CURRENT TRENDS, CHANGING TASTES AND CIRCUMSTANCES
Keen observers of the market may recognise opportunities by isolating trends and then generating ideas to follow those trends.

(9) STATE AGENCIES

Enterprise Ireland is the state agency for developing indigenous industry, together with agencies such as county enterprise boards, business associations, and IBEC. They provide information, help and advice to existing businesses and to entrepreneurs on product ideas or business opportunities.

IDEA GENERATION

This is a systematic approach to generating ideas for new products and finding new ways of serving a market.

Idea generation may involve brainstorming, visits abroad to seek new product opportunities, or monitoring the market.

New products are essential to any enterprise: there is an ever-increasing demand for new products.

Not all products are absolutely new: most are built on existing products and concepts, for example a new model of a car.

Ideas for products fall into three categories:

- new products
- replacement of existing products, which may be significantly different from those earlier products
- imitative products—copying a product already on the market.

Keeping a flow of new ideas is a necessity and a significant problem for business. In some businesses a technique called 'brainstorming' is used.

BRAINSTORMING

In brainstorming, any idea is acceptable and no idea is rejected, no matter how irrelevant it seems. Criticism is not allowed. The important thing is generating lots of new ideas. Later these ideas will be evaluated. The great majority will be rejected, but one or two may provide the answer to the problem being investigated.

REWARDING GOOD IDEAS

As an incentive for generating ideas, employees may be rewarded for those proposals adopted with financial or promotional bonuses or fringe benefits. However, this requires careful management to ensure that the reward is fair and worth while.

New product and service development process

The process of creating new products by a firm is part of its continuous product strategy. Successful product development relies on excellence in market research and in committing resources to research and development and design, together with the technical ability to turn good designs into well-engineered products or services.

Product development can be expensive and risky, because of

- lack of research
- technical problems in design or production
- errors in the timing of the product's introduction.

MARKET RESEARCH

Market research is defined as 'the systematic gathering, recording and analysing of facts relating to identifying, anticipating and satisfying customers' needs.'

Market research aims to provide the management with information on which to base its marketing and production decisions. It is a risk-reducing technique, in that it enables the firm to produce the right product or service at the right time and at the right price to satisfy demand.

REASONS FOR CARRYING OUT MARKET RESEARCH

- It helps a firm establish customers' needs and helps it produce products that satisfy those needs.
- It reduces the risk of producing a product not required by consumers, together with all the development costs involved.
- It tests customers' reaction to a new product and finds out whether it meets their needs.
- It helps in the decision-making process.
- It finds out competitors' strengths.
- It helps in finding out the weaknesses of existing products and discovering why sales are falling.

MARKET RESEARCH TECHNIQUES

There are many different types of market research, including *desk research* and *field research.*

Desk research

This relates to research information already published. Because of its general accessibility and low cost, it should always be undertaken before field research.

There are two sources of desk research, internal and external to the company.

Internal

This is internal data collected for another purpose. There is a lot of information within a firm that can be used for market research purposes, including

- records of sales volume
- importance of customers
- location of customers and sales per customer
- reports of sales personnel
- computer data-bases
- marketing reports.

Depending on the nature of the research, information would also be available on purchasing, production, distribution, and personnel.

External

This is public data collected by third parties and includes research reports, Government and trade statistics, books, directories, and commercial data-bases. Some examples include:

- *Central Statistics Office*—household budget surveys, foreign trade facts and figures, consumer price index, population statistics: age, sex, marital status, economic status

- *state agencies*—Enterprise Ireland, IDA
- *Government departments*—Companies Registration Office, Department of Enterprise, Trade and Employment, Revenue Commissioners
- *industry associations*—IBEC, ISME, SFA
- *European Commission*
- *chambers of commerce, county enterprise boards*
- *trade associations*—SIMI, ITAA
- universities and institutes of technology, local libraries
- commercial data-bases—information on specific markets available for purchase
- internet—a vast store of business information
- business magazines, trade journals, newspapers.

Desk research is useful, but it is unlikely to provide the information needed. The drawback of desk research is that it takes little account of what is happening in the market: it is often collected for some other purpose, and is usually out of date. For example, desk research might provide information about total consumer spending on cars, but to find out about customers' attitudes to a new BMW would require primary research to collect primary data.

The advantages of desk research are:

- it is relatively inexpensive, as the information is already available
- research can be done quickly.

Field research

Field research involves collecting original data directly related to a firm's products, customers or markets by making direct contact with potential consumers to find their views. Primary data is collected by carrying out fieldwork based on a structured questionnaire or interview with a sample of the population.

Field research can be expensive and time-consuming. Its objective is to present a more complete and up-to-date picture of the market.

Field research methods include:

Surveys

These involve asking people for their responses to new product ideas. They can be carried out by phone or personal interview by a researcher, using a questionnaire.

Questionnaires

A questionnaire is a document containing a series of structured questions designed to generate information required to meet the objectives of research. It is used to identify customers' needs and motivations and to gauge reaction to the product on offer.

Considerable care needs to be exercised in the preparation, development and testing of questionnaires before they are used and in interpreting the results obtained.

Questionnaires may be designed to take a highly structured form, involving detailed questions requiring direct responses—yes-or-no answers, multiple-choice questions, rating on a scale, or open-ended questions, giving respondents an opportunity to air their views.

When writing questions, the following points should be borne in mind:

- Each question should ask for only one point.
- Questions should not contain bias (for example, 'How much do you like 7-up?').
- Ask questions in the correct sequence, leaving questions such as age, address and occupation until the end.

The confidence with which results of questionnaires can be used depends on the response rate, that is, the proportion of those contacted who complete and return a postal questionnaire or who answer fully a personally conducted questionnaire.

Observation

This is a technique that requires a researcher to watch and record behaviour rather than ask questions.

SELECTING RESPONDENTS TO A SURVEY

Sampling

For research to provide absolutely accurate results it would be necessary to survey every possible consumer of a product or service. This is not possible; consequently, only a sample of the target market is chosen.

A sample is a group of respondents selected to be representative of the views of the target market as a whole. 'Representative of total market' means that the sample chosen contains characteristics of the total market: for example, the target market for an icepop might be children aged between six and twelve. If research were to be carried out into the market for icepops, the sample chosen would have to be made up almost exclusively of children in this age group.

STAGES IN THE NEW PRODUCT AND SERVICE DEVELOPMENT PROCESS

The development a new product or service goes through a number of stages.

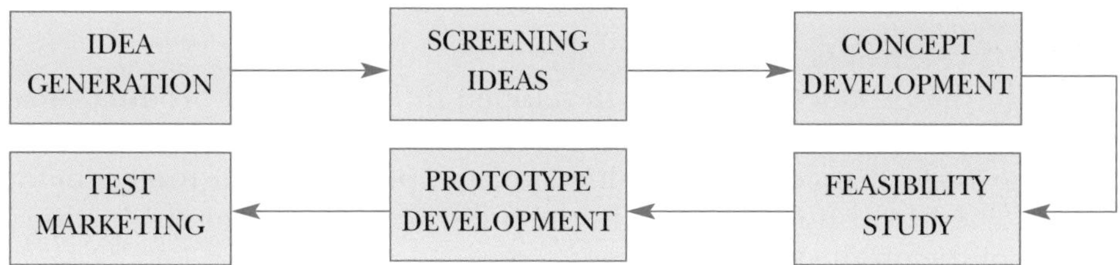

(1) IDEA GENERATION

The development of a new product starts with idea generation—the systematic search for ideas for a possible product the company can envisage offering to the market. A business must generate many ideas to find a few good ones. The technique of brainstorming may be employed here.

(2) SCREENING IDEAS

When a number of product ideas have been generated, the next stage is selecting the product or service with the greatest potential for development. The purpose of screening is to spot good ideas and to drop poor ones as soon as possible. The company wants to go ahead only with ideas that will turn into profitable products.

(3) CONCEPT DEVELOPMENT

Attractive ideas must now be developed into product concepts. A product concept is a detailed version of a new product idea stated in meaningful consumer terms. This is to ensure that the product is acceptable to customers and that it is capable of fulfilling customers' needs and requirements. It must be superior to and different from other products on the market.

This difference is called a 'unique selling-point' (USP), which is 'the feature of a product that can be focused on in order to differentiate it from all competition.' Unique selling-points should be based on a real product characteristic: for Mars the unique selling-point of one of its chocolate bars, Topic, is 'a hazelnut in every bite.'

(4) FEASIBILITY STUDY

A feasibility study will investigate the product's potential in its contribution to sales, costs, and profit. It finds out the following:
- the demand for the new product or service
- the impact of the new product or service on the environment
- the cost of producing the product or service
- what type of marketing mix will suit the new product or service.

Research will be required on:
- potential and likely sales
- effects on costs
- whether the firm has the skills and equipment to produce the product or service
- the likely profit from the product or service.

Grants for feasibility studies are available from Enterprise Ireland and from county enterprise boards.

(5) PROTOTYPE DEVELOPMENT

At this stage the product concept is developed into a physical product. A small number of experimental models is manufactured to aid in testing the production process, the performance of the product and acceptability to customers before it is decided whether or not to engage in the full-scale commercial production and marketing of the product.

Prototype development can be an expensive and lengthy phase, which ascertains
- attributes of the product—shape, size, colour, design, materials, functions
- production difficulties
- cost of production.

Product testing can now be carried out. Tests are designed to ensure that the prototype conforms to certain standards of performance and durability.

(6) TEST-MARKETING

A trial run of the new product or service is used to determine the reaction of potential buyers, who are given the product to try out so as to reduce the risk of failure.

Customers' opinions about the performance of the product, its quality and the satisfaction they derive from it are compiled, together with their reaction to a range of possible prices that could be charged. This information is used by the firm to decide whether or not to go ahead and launch the product on the market. Customers' reactions also indicate whether changes to the product would strengthen its appeal.

At this stage the management has all the information it needs to enable it to make a decision whether to produce and market the product as a full-scale commercial venture.

13. MARKETING

Marketing is defined by the Institute of Marketing as:

'the process responsible for identifying, anticipating and satisfying customer requirements profitably.'

It is the process of
- *identifying* customers' requirements through market research
- *anticipating* customers' needs
- *satisfying* customers' requirements by producing products that satisfy these needs
- *promoting* these products to customers through various marketing mix policies.

Marketing concept

The marketing concept emphasises the need for a business to adopt a customer-oriented approach. This policy is aimed at generating profit by recognising and satisfying customers' needs.

The marketing concept holds that the achievement of the company's goals depends on
- determining the needs, attitudes and wants of potential customers
- developing products with characteristics specially designed to satisfy consumers' needs
- supplying the desired product or service more effectively and more efficiently than competitors
- generating profit by creating customer satisfaction.

Many successful and well-known companies have adopted a marketing concept, including IBM, Disney, and McDonald's.

MARKETING OBJECTIVES

A firm's marketing objectives are to sell its products or services and to satisfy customers. To achieve these objectives it must use its resources effectively and apply appropriate marketing strategies.

Marketing strategy

This is a plan that lays down the best use of the company's resources and the tactics it employs to achieve its marketing objectives.

The strategy is implemented through marketing mix policies relating to the four Ps—*product, price, place,* and *promotion.*

STAGES IN DEVELOPING A MARKETING STRATEGY OR PLAN

1. **Opportunity analysis:** Investigate the market to identify business opportunities.
2. **Target market selection:** Select a target market and divide the market into categories (*market segmentation*).
3. **Market research:** Carry out market research into the needs and demands of the selected target market.
4. **Marketing mix:** Formulate a marketing mix plan relating to the four Ps—*product, price, place,* and *promotion.*

Marketing strategy includes market segmentation and target market.

MARKET SEGMENTATION

This consists of dividing a market into similar groups of customers, where each group or segment is made up of customers who have similar expectations of the product.

A firm could choose any segment as its target market and run a specialised marketing mix plan (four Ps) to satisfy the needs of that segment, for example Sensodyne toothpaste for those with sensitive teeth that react painfully to heat and cold.

The ways in which a market can be segmented are:

- *geographically*—by region, county, city, etc.
- *demographically*—by age, sex, family size, income, occupation, or education
- *psychologically*—by attitudes and tastes, social class, or life-style.

The advantage to the business is that it can target its marketing campaign more accurately and match customer categories to the products on offer.

MARKET NICHES

Gaps in the market may emerge for which a new product or service could be developed.

TARGET MARKET

Businesses recognise that it is impossible to market products that satisfy all customers. They must therefore select as their target one or more segments that offer an attractive opportunity for profit. 'The target market consists of a set of buyers sharing common needs or characteristics that the company decides to serve.'

Having selected its target market, a company can develop the correct marketing mix—product, price, place, and promotion—to reach that target market. Example: The target market for *Business Revision for Leaving Certificate* is Leaving Certificate pupils studying business.

Marketing mix

The marketing mix can be defined as 'the combination of decisions regarding product, price, place and promotion used by a firm to implement its marketing strategy.'

The marketing mix for any product or service has as its foundation customer satisfaction and a high level of product quality and service. The company must design a *product* to satisfy customers' wants, sell it at a competitive *price*, have it for sale in a *place* convenient to customers, and undertake *promotion* to communicate with the target market.

ELEMENTS OF THE MARKETING MIX

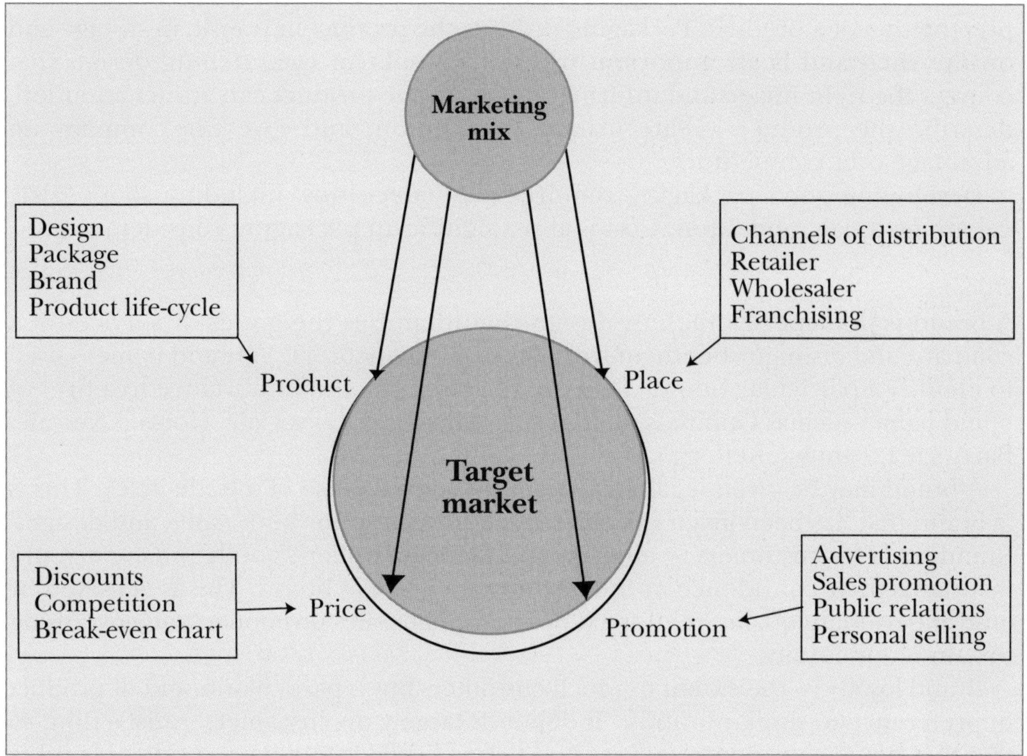

PRODUCT

A product or service is anything that can be offered to the market for use or consumption that might satisfy a need or want.

When developing products, firms must

(1) identify the needs the product will satisfy: for example, an oven provides a means of heating food;
(2) design the product with all its characteristics, quality features, brand name, and packaging;
(3) offer additional services and benefits to the customer, for example warranty, after-sales service, installation, delivery, or credit.

Product design

This is the process of designing a product, from an idea to a product that can be produced and marketed commercially.

Design determines a product's form, shape and performance and determines its marketability and cost of production.

A good designer considers appearance, safety, and ease of use. A good design will be economical to produce and service, attract attention, improve performance, cut production costs, and give the product a strong competitive advantage in the market.

Packaging

Packaging is an essential element in the marketing mix for any consumer product. It includes the activity of designing, producing and costing the protection and presentation of a product. Packaging protects the product in transit, in storage and on the shelf and is an important marketing tool. An eye-catching design that conveys the right image and information about the product can attract attention, describe the product, create instant recognition, and give the company an advantage over competitors.

Developing good packaging requires many decisions, including shape, size, colour, materials, and safety. Cost is also a significant packaging consideration.

Branding

A brand is 'a name, symbol, or design that identifies the goods or services of a company and distinguishes them from those of competitors.' A brand name is used to identify a particular brand. Think of the strength and importance to a firm of brand names such as Guinness, Ballygowan, Microsoft, Coca-Cola, Hoover, Nescafé, Barry's tea, Zanussi, Kellogg's.

A brand may be given legal protection through the use of a trade-mark. This is 'a brand that has been given exclusive legal protection for both name and design.' Branding helps customers to identify a particular supplier's goods and creates and maintains their confidence in the performance of the brand. This is achieved by ensuring constant quality, reinforced by appropriate sales promotion and advertising to gain brand loyalty.

Brand loyalty is 'the extent to which customers buy a particular brand of product in preference to similar brands.' It depends largely on customers' satisfaction, so that they buy the product regularly. A well-established brand has considerable value in giving a supplier a competitive advantage.

Own brands

Large retailers sell goods under their own brand names, for example 'St Bernard' (Dunnes Stores), 'St Michael' (Marks and Spencer). Own brands are distinctive and build up a good reputation for the retailer.

Advantages of branding

1. Customers recognise the product or business and can easily distinguish it from that of competitors.
2. It promotes customer loyalty with increased sales and profits.
3. It is easier to launch a new product on the market if it has a brand name.
4. The customer is assured that the branded product is of good quality.
5. Some brand names are so popular that the product becomes known by the brand name, for example Biro, Tippex.

PRODUCT LIFE-CYCLE

Products follow a life-cycle of six distinct stages:
(1) development
(2) introduction
(3) growth
(4) maturity
(5) saturation
(6) decline.

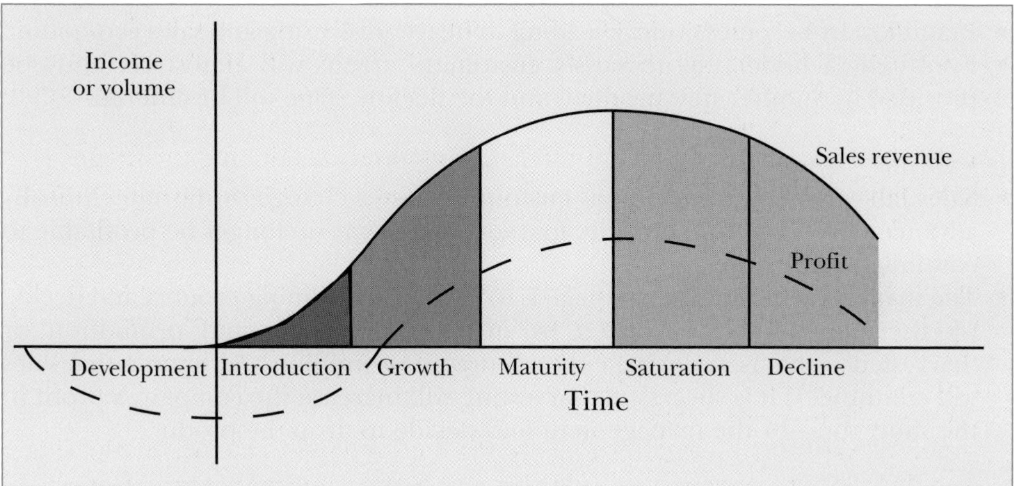

(1) *Product development*

The company finds and develops a new product idea. During the development phase, sales are nil and there is substantial negative cash flow because of expenditure on research and development, market research, product design, and production.

(2) *Introduction*

- This is a period of slow sales growth and high expenditure on advertising and promotion as the product is introduced to the market.
- Profit is non-existent at this stage.
- Advertising will be informative, to tell the public of the availability of the product.
- The price may be high, because it is a new product and there is little competition.

(3) *Growth*

- The product commands acceptance and is demanded by many customers.
- There is rapid growth in sales, a positive cash flow, and increasing profit.
- Persuasive and competitive advertising will be used to persuade customers to buy the product instead of that of competitors.
- The price may be reduced to attract a wider market.
- The search starts for a new product that will eventually replace this one.

(4) *Maturity*

- Sales and profits reach a peak and start to level off.
- Profits stabilise, as the product has achieved acceptability by most customers.
- The price may be further reduced to maintain market share.

- Other markets are sought, as are other uses for the product.
- The product is examined for further development to keep a competitive edge.
- The level of advertising and sales promotion is increased to encourage more demand.
- Those other products that will replace the product may be introduced.

(5) *Saturation*
- Sales growth slows down as the market becomes progressively saturated and the firm must compete on price to maintain its market share.
- Brand loyalty becomes critical, leading to heavy advertising and sales promotion.
- Eventually a better way to satisfy customers' needs will almost certainly be provided by another new product, and the decline stage will be entered.

(6) *Decline*
- Sales fall off and profit drops as customers' tastes change or more technically advanced products take over the market, and it may no longer be profitable to continue production.
- The management's task at this stage is to identify a declining product and decide whether it should be rescued by further advertising and promotion or 'harvested'—that is, reducing expenditure on promotion and hoping that sales will continue. If it is successful, harvesting will increase the company's profit in the short run—or the management may decide to drop the product.

Not all products follow this life-cycle. Some products are introduced and die quickly; others stay at the maturity stage for a very long time.

Every product will eventually decline and die; it is therefore necessary for firms to carry out continuous development of new products and come up with new product ideas. This should be financed from the cash flow of products at the mature stage of their life-cycle.

PRICE

Price is an important element in a purchasing decision, because the demand for products or services is influenced by price. Price affects sales volume and the amount of profit of companies.

A balance has to be arrived at between setting a price that will cover costs and earn a satisfactory profit, while at same time being attractive to consumers.

Factors that determine the price of a product

(1) *Costs of research and development and production*
All costs must be calculated and recouped over the life of the product.

(2) *Type of product*
Whether perishable or durable, mass-produced, or technically advanced.

(3) *Competition*
The price will have to be similar to competitors' to gain market share.

(4) *Economic conditions*
If the economy is booming, people will have more disposable income, and prices may be increased.

(5) *Type of customer*
Different prices may be applied to existing customers as against new customers, or for large orders as against small orders.

(6) *Legal issues*
Prices may be subject to Government price controls, for example electricity.

Pricing methods

These depend on the firm's marketing objectives. There are several different criteria for pricing products:

(1) *Cost-plus pricing*
This involves calculating all costs—research and development, production, distribution, and marketing—and adding a percentage for profit.

(2) *Psychological pricing*
This means setting a price based on customers' perceived expectations in the target market. Charging high prices for certain high-quality consumer products can convey an impression of exclusiveness: for example, buyers perceive higher-priced cars to be of higher quality.

(3) *Competitive pricing*
The price is determined with reference to what competitors are charging; a new petrol station would have to charge prices in line with local competition.

(4) *Market-skimming pricing*
This means charging a high price on entry to the market. This secures high profit margins and allows for quick recovery of research and development costs.

(5) *Market-penetration pricing*
This means setting a low initial price to penetrate the market quickly and attract a large number of customers and win a large share of the market.

(6) *Tactical pricing*
A company may adjust its basic prices to reward customers for certain responses, such as early payment of bills, volume purchases, or buying out of season. Price adjustments are called *discounts*.

Discounts

Cash discount

This is a price reduction to buyers who pay their bills on time.

Trade discount

This is a reduction from a supplier's list price given to buyers who buy in bulk. This is done to secure orders against competitors and to encourage larger orders.

Seasonal discounts

This is a price reduction to buyers who buy products or services out of season; this allows the supplier to keep production steady during the entire year. Hotels, travel agents and airlines offer seasonal discounts during their off-peak periods.

BREAK-EVEN ANALYSIS

Breaking even is when a firm is just covering its costs, making neither a profit nor a loss.

The purpose of break-even analysis is to ascertain the sales level, in units and value, that a company must achieve to break even.

(1) *Costs*

TOTAL COSTS = FIXED COSTS + VARIABLE COSTS

1. *Fixed costs* are costs that remain unchanged, irrespective of the level of production, for example rent and rates, insurance, management salaries. These costs have to be paid whether or not anything is produced.
2. *Variable costs* are costs that change directly with the level of production, for example the raw materials used and direct labour. These will tend to double if output doubles.

TOTAL VARIABLE COSTS = VARIABLE COST PER UNIT × NUMBER OF UNITS PRODUCED

(2) *Revenue*
Total revenue is the money received by a firm from the sale of its goods or services.

TOTAL REVENUE = SELLING PRICE × QUANTITY SOLD

(3) *Contribution*
This is a measure of the amount of money that each unit sold contributes towards covering the fixed costs of a business. Once fixed costs are covered, all further contribution is profit.

CONTRIBUTION = TOTAL REVENUE – VARIABLE COSTS

CONTRIBUTION PER UNIT = SELLING PRICE PER UNIT – VARIABLE COSTS PER UNIT

Break-even
This is the level of output and sales at which a firm generates just enough income to cover fixed and variable costs, earning neither a profit nor a loss.

If the selling price of a product exceeds its variable cost, each unit sold will earn a contribution towards fixed costs. If total contributions cover fixed costs, the firm breaks even.

Break-even point
The break-even point is the level of sales at which the firm breaks even, making neither a profit nor a loss.

$$\text{BREAK-EVEN} = \frac{\text{FIXED COSTS}}{\text{CONTRIBUTION PER UNIT}}$$

Margin of safety
This is the difference between sales volume and break-even point, and is the amount by which sales can fall before a firm incurs a loss.

MARGIN OF SAFETY = SALES VOLUME – BREAK-EVEN POINT

Break-even chart
All costs (fixed and variable), together with the sales income expected from the product, can be represented on a *break-even chart*, which will show the break-even point.

Drawing a break-even chart
1. Calculate the break-even point. This allows you to position the diagram properly on the page.
2. Label the horizontal axis as *Output (units)* and the vertical axis as *Costs and revenue.*
3. Decide the scale, making sure the break-even point (BEP) is positioned in the middle of the chart.
4. Draw the fixed-cost line (FC). This will be a straight line parallel to the horizontal axis at the appropriate level.
5. Draw the total-cost line (= FC + VC). This line starts at the point of intersection of the fixed-cost line and the vertical axis and slopes upwards. To draw this line it is necessary to work out the total cost at two different levels of output.
6. Draw the total revenue line. This line starts at 0 and slopes upwards. To draw this line it is necessary to work out total revenue at two different levels of output.
7. Establish the break-even point (BEP), where the total-cost line and total-revenue line intersect. Before this point the business is making a loss; after this point the business is making a profit.
8. Show the margin of safety: sales *volume – BEP.*
9. Show profit at full capacity: *total revenue – total costs.*

Sample question and solution
Illustrate by means of a break-even chart the following figures, showing (*a*) break-even point, (*b*) profit at full capacity, and (*c*) margin of safety:

Fixed costs:	€20,000
Variable costs:	€3 per unit
Forecasted output (sales):	12,000 units
Selling price:	€5 per unit
Full capacity:	15,000 units

Suggested solution
Break-even point

CONTRIBUTION PER UNIT =	SELLING PRICE PER UNIT	–	VARIABLE COST PER UNIT
=	€5	–	€3
CONTRIBUTION PER UNIT =		€2	

$$\text{Break-even point} = \frac{\text{fixed cost}}{\text{contribution per unit}} = \frac{€20{,}000}{2} = 10{,}000 \text{ units}$$

This means that 10,000 units must be sold in order to break even.

Profit at full capacity	€
Sales (15,000 units × €5):	75,000
Less variable cost (15,000 × €3):	45,000
Contribution	30,000
Less fixed costs	20,000
Profit	10,000

Margin of safety

Sales	–	break-even point
= 12,000 units	–	10,000 units
= 2,000 units		

This means that sales can fall by 2,000 units before a loss is incurred.

Workings for drawing total-cost line

The total-cost line starts at the point of intersection of the fixed-cost line and the vertical axis and slopes upwards. We must find two other points on this line and work out total cost at two levels of output.

Output (units)	5,000	15,000
Variable costs (€3)	€15,000	€45,000
Fixed cost	€20,000	€20,000
Total cost	€35,000	€65,000

Points on line are (5,000 units, €35,000) (15,000 units, €65,000)

Workings for drawing total-revenue line

The total-revenue line starts at 0 and slopes upwards. Find two other points on this line and work out total revenue at two different levels of output.

Output (units)	5,000	15,000
Revenue (€5 per unit)	€25,000	€75,000

Points on line are (5,000 units, €25,000) (15,000 units, €75,000)

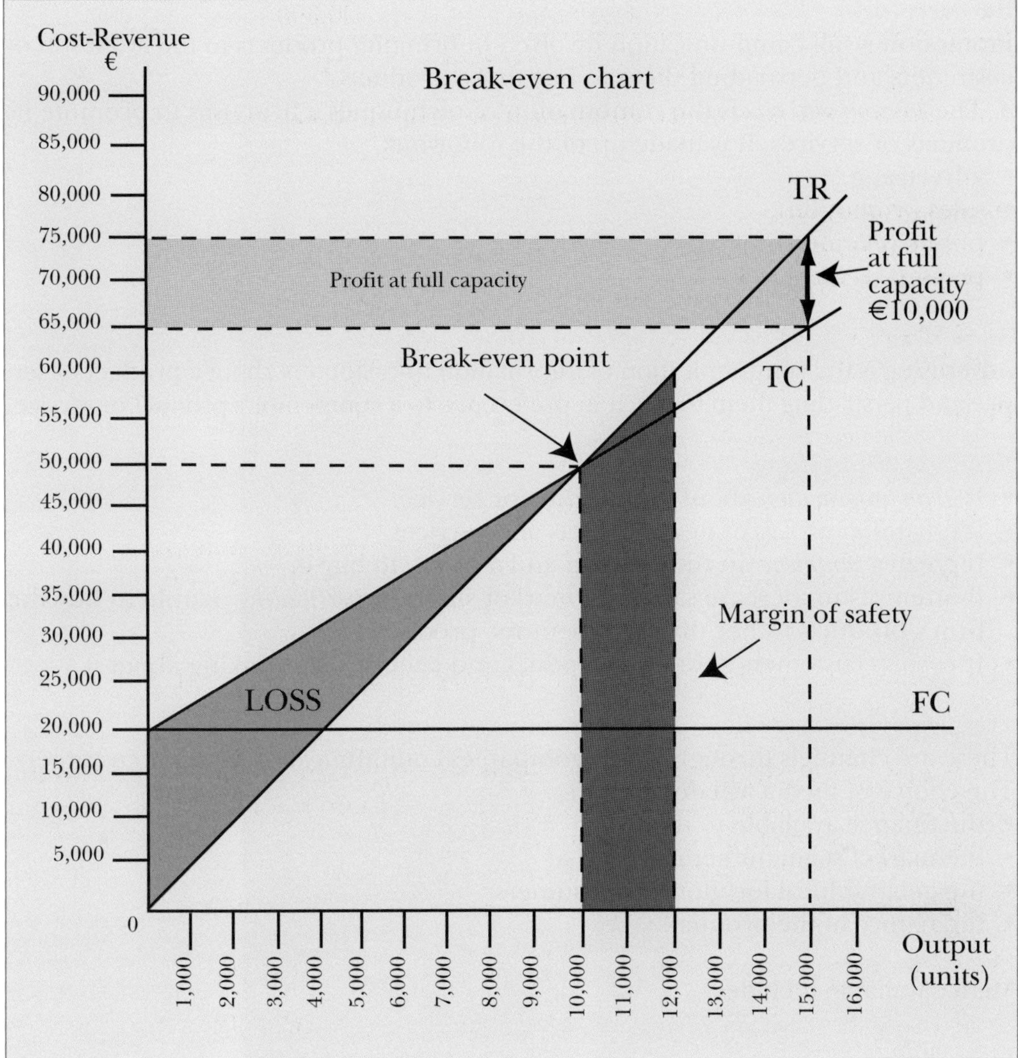

Uses of a break-even chart

- To determine the profit or loss likely to arise from a given level of production or sales.
- To show the impact of changes in fixed or variable costs on profitability.
- To show the impact of changes in the selling price on profitability.
- To show the level of activity required to generate a required profit.
- To show the margin of safety at different levels of output.
- To show the profit the firm can make if it operates at full capacity.

PROMOTION

Promotion is 'all communication involved in bringing products to the attention of customers and persuading them to buy those products.'

The *promotional mix* is the combination of techniques a firm uses to promote its products or services. It is made up of the following:

- advertising
- sales promotion
- public relations
- personal selling.

Advertising

Advertising is the communication of information to customers about a product or service and persuading them to buy it in preference to a competitor's product or service.

Functions of advertising

- It gives *information* about the product or service.
- It creates *awareness* of new products and services.
- It creates *confidence* in the product and a desire to buy it.
- It attempts to increase sales and market share by *persuading* people to buy the firm's products rather than competitors' products.
- It *reminds* customers about the product and keeps them thinking about it.

Types of advertising media

These are channels through which companies communicate with their customers. The choice of media will depend on

- the finance available to the firm
- the market segment being aimed at
- the geographical location of consumers
- the nature of the product.

Media available include:

Print media

National daily papers

These have wide distribution, broad acceptance, and low cost, for example *Irish Times, Irish Independent, Irish Examiner.*

Sunday papers

Sunday Tribune, Sunday Business Post, Ireland on Sunday, Sunday Independent.

Provincial papers

Examples: *Longford Leader, Kilkenny People, Cork Evening Echo, Kerryman.*

Magazines

These have high-quality reproduction and a long life (weekly or monthly), for example *Business and Finance, Economist.*

Journals

These have a specialist target market, for example *Farmer's Journal.*

Direct mail

Direct mail (also called junk mail) is advertising material posted directly to selected addresses.

Broadcast media

Television

This is expensive, has a large audience, and is very effective. It appeals to the senses, combining sight, sound, and motion.

Radio

National radio is costly but has a high listenership. There is audio presentation only, requiring lower attention than television. Local radio is excellent for local advertising.

Cinema

This has a local audience, and is as effective as television.

Display media

These are flexible and have low cost. They are eye-catching and attract a lot of attention. Examples: hoardings, posters, vehicles, bus shelters, railway stations, football stadiums.

Electronic media

The internet is used increasingly by business to advertise globally.

Word of mouth

This involves customers talking about products they like or dislike. Personal influence carries great weight for expensive products, for example cars: buyers seek the opinion of previous purchasers.

Advertising legislation

Consumer Information Act (1978)

- The act prohibits false or misleading claims about goods or services.
- It prohibits the publication of advertising that is false or misleading and is thereby likely to cause loss, damage or injury to members of the public.
- The act established the office of Director of Consumer Affairs, who can prosecute advertisers who make false or misleading claims about goods or services.

SALES PROMOTION

Sales promotion consists of short-term incentives to boost sales of a product or service. Advertising offers reasons for buying a product or service; sales promotion offers a reason for buying it now.

Sales promotions are used in short bursts

- to introduce a new product or brand
- to renew interest in a product whose sales have fallen
- to stimulate extra demand for a well-established brand.

A variety of techniques is used for these purposes, including:

Consumer promotions
- free trial samples
- money-off packs
- 'two for the price of one' offers
- extra quantities for the same price
- competitions offering prizes
- coupons offering gifts
- trading stamps
- in-store demonstrations

These methods can succeed only if the product being promoted is widely available, so retailers must be encouraged to stock it.

Trade promotions for the retailer
- Exhibition and trade fairs
- Sales competitions
- Extended credit
- Special offers on purchases
- Free extra quantities
- Gifts and prizes
- Merchandising

Merchandising
This is an in-store promotional service to retailers from manufacturers near the point of sale, designed to stimulate sales. Such merchandising makes considerable use of point-of-sale display material and special display stands to ensure that products are displayed in as attractive and prominent a way as possible.

PUBLIC RELATIONS
Public relations involves presenting a good image and developing a good relationship between the company and the public by obtaining favourable publicity, building up a good 'corporate image' and heading off unfavourable rumours, with a view to building up goodwill and encouraging customers to buy the company's products.

Public relations officer
Companies employ a public relations officer (PRO)
- to deal with the media
- to provide information about the company
- to represent the company at press conferences
- to ensure that favourable comments, publicity and information about the company are used in newspapers and on radio and television
- to defend the reputation of the company in a crisis, for example when there is a pollution problem.

Methods of maintaining and developing public relations include:

(1) press statements and press conferences;
(2) participating in exhibitions and trade fairs;
(3) sponsoring sports, the arts, and other events;
(4) giving grants and scholarships for educational or sports purposes;
(5) in-house magazines, annual reports and accounts, recruitment literature;
(6) information to employees and the public about the firm's activities;
(7) supporting schools and other local organisations.

PERSONAL SELLING

This is a means of increasing the sales of a product through direct contact with prospective customers. A face-to-face meeting with customers allows the sales representative to explain fully the details of the product, to advise them and to answer questions, and to demonstrate the working of the product.

Telemarketing

This means selling products or services by contacting customers by phone. An order may be taken over the phone, or interested customers may be visited by a sales representative with a view to completing the sale. Many firms use freephone (1800) numbers to encourage customers to contact them.

PLACE

This is the process of getting products to the correct place, where customers can buy them. Distribution is often done through intermediaries, such as wholesalers and retailers. The firm must select the appropriate distribution channels in order to bring a product to its selected market.

The distribution channel is the network of firms used in the physical distribution of a product from manufacturer to consumer.

MAIN CHANNELS OF DISTRIBUTION

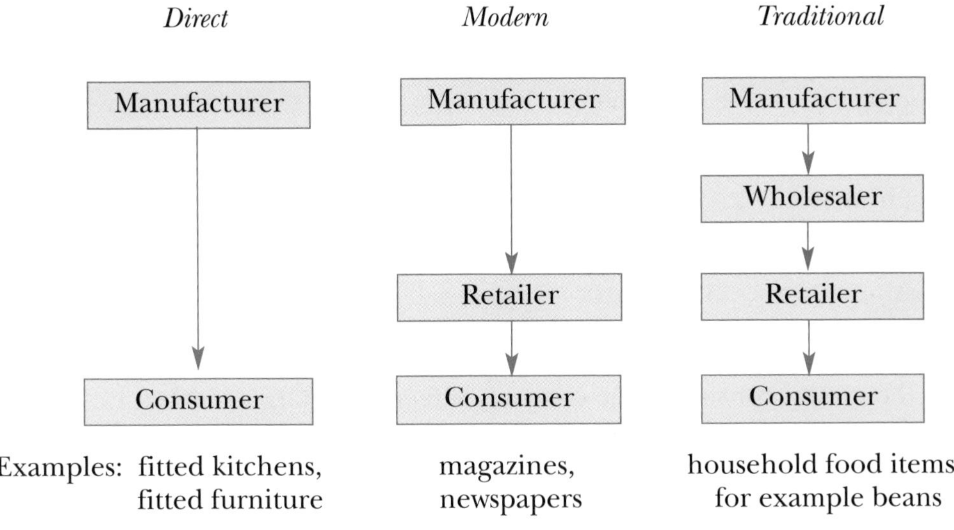

Channel 1: Direct distribution channel
This consists of the manufacturer selling directly to consumers, for example encyclopaedias, double-glazing, fitted furniture, buying from a catalogue.

Channel 2: Modern distribution structure
This channel contains one middleman: the retailer. Large retailers buy directly from manufacturers and sell to consumers, for example Dunnes Stores, Tesco.

Channel 3: Traditional distribution structure
This channel contains two middlemen: the wholesaler and the retailer. This channel is used for mass-produced goods. Wholesalers buys in bulk from the manufacturer. They stock a wide range of goods, pass on market information, provide credit, and sell to retailers.

Wholesaler
The wholesaler buys goods in large quantities from manufacturers, stores them in a warehouse, and sells them in smaller quantities to retailers. This is known as *breaking bulk.* The wholesaler acts as a middleman between manufacturer and retailer in the distribution channel.

Traditionally, the wholesaler provided retail customers with credit facilities and a delivery service, but in more recent years this has been replaced by cash-and-carry, for example Musgrave's. Wholesaling without credit or delivery has become a prominent feature of distribution systems. Retailers pay cash for the goods bought and use their own vehicle to transport them. By eliminating the costs involved in offering credit and delivery, wholesalers can offer goods at highly competitive prices.

Retailer
The retailer buys goods from a wholesaler and sells to the final consumer. Retail outlets include

- independent shops
- multiples—e.g. Dunnes Stores
- department stores—e.g. Arnotts
- supermarkets—e.g. Tesco
- shopping centres—e.g. Wilton, Cork
- franchising—e.g. McDonald's
- mail order—e.g. Argos
- street traders
- vending machines.

ANALYSING THE MARKETING MIX

PRODUCT: TOYOTA AVENSIS

Product
This is the product or service the company offers to the target market.

The Toyota Avensis consists of engine, chassis, gearbox, and thousands of other parts. Toyota offers thirteen Avensis models, ranging from 1.6 to 2-litre petrol and turbodiesel engines, available in saloon, lift-back and estate bodies. Standard safety equipment includes ABS, nine airbags, and side impact protection bars. The car carries a three-year or 100,000 km parts and labour warranty.

Price

This is the amount of money the customer has to pay to obtain the product.

Toyota calculate retail prices that dealers charge. Dealers negotiate the price with each customer, offering discounts, trade-in allowances, free road tax for one year, and low-interest finance to overcome the present competitive environment.

Toyota Avensis prices range from €25,380 to €35,450.

Place

This is where the product is available to target consumers.

Toyota operates through a body of independently owned dealerships that sell the company's models. Dealers keep a stock of Toyota cars, demonstrate them to potential customers, negotiate prices, and service cars after the sale.

Promotion

This consists of activities that communicate the merits of the product and persuade the target customer to buy.

Toyota spends millions of pounds each year on advertising to tell customers about the company and its products. An emphasis is placed on brand loyalty. There is advertising on television and in newspapers and magazines.

Toyota and dealers offer special promotion sales, low finance rates, free road tax, free insurance and membership of the Automobile Association as added incentives.

An effective marketing plan blends all the elements of the marketing mix to achieve the marketing objectives.

14. GETTING STARTED

Why people wish to set up their own business

1. They have difficulty in finding suitable employment.
2. They are stimulated by redundancy.
3. They spot an opportunity in the market.
4. They want to fulfil a long-time ambition.
5. They wish to be independent and want control over their own situation.
6. They have a need for achievement—the personal satisfaction of doing a job properly.
7. They are frustrated at the lack of recognition in their present job.
8. They wish to make more money.

OBSTACLES FACING PEOPLE SETTING UP THEIR OWN BUSINESS

(1) *Location, finance, administration*

- Finding a suitable location, premises, product, and employees
- Obtaining low-cost finance
- Managing working capital
- Keeping accounts

- Insurance and PAYE
- Credit control

(2) *Technology*

- Investment and training required in up-to-date technology (computers, fax, e-mail)

(3) *Management and marketing*

- Lack of expertise in the day-to-day management of a business or in marketing

(4) *Legislation*

- Employment legislation
- Legislation and formation procedures involved in setting up a business

(5) *Tax*

- Registering for VAT and PAYE

(6) *Business costs*

- High cost of doing business: transport, energy, communications

(7) *Competition*

- Intense competition from abroad for newly established businesses

Overcoming obstacles involved in setting up business

(1) *Information and advice*

Many organisations promote enterprise, including banks and enterprise boards. Enterprise Ireland provides information and advice on all aspects of starting up a business.

(2) *Mentor schemes*

An experienced businessperson makes available their experience and expertise. Mentor schemes are available from enterprise boards and area partnership companies.

(3) *Professional advice*

A consultant can provide advice on implementing your project, on grants and assistance.

An accountant can provide advice on accounts, tax, and sources of finance.

A solicitor can provide advice on lease agreements, formation procedures and legalities, loan agreements, contracts, and legislation.

(4) *Business plan*

A good business plan is required to describe your plan to the bank or enterprise board.

(5) *Training courses*
Many organisations, such as enterprise boards, FÁS, and institutes of technology, run courses for entrepreneurs covering bookkeeping, tax, management accountancy, costing, and budgeting.

Finance options

Start-up finance can be raised in many ways, including
- friends or relatives
- bank loan
- investors.

Most companies use a variety of sources. This range of finance sources affects the business in many ways.

IMPLICATIONS OF RAISING FINANCE

(1) INCOME AND COSTS
Borrowing creates an inflow of cash from the source. This must be balanced against costs, that is, the repayment of principal plus interest out of future income.

(2) TAX
Interest on loans is deducted before profits are calculated, that is, interest is tax-deductible. Dividends are paid out of profits after tax: they are not tax-deductible.

(3) RISK
There is a risk of not being able to meet commitments or repayments of interest and principal associated with the source.

(4) CONTROL
There is a possibility of the source of finance affecting the ownership and therefore the control of the company: a share issue brings in new shareholders, who have a degree of ownership and control.

(5) CASH FLOW
Repayments have an impact on the cash flow of the business. Will there be enough cash to pay wages, PAYE, PRSI and other bills?

Factors to be considered when choosing a source of finance

(1) PURPOSE OF LOAN
The source should be matched with the use.
- Buying stock, paying wages: short-term sources
- Buying equipment or vehicles: medium-term sources
- Financing land and buildings: long-term sources

(2) DURATION OF LOAN
This depends on the use, whether short-term, medium-term, or long-term.

(3) Security
Security may have to be provided.

(4) Conditions imposed by lender
The lender may impose conditions on the use of the money.

(5) Existing loan commitments
If a firm has existing loans, it may decide to opt for an alternative source of finance, for example to issue shares.

(6) Economic climate
If interest rates are low, borrowing will be cheaper.

(7) Use of information
Information about sources can be used to make informed decisions between the alternatives.

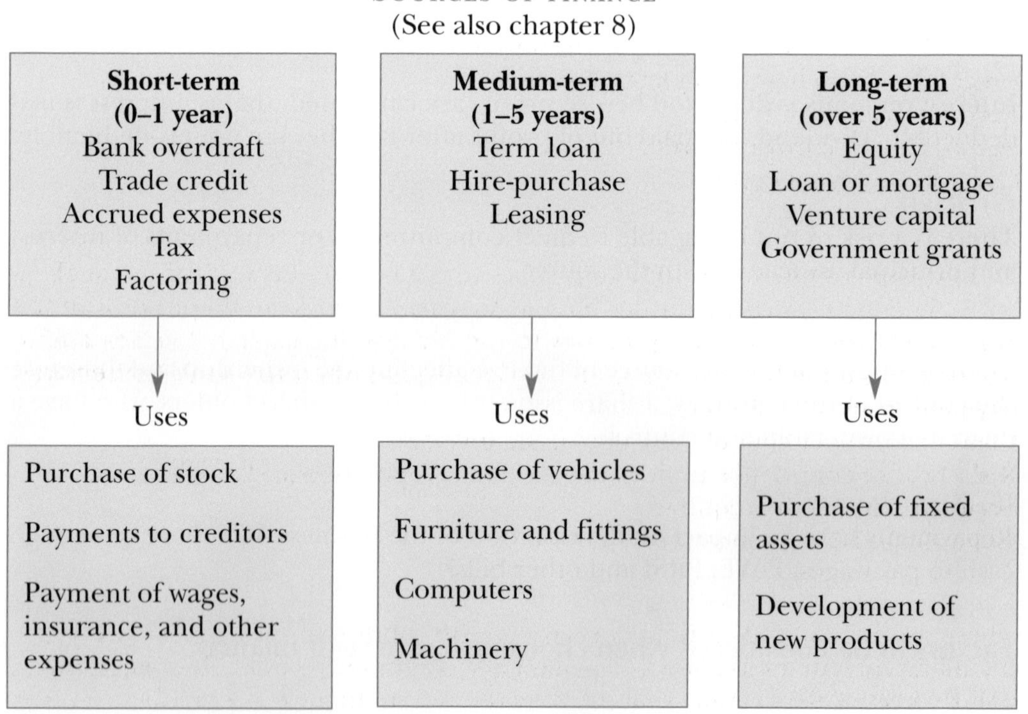

Short-term sources of finance
These are sources that must be repaid within one year. They are used to buy stock and to pay wages, pay creditors and other bills.

Bank overdraft
The company is granted permission to withdraw more than the amount of money in the current account, up to a specified limit.
Cost: Interest charged on daily overdrawn balance.

Risk: Can be recalled at any time.
Security: No security required.
Control: No loss of control.

Trade credit

This involves buying goods on credit and paying for them later.
Cost: Loss of discounts; interest is charged on overdue accounts.
Risk: Loss of credit rating if invoices are not paid on time.
Security: No security required.
Control: No loss of control.

Accrued expenses

This means delaying paying bills and using the money for other purposes.
Cost: No interest is charged; cash discounts may be lost.
Risk: Loss of credit rating and reputation if bills are not paid on time.
Security: No security required.
Control: No loss of control.

Tax

Tax collected is paid in arrears, for example VAT.
Cost: Interest is charged on late payments.
Risk: Fines and tax audit.
Security: No security required.
Control: No loss of control.

Factoring

The firm sells some of its unpaid invoices to a factoring firm, which is usually a bank. The bank usually provides immediate cash, up to 80 or 85 per cent of the customer's invoices, releasing money to use for working capital. The remaining balance, less a fee for providing the service, is paid when the bank has received payment from the customer.
Cost: About 5 per cent of the value of the invoices.
Risk: Loss of confidence in firm, damage to its reputation and credit status.
Security: No security required.
Control: No loss of control.

Medium-term sources of finance

These are best suited to financing assets with a life span of three to five years, including such items as plant and machinery, computer systems, office equipment, and vehicles. The principal sources of medium-term finance are *term loans, leasing,* and *hire-purchase.*

Term loans

Term loans are negotiated with a bank and are repaid in fixed instalments over an agreed period.
Cost: Interest is charged; the rate depends on the risk and the firm's credit status.
Risk: Loss of credit status, refusal of future loans if repayments are not made as agreed.

Security: Security may be required.
Control: Conditions attached may restrict the business, especially assets used as security.

Leasing

This means renting fixed assets in return for payment of an agreed monthly rental. The hirer of the asset never obtains ownership.
Cost: Expensive; rentals are tax-deductible; loss of depreciation write-off in profit and loss account; loss of Government grants (as the asset was not purchased).
Risk: No risk if rentals are paid on time.
Security: No security required.
Control: No loss of control.

Hire-purchase

This means purchasing an asset by means of an initial deposit and the balance in the form of regular instalments paid over an agreed period.
Cost: Very expensive; interest rates are high.
Risk: Repossession of the asset if instalments are not paid.
Security: To an extent the asset is the security, as it can be lost if payments are not made.
Control: No loss of control.

LONG-TERM SOURCES OF FINANCE

These include money provided by the owners (*equity*) or *venture capital* from external sources, *long-term bank loans*, or *Government grants*.

Equity (share capital)

Equity is provided by the owners or shareholders and is the capital of the company. It remains as a permanent source of finance as long as the company remains in existence. Shareholders get a *dividend* from the company's profits.
Cost: Cost of share issue, cost of dividends.
Risk: Loss of investment if venture fails.
Security: No security required.
Control: Loss of voting control to new shareholders. Control of the business will have to be shared with new shareholders.

Venture capital

This is finance provided as start-up capital to new firms that are considered to be especially risky and unable to raise finance from more conventional sources. Capital is provided through a loan or through purchase of shares, or both.

A venture capital company usually appoints one of its staff to the board of directors of the new enterprise to oversee the operations. Examples of venture capital companies: Allied Irish Investment Bank, Industrial Credit Company.

Long-term loans (debentures)

These are provided by banks. They carry a fixed rate of interest, and there is a specific repayment schedule.
Cost: High interest payments, which may be substantially reduced as interest is tax-deductible.

Risk: Loss of assets put forward as security if the loan is not repaid.
Security: Fixed assets are required as security.
Control: The lender may impose restrictions on the management's freedom to act independently as part of a loan agreement.

Government grants
These usually have conditions attached. The project must be viable in the long run and must create jobs. Grants are available from Enterprise Ireland and from county enterprise boards.
Cost: No interest or cash repayments nor dividend payments.
Risk: If the conditions attached are not met, the grant may be recalled.
Security: No security required.
Control: The body advancing the grant may look for share ownership to make sure the grant is used in accordance with the agreement.

THE MANAGEMENT OF WORKING CAPITAL

Liquidity
This is the ability of the firm to pay short-term debts as they fall due.

Working capital
This is the day-to-day finance available for running the business. It is the excess of current assets over current liabilities.

Working capital keeps the business going from day to day. If working capital is positive, the business is *liquid.*

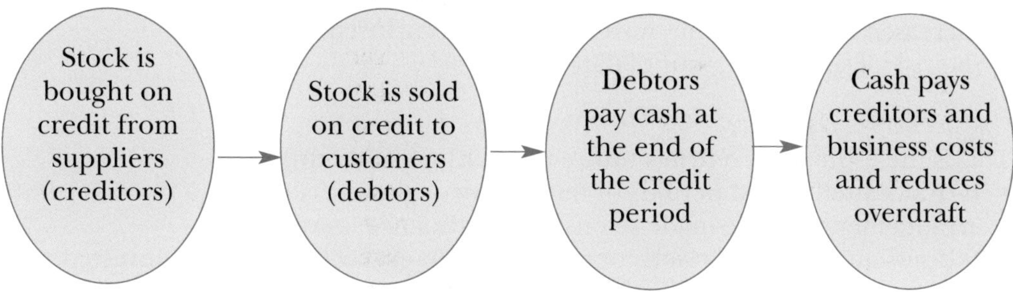

THE WORKING CAPITAL CYCLE

Overtrading
If working capital is negative—that is, if current liabilities are greater than current assets—the business is said to be *overtrading.*

When working capital is negative the following difficulties may arise:
- inability to pay debts when they become due, with a consequent loss of goodwill and creditworthiness
- inability to take advantage of discounts for prompt payment
- stock withheld by a supplier until payment is made in cash
- the firm may be forced to sell goods at reduced prices to obtain funds quickly
- the firm may be forced to buy goods in small, uneconomical quantities.

CREDIT CONTROL (See also chapter 7)

Control is exercised by a firm over its trade debtors to ensure that customers pay their debts on time, to minimise the risk of bad debts.

Credit control involves establishing a credit policy:

- assessing the creditworthiness of customers
- encouraging prompt payment by offering cash discounts
- monitoring and recording payments due
- recovering bad debts and pursuing overdue accounts
- minimising the amount of money tied up by debtors, improving liquidity and profitability.

Bad debts

Bad debts are amounts owed by debtors that are unlikely to be paid, for example when a customer becomes insolvent. Bad debts are written off as a business cost to the profit and loss account for the period.

STOCK CONTROL (See also chapter 7)

Stock is controlled so that the firm has the correct amount at all times to satisfy customers' demands—never too much, never too little.

Too little stock means

- lost orders
- loss of goodwill
- production difficulties.

Too much stock means

- cash tied up in stock
- increased insurance, rent, warehouse and security costs
- the risk of stock going out of date.

CASH FLOW FORECAST (See also chapter 8)

This is the estimate of a firm's future cash inflows and outflows.

- It draws attention to periods of temporary negative cash flow, so that overdraft arrangements can be made to ensure that finance is available.
- It draws attention to periods of surplus, when excess funds can be invested.

TAX IMPLICATIONS OF BUSINESS START-UP

Businesses are subject to the following taxes:

(1) *Income tax*

Sole traders and partnerships are liable to income tax on profits. They must register under the self-assessment system, submit their own estimate of tax liability, and send the amount to the Revenue Commissioners.

(2) *Corporation tax*

Limited companies pay corporation tax on profits.

(3) *Value-added tax (VAT)*

All traders whose annual turnover exceeds a specified amount must register for VAT. The trader pays VAT on goods and services purchased, and charges VAT on goods and services supplied.

If the tax collected exceeds the amount of tax paid, the difference must be paid to the Collector-General. If the tax paid exceeds the amount of tax collected, the Collector General refunds the excess.

(4) *Pay-as-you-earn (PAYE) income tax*
Employers must deduct income tax at a specified rate from employees' wages and send it to the Revenue Commissioners.

(5) *Pay-related social insurance (PRSI)*
Employers are obliged to deduct PRSI from employees' wages. PRSI is made up of social insurance and a health levy. The employer pays a contribution towards PRSI for each employee.

Ownership options

When starting a business, an entrepreneur has a choice of many different types of business structure through which to conduct business, including
- sole trader
- partnership
- limited company.

SOLE TRADER
Sole traders set up a business of which they are the sole owner. This is an attractive route for a person who is concerned with retaining ownership and control of their own business.

PARTNERSHIP
A partnership is an agreement between two or more people (up to a maximum of twenty) to go into business together with a view to making a profit.
- Extra capital is available to finance the business.
- Profits and losses are shared between the partners.
- Risk and responsibility are shared.

LIMITED COMPANY
A limited company is a legal entity separate from its owners. The shareholders have *limited liability* and are not personally liable for the debts of the company: they can lose only the amount of their investment.

A private limited company has a minimum of one shareholder and a maximum of fifty.

Shareholders buy shares in the company, and this forms its share capital. Profits are divided among shareholders through *dividends.*

Production options

Having decided what products to produce, a firm must choose a method of production. There are three main methods: job production, batch production, and mass production.

JOB PRODUCTION

This involves producing one-off items to suit specific customers' orders.

CHARACTERISTICS

1. The product is produced to a customer's order: goods are not held in stock.
2. Production involves skilled work, with an emphasis on craftsmanship, not the quantity produced.
3. Raw materials, machinery and equipment are expensive.
4. The cost of production is high, and the product is therefore expensive.
   Examples: Hand-crafted furniture, shipbuilding, suit of clothes, wedding dress, hand-cut crystal, building a house.

BATCH PRODUCTION

This involves the manufacture of a number of identical products in batches rather than continuously. A furniture manufacturer might produce tables in week 1, chairs in week 2, and wardrobes in week 3, with machines generally being reset after each batch, ready to process the next batch.

CHARACTERISTICS

1. Within each stage of the production process, work is completed for the whole batch before the next batch is started.
2. Because of the larger quantity of goods produced, efficient production planning and control are necessary.
3. Labour is skilled (trained in a trade) or semi-skilled (trained to do a particular task).
4. The products produced are of average price and are held in stock in anticipation of customers' demands.
   Examples: books, bread, clothes, tinned vegetables, furniture.

MASS PRODUCTION

This involves manufacturing large numbers of an identical product in a continuously moving and highly automated process.

CHARACTERISTICS

1. High capital expenditure is involved in setting up an assembly line, which depends on efficient plant layout as well as good product design to minimise the unit cost.
2. The production process is geared to producing one standardised product, and product design remains the same over long periods.
3. Goods are produced and held in stock; large demand is essential.
4. More machinery than labour (skilled or semi-skilled) is used.
   Examples: cars, computers, tins of peas, domestic appliances, electricity.

Developing a business plan

A business plan is a statement of objectives, proposed operations, marketing strategy, financial requirements and financial forecasts for a business. It is an essential document for raising capital or loans.

PURPOSE OF A BUSINESS PLAN

1. It states the goals and objectives and sets out how these are to be achieved.
2. It ascertains whether the project is a good one and whether it is likely to provide an adequate profit for the owners.
3. It is required by financial institutions when finance is being sought and also by county enterprise boards when assistance is being sought.
4. It is useful to a person starting a business in mapping out the route to be taken and in becoming focused.

IMPORTANCE OF A BUSINESS PLAN

A business plan is important in enabling a company—

(1) to ensure that the owners and managers understand clearly what is required to make a success of the venture;
(2) to raise finance for the business, for example loans from financial institutions and potential investors, grants from state agencies or the European Union;
(3) to set targets that provide a yardstick by which to measure the company's performance;
(4) to formulate the company's future business strategies;
(5) to help the owners and the managers anticipate problems and prepare solutions to them.

BUSINESS PLAN

MICHELLE MORAN CATERING SERVICE LTD

Company ownership and management structure

Name of company:	Michelle Moran Catering Service Ltd.
Formed:	1 January 2015.
Shareholders:	Michelle Moran, Audrey Griffin.
Registered office:	45 O'Connell Street, Killarney, Co. Kerry.
Solicitors:	Keane and Irwin, Killarney.
Accountants:	Ferguson and Keegan Ltd, Killarney.
Bankers:	Allied Irish Bank, Main Street, Killarney.
Managing director:	Michelle Moran.
Education:	Business studies degree, University of Limerick.
Work experience:	Ten years' experience in catering industry.

Product or service

Salad rolls, sandwiches, sausage rolls, soup, scones, cakes.

Unique selling-points: Home-made products, prompt delivery, personal service and quality.

Marketing and marketing strategy

Target market:	300 small businesses, including factories and schools without canteen facilities requiring supplies.
Market niche:	Schools, colleges, and factories.
Competition:	Confectioners, bakeries, and delicatessens.

→

Targets: 100 customers after six months.
Pricing policy: 10 per cent lower than competitors.

Sales and distribution
Advertising and promotion: Brochures, newspapers, leaflets, local radio.
Distribution: Local morning delivery service.

Financing

Requirements:	Ten-year lease of premises		€20,000
	Equipment		€10,000
	Motor vehicle		€15,000
	Working capital		€5,000
			€50,000
Finance available:	Own investment (equity)	€10,000	
	Grant (CEB)	€5,000	€15,000
	Finance required:		€35,000

Financial projections
See projected profit and loss accounts and balance sheet (three years), cash flow forecast and break-even charts (three years) enclosed.

Michelle Moran

Michelle Moran

15. EXPANSION

STAGES OF BUSINESS GROWTH

Four stages of business growth can be identified:
(1) Commencement
(2) Survival
(3) Growth
(4) Maturity.

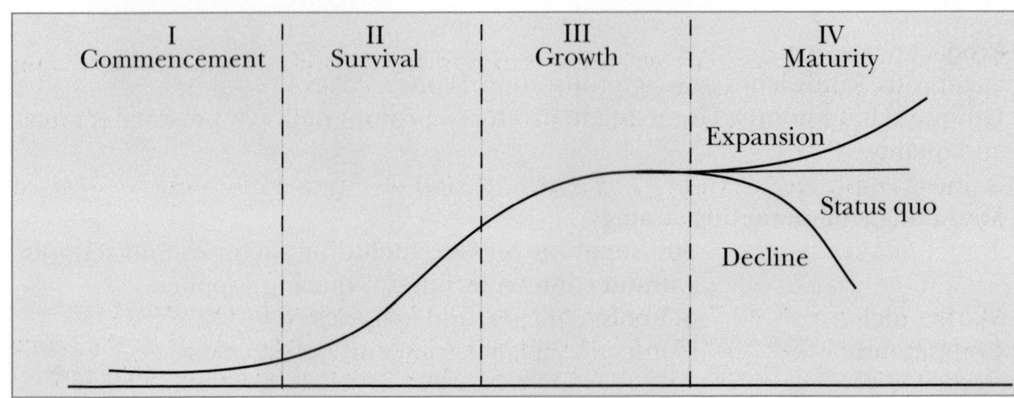

Commencement
The firm is concerned with having enough cash to meet demands and enough customers to make the business viable.

Survival
The main problem at this stage is cash flow. There must be enough cash to break even and cover costs and to finance enough growth to earn a reasonable return on investment.

Growth
The firm at this stage is large enough to ensure profitability. It usually has the need to expand further; but care must be taken not to expand too quickly, which might affect profits.

Maturity
The firm at this stage has reached its full potential in size and has adequate financial resources and experienced management.

Reasons for expansion

(1) *Economies of scale*
There is a reduction in the cost of production and distribution of the product as the size of the firm increases and output increases.

(2) *Diversification*
This involves moving into different product areas. Greater security can be achieved by moving into other areas of business and other products.

(3) *Elimination of competition*
Competition can be eliminated by a merger or the take-over of a competitor.

(4) *Increased sales and profits*
Increased sales, better use of resources and lower costs may lead to increased profits.

(5) *Specialisation in management*
Size allows specialisation in management. Large firms are able to afford specialists —offering good working conditions, promotion prospects, and fringe benefits.

(6) *Safeguarding raw materials*
The firm may want to secure its source of raw materials, and so it expands by taking over its supplier.

(7) *Psychological reasons*
Businesspeople are ambitious and like challenges and continuously strive to expand their business.

(8) *Synergy*
This is where the profit is greater than the sum of its parts (the so-called '2 + 2 = 5' effect). In the case of a merger, one firm may be good at production, while the other excels at marketing. Joining the two can make the combined firm more effective.

Finance for expansion

The following are the main sources of finance for business expansion:

(1) EQUITY CAPITAL

The company issues shares for cash, which is used to expand the business. This is referred to as *share capital* or *risk capital,* because of the uncertain nature of business.

Ordinary shareholders have voting rights and a say in policy-making. Capital is repaid only on the winding up of the company.

Shareholders hope to earn a profit on their investment by receiving dividends. They expect improved profitability and an increase in the value of the business because of expansion, and therefore the value of shares held should increase.

The principal sources of equity capital are *personal sources* and *corporate sources.* Personal sources include the promoters' equity, including family and friends and other individuals. Corporate sources are usually businesses that specialise in providing finance to business. They invest money for a share in the business.

(2) RETAINED EARNINGS

This is an amount of profit re-invested in the business for expansion purposes, rather than distributed as dividends. It is used for buying assets or acquiring other firms.

- No cost is involved.
- There is no loss of control.

(3) LOAN CAPITAL

This is long-term finance from financial institutions.

DEBENTURE LOANS

These are long-term loans to a company. They usually carry a fixed rate of interest and a specific repayment date.

Security is normally required, which may be some specific asset or a charge on all assets of the business. The company must pay debenture interest, irrespective of profitability.

- Interest is tax-deductible.
- Control of the business is not affected.

COMMERCIAL MORTGAGES

Banks provide long-term mortgages for the purchase or expansion of commercial premises. They operate like ordinary mortgages, though interest rates differ from those applying to house mortgages.

- The title deeds of the premises are usually given as security.

(4) GRANTS

Grants are an important long-term source of finance for growth and expansion.

The main provider of grant assistance is the state agency Enterprise Ireland. The European Union may also provide grants to assist expansion in developing firms. Many businesses can also apply for grants from county enterprise boards.

COMPARISON OF EQUITY CAPITAL AND LOAN CAPITAL

	Equity capital	**Loan capital**
1	A firm financed by equity is said to have low gearing or low risk.	A company financed by long-term debt (loan capital) is said to have high gearing or high risk.
2	The company is not obliged to pay dividends to shareholders if no profit is made.	Loan interest must be paid, irrespective of profits.
3	The company can decide on the level of dividends.	Fixed interest must be paid annually.
4	Capital does not have to be repaid unless the company is being liquidated.	Capital must be repaid at some future date.
5	No security is required.	Security is required.
6	Dividends are not tax-deductible.	Interest is tax-deductible.
7	Issuing ordinary shares reduces control over the company.	The loan does not affect the control of the company.

Implications of expansion

Expansion has many implications. Some effects will occur in the short term, others will appear in the long term.

(1) SHORT-TERM IMPLICATIONS

SHARE PRICE
The share price should increase because of increased demand for shares in anticipation of a bigger and more successful business.

PRODUCT MIX
There should be an increased product mix.

COMPANY STRUCTURE
A formal structure must be set up with a clear line of authority and a definite chain of command. Functional responsibilities, such as production and marketing, must be delegated.

FINANCIAL STRUCTURE
Finance in the form of equity capital and loan capital must be raised.

RESOURCES
There should be an increased demand for raw materials, transport and other resources as a result of expansion.

SUPPLIES
Economies of purchase mean that large-scale purchases can obtain better credit terms, discounts, and prompt delivery.

PROFITS
The high costs involved in expansion may lead to a reduction in profit.

DIVIDENDS
There may be reduced dividends because of reduced profit.

EMPLOYEES
Employees' uncertainty about the future may lead to poor motivation and lack of performance. Human resource policies and procedures must be implemented to cope with increased staff levels on expansion.

CUSTOMERS
Economies of scale should provide customers with more competitively priced products.

(2) LONG-TERM IMPLICATIONS

SHARE PRICE
Increased confidence and interest in the business, increased profits and an increase in the value of the business in the long term will lead to an increased share price.

PRODUCT MIX
Because of continuing market research and product development, there will be a wider product mix.

COMPANY STRUCTURE
As the business grows, further delegation is required. This brings in the knowledge, experience and expertise of many more people.

FINANCIAL STRUCTURE
Increased confidence in the management's ability to successfully manage the business means that shareholders will be more willing to invest and the bank more willing to lend. This should provide the company with a sound financial base.

RESOURCES
Increased production capacity may be required to cope with increased demand by customers.

SUPPLIES
Creditors' increased confidence in the business will lead to better purchasing terms, increased discounts, and extended credit.

PROFITS
Increased efficiency and the success of expansion will lead to increased profit in the long term.

DIVIDENDS
Increased profits will allow increased dividends to be paid to shareholders.

EMPLOYEES
Employees can be provided with better wages, better working conditions, promotion prospects, and training and development opportunities.

CUSTOMERS
Customers benefit from better prices but lose personal contact with the owners, which may ultimately affect customers' confidence.

Methods of expansion

The main methods of expansion are:
(1) **internal growth** (organic growth)
  (*a*) increasing market share
  (*b*) market development;

(2) **external growth** (inorganic growth)
  (*a*) strategic alliance or joint venture
  (*b*) merger or amalgamation
  (*c*) take-over or acquisition.

(1) INTERNAL GROWTH (ORGANIC GROWTH)

This is growth that is self-generated, that is, expansion from within, rather that achieved externally through mergers and take-overs. Finance for expansion will come from internal sources rather than from shareholders or loans; as a result, it is likely to be steady, slow, and very secure.

A company can expand internally in the following ways:
- **increasing market share**—expanding existing markets
- **market development**—finding new markets for existing products, usually by introducing products into a new geographical area.

  New markets can be entered by:
    exporting—selling products or services into foreign markets;
    licensing—where the holder of a patent or copyright allows other firms to use its technology and distribution network to produce its products in return for a fee or royalties.
    franchising—this is the granting by one firm to another of the right to supply its products. It is a contractual arrangement entered into for a specified period, with the franchisee paying royalties. Examples: McDonald's, Burger King, Kentucky Fried Chicken. (See also chapter 7.)

(2) EXTERNAL GROWTH (INORGANIC GROWTH)

This is business growth that involves a firm expanding its activities by alliance (joint venture), merger, or take-over. It allows a firm to expand more rapidly.

External growth has some attractions: for example, a merger or take-over of a competitor can allow a firm to increase its market share while availing of the economies of scale through the rationalisation of the two firms' operations.

Merged or acquired firms have to be integrated into one company, which may mean the streamlining of operations, managerial problems, or the creation of new managerial structures. If it is not done effectively, efficiency can be impaired and financial resources stretched.

STRATEGIC ALLIANCE (JOINT VENTURE)

This is an arrangement whereby two or more companies work together for the benefit of both, perhaps to increase sales or profits: for example, one company produces the product and the other company markets and distributes it.

The alliance is designed to build on the expertise and skills of each member so that they complement each other.

It is a less expensive way of expanding a firm's business than undertaking a full merger or take-over, and it allows a firm to withdraw from the activity more easily.

MERGER (AMALGAMATION)

This is an agreement between the management and shareholders of two or more firms to voluntarily form a single business, with a new board of directors. All parties to the combination participate in the management of the new company.

The combining firms are relatively equal in size, as for example in the merger of Irish Life and Irish Permanent to become Irish Life and Permanent.

TAKE-OVER (ACQUISITION)

This means obtaining control of another firm by buying 51 per cent or more of its share capital.

A take-over is often resisted by the management of the target firm; the bidder must convince the shareholders that selling is of benefit to them.

A 51 per cent stake in the target company would give the acquiring company control. Generally it would wish to take full control to be free from interference by minority interests.

INTEGRATION

The process of combining two firms is called integration. It can be either *horizontal* or *vertical.*

Horizontal integration

This is when a firm takes over or merges with another firm at the same stage of production, for example two breweries.

Vertical integration

This is when two firms in the same industry but at different stages of production join together, for example a manufacturer joining with a supplier.

CONTROL OF BUSINESS GROWTH

Control of business growth is monitored by competition law and by EU competition policy.

Competition law

The Competition Act (1991) established the Competition Authority. This was set up

- to prevent business activity that reduces competition, for example cartels
- to prevent unfair business practices, for example price-fixing
- to investigate mergers and take-overs and to decide whether they should be allowed to proceed or be stopped.

EU competition policy

EU competition policy applies to practices that may affect trade between member-states. It takes precedence over national law.

Large mergers or take-overs must be approved by the EU Commissioner for Competition to ensure that they do not breach EU competition policy.

KEY TERMS

These are some of the more important terms introduced in unit 5:

acquisition	market research
advertising	mass production
batch production	multiples
branding	own brands
break-even	personal selling
business plan	product life-cycle
cash flow forecast	prototype
channels of distribution	public relations
desk research	questionnaire
equity	retailer
exporting	sales promotion
feasibility study	take-over
job production	wholesaler
limited liability	working capital management
marketing mix	

LEGISLATION DISCUSSED IN UNIT 5

Consumer Information Act (1978).

ON COMPLETION OF UNIT 5 YOU SHOULD BE ABLE TO

- explain the importance of researching business ideas
- identify techniques for developing business ideas and researching them
- contrast the main sources of new product ideas
- identify and explain the elements involved in setting up a new business
- explain the stages involved in setting up a new business
- identify the main elements of a marketing strategy
- explain the elements of the marketing mix
- list the main sources of finance available for setting up a new business
- identify the elements of production processes
- illustrate the central role of the business plan

- identify the reasons for and methods of expansion
- identify three main sources of finance for expansion
- analyse the importance of business expansion in the domestic and foreign markets **(HL)**
- compare and contrast equity and loan capital as sources of finance for expansion **(HL)**
- evaluate the elements of the marketing mix **(HL)**
- apply the main sources of finance available for setting up a new business **(HL)**.

Practice questions—Section 1

1. List five headings usually contained in a business plan.
   (i) ____________________
   (ii) ____________________
   (iii) ____________________
   (iv) ____________________
   (v) ____________________

2. (*a*) Illustrate the various channels of distribution available for getting a product or service to the consumer.
   (*b*) Give an example of a product or service suitable to each channel.

Channel 1	Channel 2	Channel 3
____________	____________	____________
		____________
		____________
		____________

Example

3. Illustrate fully, with the aid of a suitable diagram, the stages of a product life-cycle.

Examination-style question and solution

Marketing

The marketing mix should be based on customers' needs and should support the required image for the product or service.

(**A**) Select a product or service of your choice and analyse the elements of the marketing mix. **(30 marks)**

(**B**) For a business to survive it must meet its costs. Illustrate, by means of a break-even chart, the following figures, showing:

(i) the break-even point.

(ii) the profit at full capacity

(iii) the margin of safety.

(20 marks)

Fixed costs: €10,000
Variable costs: €3 per unit
Forecast output (sales): 7,000 units
Selling price: €5 per unit
Full capacity: 10,000 units

(**C**) Describe two uses of a break-even chart. **(10 marks)**

Suggested solution

(A) *Elements of the marketing mix to be analysed: product; price; promotion; place.*

Product: *Nissan Primera*

This is one of a range of Nissan cars. It includes a driver's airbag among its many safety features. It carries a six-year anti-rust warranty.

Price

It is the top model in its price range and is competitively priced at €25,000 (list price). Customers can avail of an additional €3,000 discount. It is aimed at middle-income earners. The price includes free membership of the Automobile Association for one year.

Promotion

The emphasis is placed on brand loyalty. It is advertised on television and in magazines. Nissan sponsors many prestige events. There is free testing at any main Nissan garage.

Place

Main Nissan garages throughout the country, which buy from the main Nissan importer in Dublin. The Primera is imported from Japan.

(B) *Calculations*

(i) Break-even point—units

$$\frac{\text{FIXED COSTS}}{\text{contribution per unit}} = \frac{€10{,}000}{€2} = 5{,}000 \text{ units}$$

Break-even point—sales

5000 units × €5 = €25,000.

(ii) Profit at full capacity:

	€
Sales (10,000 × €5)	*50,000*
Variable costs (10,000 × €3)	*30,000*
Contribution	*20,000*
Fixed costs	*10,000*
Profit	*10,000*

(iii) Margin of safety

sales volume (units) – break-even point (units)

7,000 – 5,000

= 2,000 units

Summary of Figures

(1) Break-even point:

— Units: 5,000

— Sales: €25,000

(2) Profit at full capacity: €10,000

(3) Margin of safety: 2,000 units.

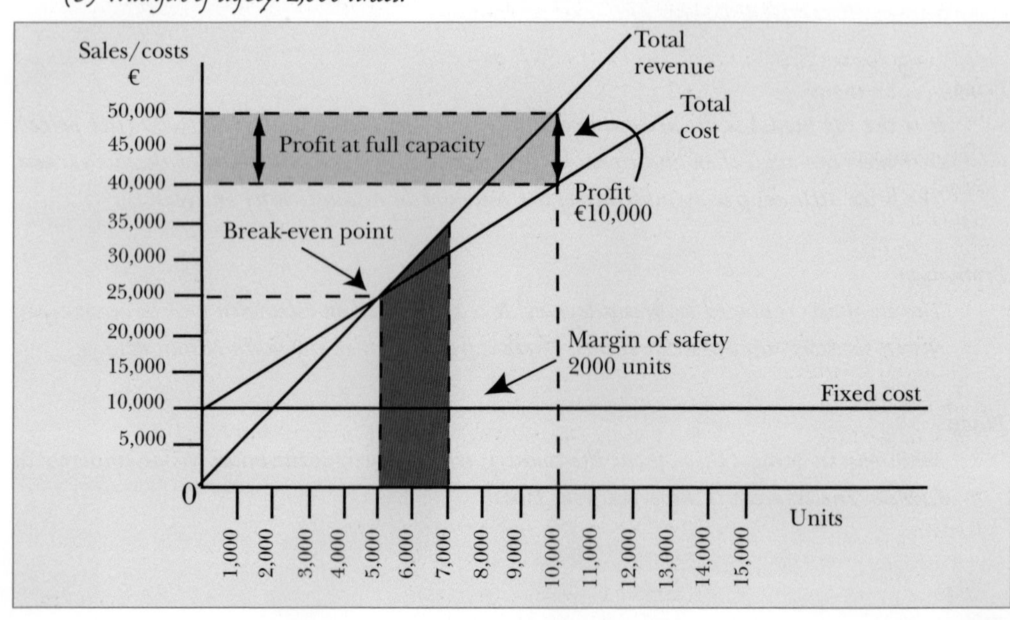

(20 marks)

(C) *Two uses of a break-even chart include:*
  (1) *it highlights the relationship between costs and profit for management decisions, for example pricing and production quantities;*
  (2) *enabling a decision to be made whether to produce or buy in.*

Examination-style question and solution

Getting started

Aileen Blake is a 26-year-old business graduate who has been working in human resource management for four years. She feels she can succeed in her own business doing consultancy work, and has asked for your help in writing the business plan.

(**A**) Explain the importance of a business plan. **(15 marks)**
(**B**) Draft a business plan for Aileen's venture under five appropriate headings. Make all relevant assumptions where necessary. **(45 marks)**

Suggested solution

(A) *A business plan is important in enabling a company to*
—formulate its future business strategies;
—provide a yardstick against which to measure the company's performance;
—seek grants from state and EU agencies and loans from financial agencies and potential investors.

(B)

Business plan for AB Management Consultants Ltd

Company ownership and management structure

Name of company	*AB Management Consultants Ltd.*
Formed	*31 May 2014*
Shareholders	*Aileen Blake, Mary Clarke*
Registered office	*Newtown, Waterford*
Solicitors	*Kerry Ltd*
Accountants	*Mayo Ltd*
Bankers	*TSB*

AB Management Consultants Ltd, specialists in human resource management

Managing director:	*Aileen Blake, aged 26*
Education:	*Business graduate*
Work experience:	*Four years' experience in human resources management.*

Product or service

Service	*Business recruitment and training* *Consultancy rooms available.*
USP	*Conflict resolution specialists.*

→

Marketing and marketing strategy

Market	*Two hundred small businesses requiring service. Fifteen customers on books.*		
Market niche	*Staff training and conflict resolution.*		
Competition	*Two recruitment agencies.*		
Target	*One hundred and fifty customers after two years.*		
Pricing policy	*20 per cent above standard rates for the industry.*		

Sales and distribution

Advertising and promotion:	*Specialist brochures; personal contacts; word of mouth. Twice-weekly local radio programme.*		

Financing

Requirements	*Ten-year lease of office block*	*€30,000*	
	Equipment	*€15,000*	
	Working capital	*€25,000*	*€70,000*
Finance available	*Own investment (equity)*	*€35,000*	
	Grant	*€10,000*	*€45,000*
	Finance required		*€25,000*
Financial projections	*See projected profit and loss accounts and balance sheets (three years). Cash flow forecasts and break-even charts (three years) enclosed.*		

Aileen Blake

Revision question

Business in action

The contribution of marketing techniques to the success of products and services is very great.

(**A**) Demonstrate a method of carrying out marketing research. **(10 marks)**

(**B**) Distinguish between the marketing concept and the marketing strategy. **(20 marks)**

(**C**) Evaluate the marketing mix for a product or service of your choice. **(30 marks)**

[60 marks]

SECTION C: ENVIRONMENT

Unit 6: Domestic Environment

Business does not operate in a vacuum: it is part of the wider economic system. This section looks at the different types of industry and business in the local and national economy. It also examines the relationship between business and the Government.

Objective: To enable pupils to understand the interaction between business firms, the local community, the Government, and the economy.

16. Categories of Industry

An **industry** is a number of firms producing similar goods or services, for example the brewing industry. They use similar raw materials and production systems.

The main categories of industry are the *primary sector* (agriculture and natural resources), *manufacturing*, and *services*.

Natural resources

The main natural resource industries are **agriculture, forestry, fishing, mining, energy,** and **scenic landscape**.

Agriculture

IMPORTANCE OF AGRICULTURE IN THE ECONOMY

1. Agriculture employs 12 per cent of the labour force.
2. It is a source of raw materials for many industries, for example food-processing, brewing.
3. It provides a market for a wide variety of industrial products: farm machinery, fertilisers, farm chemicals, services.
4. It provides food for the population: meat, milk, fruit, vegetables.
5. Home-produced food reduces the need to import, while surplus food can be exported: approximately 80 per cent of output is exported, helping the balance of payments.

TRENDS IN AGRICULTURE

(1) A DECLINE IN THE NUMBERS WORKING IN AGRICULTURE because of mechanisation, fluctuating prices, etc.

(2) OVERPRODUCTION because of increased productivity and guaranteed minimum prices.

(3) EU SUPPORTS: livestock subsidies (beef premium), structural grants (agri-tourism grants, development of organic produce, early retirement scheme).
(4) THE MOVE TO ALTERNATIVE ENTERPRISES, for example deer farming, ostrich farming.
(5) ENVIRONMENTAL CONCERNS: rural environmental protection scheme (REPS). Farmers must farm in accordance with an agri-environmental plan, controlling waste effluent, etc.
(6) QUALITY AND FOOD SAFETY: BSE, pesticide residues and the unlawful use of antibiotics have heightened people's awareness of food safety.
(7) ALTERNATIVE EMPLOYMENT: part-time employment in factories to increase income.

Forestry

THE IMPORTANCE OF FORESTRY

1. It provides direct employment.
2. It provides indirect employment, for example furniture manufacturing.
3. It provides raw material for industry.
4. It helps promote tourism.

TRENDS IN FORESTRY

1. Forests are mainly owned, run and developed by a state agency, 'Coillte', whose primary function is to maximise returns from state forests and promote their development.
2. With falling profits from farms, forestry has become an attractive option for many farmers. This growth in afforestation has been boosted by state and EU grants.
3. To encourage private afforestation, there is a planting grant scheme. This helps overcome the initial costs associated with planting trees.
4. All profits from forestry, including grants, forest premium payments, and timber sales, are exempt from income tax. This is an incentive to anybody considering private forestry.

Fishing

IMPORTANCE OF FISHING IN THE ECONOMY

1. It provides food—an important source of protein, vitamins, and fats.
2. It provides direct employment—mainly in the south-west, west, and north-west.
3. It provides indirect employment in processing, distribution, and servicing vessels.

TRENDS IN FISHING

(1) *Overfishing and depletion of fishing stocks*

Large and modern boats have increased fish catches and have given rise to problems of overfishing. Fishing vessels from other EU countries fishing in Irish waters have led to a reduction in fish stocks.

(2) *Pollution*

This is caused by oil spills and discharges from land containing residues of pesticides, insecticides, fertiliser, and industrial waste.

(3) *Increased demand*
Following the outbreak of BSE, there has been increased demand for fish.

(4) *Fish processing and marketing*
This has grown in significance, and the potential remains for further development.

(5) *Aquaculture*
The increased demand for fish has encouraged the commercial development of fish-farming or aquaculture. The main products are mussels, oysters, trout, and salmon.

(6) *The future*
The Government considers that the fishing industry has considerable potential and should be promoted more effectively.

Mining and energy

THE IMPORTANCE OF MINING AND ENERGY IN THE ECONOMY

1. Mining is a source of raw materials for industry: iron, copper, lead, tin, zinc, and gypsum.
2. It is a source of energy: coal, gas, turf.
3. It creates employment—direct and indirect.

MINING

Ireland has a varied geographical framework, which contains a wide selection of base and precious metals as well as industrial mineral deposits. The majority of Irish mining produce is exported.

ENERGY

Natural gas
1. The transmission of gas is the responsibility of An Bord Gáis.
2. Natural gas off the coast has been brought ashore and piped around the country.

Turf
Ireland has large reserves of turf, whose development is handled by the state company Bord na Móna. Virtually all the produce goes to serve two main markets: the generating stations run by the ESB and the domestic heating market.

Oil
Exploration wells have been drilled in the sea, with encouraging flows being recorded and a number of licences awarded.

Water
This is the cleanest and cheapest source of electricity.

Wind
Wind farms are becoming common in upland areas in the west of Ireland.

Scenic landscape

Ireland has a beautiful and relatively unspoilt landscape, with rugged mountains, cliffs, beaches, and numerous historical features, such as Newgrange, the Rock of Cashel, and Blarney Castle, all a major attraction to tourists.

Fáilte Éireann is the state body with responsibility for the development of tourism.

Manufacturing industry

Manufacturing industry converts a raw material into a finished product. Examples of manufacturing industry include:

CHEMICAL INDUSTRY—produces agricultural chemicals, fertilisers, nitric acid, citric acid, for example Monsanto.

PHARMACEUTICAL INDUSTRY—produces drugs for human and animal needs, for example Pfizer, Schering-Plough, GlaxoSmithKline.

ELECTRONICS INDUSTRY—produces electronic components, for example Boston Scientific.

FOOD PROCESSING—produces dairy products: cheese, butter, yoghurt, for example Kerry Group PLC, Glanbia PLC.

BREWING INDUSTRY—produces beer and spirits, for example Guinness, Murphy, Beamish and Crawford.

TECHNOLOGY INDUSTRY—produces computer hardware and software, for example Hewlett-Packard, Dell, Apple, Microsoft, Lotus.

IMPORTANCE OF MANUFACTURING IN THE ECONOMY

1. It provides direct employment.
2. It provides indirect employment in industries supplying raw materials.
3. It earns foreign currency through exports.

In Ireland, manufacturing industry is carried on by
(*a*) indigenous firms,
(*b*) transnational companies, and
(*c*) agri-businesses.

INDIGENOUS INDUSTRY

Indigenous companies are those set up, owned and managed by Irish people and with their principal place of business in Ireland.

Ireland has been overdependent on foreign firms for creating employment, so the Government established a state body, called Enterprise Ireland, with the responsibility for developing indigenous industry.

TRANSNATIONAL COMPANIES

Transnational companies have their head office in one country but manufacturing plants in many countries.

The IDA has the role of attracting foreign industries to set up in Ireland. Many transnationals have set up here; examples include Coca-Cola, Microsoft, Intel, and IBM.

They receive grants, advance factories, and tax incentives. Most of their output is exported to member-counties of the European Union.

AGRI-BUSINESS

This refers to those industries that use agricultural produce, such as beef and milk, as their raw material. The main products include cheese, yoghurt, butter, dairy products, beer, and flour.

Agri-business has been developed by the former agricultural co-operatives, including Kerry Group, and Glanbia.

TRENDS IN MANUFACTURING INDUSTRY

1. There is a shift away from traditional manufacturing industry to high-technology industry.
2. Industries are becoming more capital-intensive; technological developments, such as CAD and CAM, require less labour.
3. More transnational companies are establishing in Ireland to gain access to European markets, particularly in the technological, computer and scientific areas, for example Johnson and Johnson, Boston Scientific.
4. Many labour-intensive textile companies have closed because of competition and low wage levels in other countries, for example China.
5. Many companies with high-quality products have large export niche markets, for example Waterford Crystal and Blarney Woollen Mills, exporting to the United States, where quality is more important than price.
6. There is a trend towards producing environmentally responsible products in response to customer demand.
7. There have been many mergers and take-overs among the agri-business companies to enable them to compete in the global market: for example, Waterford Foods merged with Avonmore Foods, now called Glanbia.
8. Co-operatives have been converted into public limited companies, for example Kerry Group PLC.

THE CONSTRUCTION INDUSTRY

The construction industry involves the building of the country's infrastructure: roads, bridges, schools, hospitals, factories, offices, shops, and housing.

IMPORTANCE OF THE CONSTRUCTION INDUSTRY IN THE ECONOMY

1. It is a labour-intensive industry, providing thousands of jobs.
2. It uses Irish raw materials and natural resources.
3. It reflects the state of the economy. If there is economic growth, the construction industry will expand and prosper.

TRENDS IN THE CONSTRUCTION INDUSTRY

1. There is considerable growth in the industry, with a huge demand for housing.
2. Large infrastructural projects have been aided by finance from the EU structural fund, for example the Lee Tunnel in Cork.
3. The construction industry is greatly influenced by interest rates and Government capital spending.

Services

The services sector provides all other industries with a wide range of services, including financial and business, leisure and tourism, catering, retailing, wholesaling, distribution, communication, and professional and personal services.

Growth in the services sector

Forfás forecasts that many of the new jobs created in the future will be in services. Because of the growing importance of services, the Government is placing the emphasis on the creation of jobs in this area.

Locally provided services will be a significant job provider in the future. This growth will be in

- commercial services—business, communications, tourism
- personal services—entertainment, child-minding, restaurants
- professional services—accountancy, law, education, health.

Internationally traded services will also be a significant provider of jobs, including services such as financial, software, consultancy.

Because of the rapid advances in information and telecommunications technologies, opportunities for growth exist.

Service industry and new technology

Many new services have evolved in recent years as a result of changes in technology.

- In banking there are ATMs (cash-dispensing machines) and phone-in banking services, with access to accounts and loan applications over the phone.
- There are advances in education and training through multimedia and software programs.
- Wholesale and retail trades have become more efficient through using scanners at the point of sale, with improved stock management.
- Technology has transformed Government services, transport, and health services.
- The internet will become the norm for transacting business.
- Business will have employees operating from home (teleworking).

Reasons for the growth in services

1. There has been a development and expansion of education.
2. Expanded Government services have led to increased employment in the public sector.
3. The development of the economy has led to employment opportunities in business.
4. More disposable income leads to increased demand for leisure—holiday, travel, entertainment.
5. There has been growth in internationally traded services—services that can be exported: for example, financial consultancy has led to many new firms being set up to exploit opportunities.

Changing trends in product development

Companies deciding on new products must be aware of changes and trends in the economy that affect the demand for certain types of goods and services. Business must react to changes and provide goods and services to meet customers' demands.

Changes and trends include

- greater participation in education
- a general rise in living standards; more disposable income
- an increase in the number of women employed full time; a demand for convenience food
- a decreasing birth rate; smaller families
- an increased demand for housing; smaller houses to meet the needs of smaller families and first-time buyers
- an increased interest in fitness and health
- an increase in the amount of leisure time available to people, leading to an increase in entertainment services, for example restaurants, cinemas, video games, internet cafés.

17. TYPES OF BUSINESS ORGANISATION

Sole trader

This is a business owned and controlled by a single person. It is a common form of business, and the method by which many businesses start. It is most favoured by the owners of small retail units and by farmers, publicans, and service firms.

CHARACTERISTICS

The owner provides the capital for setting up and running the business. He or she may borrow from family, friends, or a bank. The owner has direct and personal control over the business. Decisions can be made quickly.

The owner usually works full time in the business. They may have paid employees.

The owner receives all the profits and bears all the risks of losses.

FORMATION

It is easy to set up and subject to minimal regulation. There are almost no legal formalities, apart from registering with the Registrar of Business Names if the business name is not the proprietor's name. Anyone wishing to operate a pub must obtain a licence.

The business must register for PAYE, PRSI and VAT if relevant.

ADVANTAGES

1. Relations with customers and employees are usually good. Customers are known personally to the proprietor; employees work alongside the owner.
2. A sole trader is not obliged to disclose financial accounts or any information on the business except for tax purposes.
3. It is possible to change the business structure later to that of a limited company.
4. There are no costly reporting or registration costs.

DISADVANTAGES

1. Sole traders sometimes work long hours, with few holidays and limited leisure time.
2. Should the business fail, the owner alone is liable for debts. Creditors may seize not only business assets but also personal possessions, such as a house. This is called *unlimited liability*.
3. Sole traders generally have little capital for expansion and are heavily reliant on their own personal commitment to make the business a success.
4. Raising finance may be a problem, as the bank may doubt whether the person has all the necessary qualities for success.
5. The business usually stays small, because of problems of working capital and cash flow.
6. The business is dependent on the owner's continuing good health.
7. Problems with succession often mean that the business dies on the retirement or death of the owner.

Partnership

This is an agreement between two or more people to go into business with a view to making a profit. Membership of the firm is between two and twenty; exceptions are accountants and solicitors, who may have more, while a banking partnership is limited to ten.

Partnerships are common among doctors, solicitors, architects, accountants, and surveyors.

FORMATION

Few legal formalities are required to set up a partnership.

The firm must register its business name if this is different from the partners' names. Partnerships are governed by the Partnership Act (1890).

All partners should sign a written agreement (*deed of partnership*), which sets out

(*a*) how the business should be financed,
(*b*) the partners' salaries,
(*c*) how profits and losses are to be shared, and
(*d*) what happens if a partner decides to leave.

Having this agreed in advance may avoid serious problems later.

ADVANTAGES

1. Extra capital is available to finance the business.
2. The partners can specialise, for example one partner buying and another selling, as they may have different skills and experience.
3. Decision-making is shared.
4. Risk and responsibility are shared.
5. Financial results are not open to public inspection.

DISADVANTAGES

1. Each partner is personally liable for all the debts of the business: they have *unlimited liability*, like a sole trader.

2. The partners are responsible not only for their own actions but also for those of the other partners.
3. Partners may turn out to be incompatible: difficulties may arise if there is a dispute among them, or if one partner wants to withdraw their investment.
4. Death, insanity or bankruptcy will result in the termination of the partnership.
5. The profits must be shared between partners.

Private limited company

A private limited company is a firm in which a number of people—the *shareholders*—contribute funds to finance the firm in return for shares. The minimum number of shareholders is one; the maximum is fifty.

The shareholders have *limited liability*, so they can lose only whatever amount they invest. Once a company is formed it becomes a separate legal entity, distinct from its shareholders. The company has the word *Limited* or *Teoranta* as the last part of its name.

Shares cannot be bought and sold on the stock exchange.

The company is managed by a board of directors appointed by the shareholders. The directors must report on the progress of the company to its shareholders at the AGM, where shareholders can vote to remove directors if they are dissatisfied with their performance.

SINGLE-MEMBER PRIVATE LIMITED COMPANY

Under an EU regulation issued in 1994 a person can form a single-member private limited company. There will be only one name in the memorandum of association; but there must be two directors.

ADVANTAGES OF A PRIVATE LIMITED COMPANY

1. Limited liability ensures that the personal assets of shareholders are safe if the company goes into liquidation. This assumes that personal guarantees have not been given to any person or institution to whom the company owes money.
2. Obtaining credit from suppliers and finance from financial institutions (*debt capital*) is easier when trading as a private limited company as compared with a sole trader.
3. The company can have up to fifty shareholders who can invest money in the company (*equity capital*).
4. The company's profits are subject to much lower rates of tax. From 1 January 2003 the corporation tax rate has been $12\frac{1}{2}$ per cent.

DISADVANTAGES OF A PRIVATE LIMITED COMPANY

1. It is more difficult to set up: there are many legal regulations to be followed.
2. Substantial costs are involved in forming a private limited company and in complying with the Companies Acts.
3. As a company is a separate legal entity, the freedom to withdraw money from it is restricted.
4. The company is required by law to carry out an annual audit. Accounts must comply with the Companies Acts and the Auditing and Accountancy Standards.

5. The cost of completing accounts is significantly higher than for a sole trader or partnership.
6. An annual return and accounts must be made to the Registrar of Companies. Companies must also make a tax return and pay corporation tax on profits.
7. Profits are shared among the shareholders.

FORMATION OF A PRIVATE LIMITED COMPANY

The formation procedure for a private limited company is laid down in the Companies Acts (1963–1990).

One or more people may form an incorporated company by subscribing their names to a *memorandum of association* and complying with the requirements of the Companies Act (1990).

FORMATION PROCEDURE

The formation of a limited company requires the drawing up of the following documents:

MEMORANDUM OF ASSOCIATION

This governs the external relationship between the company and the public. It contains

(1) the name of the company, with *Limited* or *Teoranta* as the last word;
(2) the objectives of the company;
(3) a statement of the amount of share capital with which the company proposes to be registered and its division into shares;
(4) a statement that the liability of its members is limited;
(5) the signature of each subscriber, opposite the number of shares they purchase.

The memorandum must be printed, must bear the same stamp as if it were a deed, and must be signed by each subscriber in the presence of at least one witness.

If a company carries out an act that it is not empowered to do it is said to be acting *ultra vires.*

ARTICLES OF ASSOCIATION

These set out the internal rules under which the company will operate and its relations with its shareholders. The articles must state:
(1) the share capital and its division into classes of shares;
(2) procedures for calling a company meeting;
(3) the procedures at company meetings;
(4) voting procedure at meetings;
(5) the powers and duties of directors;
(6) procedures for appointing and removing directors.

There are sample articles in Table A of the Companies Acts (1963–1990). Companies may adopt any or all of the regulations in Table A.

A STATEMENT OF THE AMOUNT OF AUTHORISED CAPITAL

A DECLARATION OF COMPLIANCE WITH THE PROVISIONS OF THE COMPANIES ACTS (1963–1990)

This is contained in form A1. Form A1 also requires a company to state:

(1) the company name;
(2) the address of its registered office;
(3) particulars of the first company secretary;
(4) particulars of those willing to act as first directors.

All these documents and the fees are delivered to the Registrar of Companies. If the registrar is satisfied that the documents are in order, a *certificate of incorporation* is issued. This is the birth certificate of a limited company, which may then begin trading.

The company is now a separate corporate body in the eyes of the law. It can enter into contracts, sue, and be sued.

Public limited company

The shares of a public limited company are quoted on the stock exchange and are freely transferable, so they can be bought and sold by members of the public.

The company must issue a *prospectus* (a history of the company), inviting members of the public to subscribe for shares. There must be a minimum of seven shareholders; the maximum depends on the number of shares issued.

The name of a public limited company must end with the initials *PLC* or *CTP*. The company cannot start trading until it is issued with a *trading certificate* by the Registrar of Companies.

A public limited company must have an audit and must submit audited financial statements to the Registrar of Companies.

A public limited company must submit an annual return to the Registrar of Companies containing a list of the shareholders, particulars of the directors and secretary, the amount of the company's total indebtedness in respect of mortgages, and other statutory information. Audited financial statement must be attached to the annual return.

FORMATION OF A PUBLIC LIMITED COMPANY

1. A private limited company is first formed.
2. The company must have a minimum of seven shareholders; there is no maximum requirement.
3. It must submit a statutory declaration to the Registrar of Companies relating to
    - the authorised share capital
    - any benefit given to a promoter of the company
    - the amount of share capital issued and paid for
    - expenses incurred in setting up the company.
4. If the Registrar is satisfied with the statutory declaration, a trading certificate is issued.
5. Before a public limited company starts trading it must have a certificate of incorporation and a trading certificate issued by the Registrar of Companies.

ADVANTAGES OF PUBLIC LIMITED COMPANIES

1. There is limited liability for the shareholders.
2. The company has access to large amounts of capital, as its shares are sold on the stock exchange.
3. Top-quality management can be recruited.
4. Public limited companies have a higher credit rating, making it easier to obtain finance from financial institutions.
5. There is continuity of existence: if a shareholder or a member of the board of directors dies, the company continues.

DISADVANTAGES OF PUBLIC LIMITED COMPANIES

1. Formation expenses are high; the company must meet the requirements and regulations of the stock exchange.
2. There are many legal requirements to be followed; companies are governed by the regulations of the Companies Acts (1963–1990).
3. Annual accounts must be audited and published.
4. The owners or shareholders may have little say in the running of the business, as most decisions are made by the management.
5. Profits must be distributed among shareholders in the form of dividends.

Business alliances (joint ventures)

Joint ventures combine the skills and resources of two or more firms in a particular line of activity, but they continue to function separately in all other respects. Combining the resources of two firms may facilitate the establishment of a more large-scale operation, giving the joint venture access to economies of scale and increased market penetration.

Joint ventures are popular, as companies co-operate with each other in foreign markets to share costs and market information, to exploit new technology, human resources, and management expertise, or to gain access to new markets.

Alliances can take a number of forms:

- one firm contributing new technology and products and the other providing marketing expertise and distribution channels
- joint research and development
- a transnational enterprise forming an alliance with a local partner as a means of entering unfamiliar markets.

ADVANTAGES OF ALLIANCES

1. They are easy to establish: there are few legal formalities.
2. Each firm benefits from the skills and expertise of the other.
3. There is an improved image for the firm if it forms an alliance with certain well-known companies.
4. Alliances avoid the need for a complete merger, with all the managerial problems that follow.

DISADVANTAGES OF ALLIANCES

1. Agreement must be secured between the partners on how the business should be managed and developed.

2. Control is shared by the partner firms.
3. Disagreements may lead to the alliance ceasing.
4. The common interest that brought the firms together may disappear, leaving a problem.

Franchising

This is a business arrangement whereby the owner (*franchiser*) of a product, service or trade name grants a licence in return for a fee allowing a person or company (*franchisee*) to trade using the same name, product, or service.

A franchise is a contract entered into for a specified period, with the franchisee paying an initial fee and royalties to the franchiser.

The franchisee agrees to

- invest capital in the business
- pay royalties based on a percentage of turnover
- conform to specified standards
- design their premises exactly as laid out by the franchiser
- buy all supplies from the franchiser
- sell only the franchiser's products.

Examples of franchises include McDonald's, Burger King, Kentucky Fried Chicken, Tie Rack, Benneton, Prontaprint, Body Shop, Pronuptia, Abrakebabra, Dunkin Donuts, O'Brien's Sandwich Bars.

ADVANTAGES OF FRANCHISING

1. The trading strategy and methods have been tested and proved elsewhere, which reduces the risks in setting up a new business or expanding an existing one.
2. It offers instant brand recognition and reputation—names and trade-marks have wide recognition and customer loyalty, guaranteeing high demand from the outset.
3. Unit costs can be reduced through bulk buying.
4. At the start-up stage the franchiser provides valuable assistance, including selection of sites, market analysis, interior design, equipment, operating methods and standards, training of employees, and continuing support.
5. Market research, advertising and product development are usually undertaken by the franchiser.

DISADVANTAGES OF FRANCHISING

1. There is little scope for the franchisee's initiative in the areas of product or service development or branding and design.
2. The franchise is not transferable: the goodwill remains the property of the franchiser.
3. Setting-up costs are high—an initial fee together with continuing royalties to the franchiser.
4. There is pressure on the franchisee to achieve the high standards set.

Transnational corporations

These are large companies that have their head office in one country and manufacturing or assembly plants in other countries, so as to secure supplies of raw material, use cheap labour, serve local markets, and bypass trade barriers.

They are a very efficient form of organisation, manufacturing and marketing in a number of countries. They raise funds in different countries and tend to be quoted on a number of stock exchanges.

Decisions are made on an international scale not easily controlled by the rules of any one country: for example, a transnational might decide to close a factory in one country and open in another country where wages are lower.

The head office of a transnational is usually in a large city, where communications and other services are best developed. In contrast, plants are usually established in less urbanised countries, such as Ireland, or in depressed industrial areas, because of the availability of land, low wage rates, and government incentives.

Examples of transnational corporations include Jefferson Smurfit, which has plants and markets in Ireland, Britain, continental Europe, the United States, and South America. Other examples include Shell (Britain and Netherlands), Philips (Netherlands), Nestlé (Switzerland), Nokia (Finland), Siemens (Germany), Volkswagen (Germany), Toyota (Japan), Coca-Cola (United States), Intel (United States).

ADVANTAGES OF TRANSNATIONALS

1. They provide employment, income, and increased living standards. Workers spend their income in the community and pay income tax and social insurance on their wages.
2. Imports are reduced, as goods that were not previously produced in the host country are now available to satisfy local demand; this improves the country's balance of payments.
3. Exports may be increased by a transnational's overseas sales effort.
4. Competition in the host country is increased, with beneficial effects on prices, efficiency, and innovation.
5. Better management and product techniques by transnationals will force domestic producers to improve their own standards to survive.
6. Transnationals provide revenue for the exchequer in the form of corporation tax and VAT.
7. The presence of transnationals in Ireland enhances Ireland's reputation as a business location and may bring further investment to the country.

DISADVANTAGES OF TRANSNATIONALS

1. Profits are repatriated to the home country.
2. Transnationals have been known to exert political pressure in host countries.
3. Some have excessive power and are able to exploit host countries, especially in the 'Third World', where they are able to operate with low health and safety levels and inadequate pollution control.
4. Transnationals are able to adjust their affairs so that profits are declared in those countries where the tax system is most advantageous.

5. They can cause economic problems and local unemployment if they close down a plant.

INCENTIVES FOR ATTRACTING TRANSITIONAL COMPANIES TO IRELAND

IDA Ireland is responsible for promoting overseas investment in Ireland. It offers

- generous grants for setting up, research and development, training workers, and building factories
- favourable corporation tax rates
- educated and skilled workers
- a modern communication system and well-developed infrastructure.

Co-operatives

A co-operative is a business owned and run by a group of people, each of whom has a financial interest in its success and an equal say in how it is managed.

Co-operatives exist mainly in the agricultural industry, with a growth in agri-business and a tendency to compete internationally. The trend is towards larger organisations, with a lot of merger activity.

Co-operatives are registered under the Industrial and Provident Societies Act and must make an annual return of their accounts to the Registrar of Friendly Societies. The Irish Co-operative Organisation Society Ltd (ICOS) co-ordinates the activities of co-operatives.

DISTINCTIVE FEATURES OF CO-OPERATIVES

1. They are voluntary and have an open membership; shares are not transferable.
2. Each member has one vote, and each member holds one share in the business.
3. The surplus is distributed among the members in proportion to the amount of business they conduct with the co-operative.

FORMATION OF A CO-OPERATIVE

At least eight people buy one share each in the co-operative. A copy of the rules of the co-operative is submitted to the Registrar of Friendly Societies.

If the rules are in order, the registrar issues a *certificate of registration.* The co-operative can then begin trading.

TYPES OF CO-OPERATIVE

(1) PRODUCER CO-OPERATIVE

In a producer co-operative a group of producers, for example farmers, sets up a business to process and market their produce. The farm produce, for example milk or beef, is processed and sold as cheese, cream, beefburgers, etc.

Producer co-operatives are mainly found in agriculture.

(2) WORKER CO-OPERATIVES

This is a co-operative that is owned and controlled by those who work in it. Many worker co-operatives are formed because of redundancy and the difficulty of finding employment. The members put the finance together and start a business.

Worker co-operatives may suffer from a lack of capital and lack of management skills.

(3) CREDIT UNIONS

Credit unions are financial co-operatives owned and run by their members. The members live in the same area or are employed in the same company.

Credit unions encourage saving and provide loans at favourable interest rates. They are managed by a board of directors elected by the members. The members get an annual dividend out of the surplus.

CO-OPERATIVES BECOMING PUBLIC LIMITED COMPANIES

Some co-operatives have changed their structure to that of public limited companies, mainly to raise finance for expansion, generate publicity, and increase sales in other countries, for example Kerry Group PLC, Glanbia PLC.

ADVANTAGES OF CONVERTING TO PUBLIC LIMITED COMPANY

1. Finance is available by selling shares to the public.
2. Shareholders can sell their shares on the stock exchange.
3. Public limited companies attract better-quality management.
4. It is easier to obtain finance from banks etc.
5. Converting from co-operative to public limited company generates much favourable publicity, increasing sales and profits.

ADVANTAGES OF CO-OPERATIVES

1. The members have limited liability.
2. Each member has an equal say in running the business.
3. There is a great incentive for members to do business with the co-operative, as the amount of dividends depends on the business transacted.
4. Producer co-operatives provide a market for the output of the agricultural and fishing industries.

DISADVANTAGES OF CO-OPERATIVES

1. A lack of finance from the members leads to borrowing or to some co-operatives converting to limited companies to raise additional finance.
2. Limited return on capital invested by members.
3. An annual return must be made to the Registrar of Friendly Societies.

State enterprises

These are enterprises set up, financed and controlled by the Government. The Government provides the share capital and subsidies. Income is generated through the sale of products or services.

They are large organisations, so they have excellent credit ratings with financial institutions.

FORMATION

Statutory corporations are formed by an act of the Oireachtas, for example CIÉ, ESB, RTÉ.

State-owned companies are set up as limited companies registered under the Companies Acts but with the Government as majority shareholder.

REASONS FOR STATE INTERVENTION

1. State enterprises provide essential services, such as electricity (ESB), health insurance (VHI), and postal services (An Post).
2. They provide employment and safeguard existing employment.
3. They promote industrial development, for example IDA Ireland, Enterprise Ireland.
4. They undertake the development of natural resources, for example Bord na Móna, Coillte.
5. They finance organisations where the capital required is outside the capacity of private enterprise.
6. They promote the development of business through education and training, for example FÁS.

STATE ENTERPRISES CLASSIFIED

MARKETING	TRANSPORT	TRAINING	PRODUCTION	DEVELOPMENT	SERVICES
Bord Iascaigh Mhara An Bord Bia Fáilte Éireann	CIÉ	FÁS Teagasc	Bord na Móna Coillte ESB	Enterprise Ireland IDA Ireland	An Post VHI RTÉ An Bord Gáis

ADVANTAGES OF STATE ENTERPRISES

1. They provide employment.
2. They provide essential services.
3. They promote industrial development.
4. They develop the country's infrastructure.

DISADVANTAGES OF STATE ENTERPRISES

1. Some state firms may suffer losses, which are borne by the taxpayers.
2. The absence of a profit motive may lead to inefficiency.
3. Many state enterprises lack adequate capital, which leads to heavy borrowing.
4. The directors may lack management expertise.

Indigenous firms

These are firms founded in Ireland and owned by Irish people. Such businesses are being promoted by the Government so as to compete with foreign-owned firms in Ireland.

Enterprise Ireland was established by the Government in 1998 as the organisation with responsibility for helping to expand the sales, exports and employment of Irish companies.

ADVANTAGES OF INDIGENOUS FIRMS

1. They set up and remain in Ireland and provide employment.
2. The profits belong to Irish people.
3. Much of their output is exported, helping the balance of payments.

4. Much of the profit earned is re-invested in the business.
5. If indigenous firms are successful it may stimulate other entrepreneurs to set up in business.

DISADVANTAGES OF INDIGENOUS FIRMS

1. There is a high failure rate among new businesses.
2. They are heavily assisted by grants.
3. It is difficult for them to compete with transnationals.
4. They must export, because of the limited size of the Irish market.

Changing trends in the ownership and structure of business

The following are some of the changes taking place in the ownership and structure of business.

1. Producer co-operatives converting to public limited companies to enable them to raise more finance, for example, Waterford Co-op became Waterford Foods PLC; Avonmore Co-op became Avonmore PLC; Waterford and Avonmore PLCs merged to form Glanbia PLC.
2. An increase in the number of firms entering into alliances with firms at home and abroad to share skills and expand.
3. The privatisation (selling to private owners) of state enterprises, for example, in 1999 Telecom Éireann was privatised and is now called Eircom PLC. Aer Lingus was privatised in 2006.
4. Building Societies converting to public limited companies, for example, Irish Permanent. Insurance companies converting to public limited companies, for example, the state-owned life assurance company Irish Life was privatised and operated for a time as Irish Life PLC; it them merged with Irish Permanent to become Irish Life and Permanent PLC and a further merger involving TSB brought about Permanent TSB.
5. The expansion of companies abroad, for example, AIB and Bank of Ireland have expanded into Britain and the United States. Jefferson Smurfit now operates throughout the world.
6. Transnational corporations setting up in Ireland, for example, Intel, Dell, GlaxoSmithKline.
7. An increase in the number of franchises being entered into as an easy method of starting a business with a low risk of failure.

REASONS FOR CHANGING STRUCTURES IN BUSINESS

(1) RAISING FINANCE

- Raising finance for expansion.
- Changing from a private limited company to a public limited company.
- Changing from a co-operative to a public limited company.
- Raising finance through the sale of state companies to private owners.

(2) REDUCING RISK
- Availing of the protection of limited liability, for example a sole trader converting to a private limited company.
- Entering into a franchise agreement rather than setting up a business from scratch.

(3) GROWTH
- Changing a business structure to bring in new skills and allowing increased finance to be raised, which facilitates growth.

(4) MARKETING
- Becoming a public limited company enhances the company's reputation and image, making it easier to market goods and services.
- Forming an alliance with a foreign firm, allowing a business to market and distribute goods abroad.

(5) INTRODUCING SKILLS
- Changing the structure to bring in new skills, for example a sole trader entering into a partnership to avail of the partners' skills.
- Forming alliances to allow the firm to share skills and resources.

(6) ATTRACTING TOP MANAGEMENT
- Changing from a private limited company to a public limited company to attract top management.

18. COMMUNITY DEVELOPMENT

The community and business

'Community development' refers to the development of communities by setting up enterprises that provide goods and services.

HOW COMMUNITIES BENEFIT FROM LOCAL BUSINESS

(1) EMPLOYMENT

There is direct employment in business and also indirectly in the services required to run a business efficiently, for example banking, transport.

(2) WEALTH CREATION

Money earned by employees will be spent in the community, which creates enterprise opportunities, leading to the creation of wealth, with better infrastructure and services.

(3) STANDARD OF LIVING
The quality of life of everyone in the community is improved.

(4) JOB SECURITY
The job security of people in the community allows planning for the future development of the area.

REASONS FOR COMMUNITY DEVELOPMENT

(1) To tackle unemployment; enterprise creates jobs.
(2) To promote an enterprise culture and encourage the growth of entrepreneurs and the development of local enterprise.
(3) To improve the local infrastructure and local services.
(4) To give power and control to local people so they can solve problems in their own community.
(5) To solve local problems, resulting in a better quality of life for local people.

Community initiatives

Many initiatives are available to communities to help with economic development, including:

COUNTY ENTERPRISE BOARDS

County enterprise boards have a responsibility for enterprise development and specifically provide a range of business services to enterprises employing up to ten people, including service industries. Each board works to stimulate business activity and to support enterprise in its own locality.

The purpose of county enterprise boards is to encourage local initiatives and to support small enterprise projects that have the potential to create jobs.

Each board has access to an enterprise fund, established to assist small projects. The following grants are available:

- capital grants—a maximum of 50 per cent of the cost of assets, up to a limit of €75,000
- feasibility study grants—a maximum of 50 per cent of the cost of preparing a feasibility study or business plan, subject to a limit of €5,100 in the case of a single project
- employment grant—amounting to €7,500 for each additional employee.

County enterprise boards may take equity in a business or request that a portion of the grant be repaid over a period. Enterprise boards promote the development of small business through access to advice, information, guidance, and counselling, that is, how to covert an idea into a business and to develop a business plan.

Enterprise boards run their own finance, training and marketing courses to assist new enterprises in developing their business. They provide a 'mentoring service', using an experienced business person who makes available their experience and expertise to small businesses.

The *management development programme* enhances the management capability of small businesses to improve the general level of management and to lessen the risk of business failure.

LEADER PLUS

This is a community initiative for rural development that enables local groups to implement their own business plans for the development of their areas. It replaced the Leader II initiative in 2001.

The Leader programme is administered locally through community companies that have established development plans that adhere to guidelines as set by the Department of Agriculture, Food, and Rural Development. Its primary objective is to demonstrate the importance of direct support for local initiatives in the development of communities.

Financial and technical assistance can be provided within the following range of eligible measures:

Technical support and project pre-development

This includes feasibility studies, market research, and consultancy.

Vocational training

Leader has introduced and financed a range of training schemes to enhance local skills and competence. Initiatives are aimed at encouraging innovative thinking in the creation or expansion of local enterprise.

Rural tourism

This includes the development of new tourist facilities, accommodation, amenities, niche products, and marketing.

Small enterprises, crafts, and local services

This includes new product development or diversification, business creation or expansion, marketing, and the development of local services.

Exploitation and marketing of farm, food, forestry and fisheries products

This includes the development of alternative farm enterprises, natural resources, and the development and marketing of food and fisheries produce.

Preservation and presentation of local cultural heritage

This includes the enhancement of amenities, the preservation of local architecture, cultural creativity, and the preservation of local heritage, village renewal, and environmental works.

Financial assistance

Grants are available for eligible projects as follows:

- capital and marketing grants of up to 50 per cent of investment
- employment grants
- technical or feasibility study grants.

FÁS COMMUNITY ENTERPRISE SCHEME

FÁS is the state agency set up to provide training for people in industry to create employment. It provides a full range of support services to industry and to groups setting up a business. It also provides assistance to those trying to establish a community-based project.

The community enterprises scheme is run by FÁS to help community groups develop enterprises in their locality. It provides a range of services:

- management training courses
- advisory service on a range of issues, such as training, recruitment, ownership options, and tax issues
- assistance with the selection and recruitment of employees
- grants for project development; the project must be commercially viable and must create employment.

AREA PARTNERSHIP COMPANIES (APCs)

These are an alliance of social partners in a locality (voluntary associations, state agencies, farmers' organisations, trade unions, employers, local authorities, etc.). APCs are directed at areas of high unemployment in disadvantaged areas. The aim is to create businesses that will last.

APCs are financed by grants from the Government and the European Union. They provide a service similar to that of county enterprise boards within their locality.

APCs work to a local action plan. They do not displace existing businesses.

19. BUSINESS AND THE ECONOMY

An economy is a system that uses the four factors of production—land, labour, capital, and enterprise—to produce goods and services demanded by consumers.

Land—natural resources
Labour—human effort of workers
Capital—machinery, factories, stocks
Enterprise—risk and initiative

Impact of the economy on business

The performance of the economy affects business. The economy is affected by the following economic variables: inflation, interest rates, tax, grants, unemployment, and exchange rates.

INFLATION

Inflation is an increase in the general level of prices that is sustained over time. The rate of inflation can be measured using the *consumer price index*, which shows the annual change in consumer prices.

IMPACT OF HIGH INFLATION ON BUSINESS

(1) *More difficult to sell abroad*
Increased costs lead to increased prices. If Irish prices rise above those of competitors abroad, they will be priced out of the market.

(2) *Loss of confidence in currency*
Rising prices mean a fall in the value of money and a loss of confidence in the currency.

(3) *Less capital available for investment*
Wealth is eroded by inflation, therefore less capital is available for investment.

(4) *Balance of payments problems*
Exports become dearer and less competitive in foreign markets; exports therefore decrease. Imports become more competitive on the home market; imports therefore increase.

(5) *Decline in sales*
The purchasing power of consumers declines, and wages will buy fewer products and services. High prices decrease consumption with a decline in sales.

(6) *Reduction in profits*
Increased costs of raw materials and other costs will reduce profits.

(7) *Industrial relations problems*
Employees will look for pay increases to keep up with inflation.

IMPACT OF LOW INFLATION ON BUSINESS

(1) *Stability*
With low inflation, prices, costs and wages will be stable, and business planning will be easier.

(2) *Lower wage demands*
Low inflation results in lower wage demands.

(3) *Improved competitive position*
Low inflation will increase the competitive position of Irish goods abroad, leading to more goods being sold, with an increase in production and jobs.

INTEREST RATES

The rate of interest is the price a person or a business pays for borrowing money, that is, the price paid for the use of money.

The interest charged depends on the purpose and duration of the loan, the amount borrowed, the collateral offered, and the creditworthiness of the borrower.

The rate of interest in a country depends on the forces of supply and demand for finance. When there is not enough money to meet demand, interest rates rise; when money becomes plentiful, interest rates fall.

From 1 January 1999 Irish interest rates, together with the interest rates of other euro countries, were set at the same level and are controlled by the European Central Bank.

IMPACT OF INTEREST RATES ON THE ECONOMY

HIGH INTEREST RATES

- *discourage new investment*: borrowing for expansion will be more expensive
- *reduce consumer demand,* because of the high cost of borrowing; sales will fall
- *increase business costs,* leading to reduced profit; increased costs make exports less competitive
- *attract foreign investors,* who will be able to invest their deposits in Irish banks and avail of the high interest.

Falling sales and reduced profit will put pressure on business to repay interest plus loans and may result in business closures and job losses.

LOW INTEREST RATES

- *encourage new investment and enterprise,* as borrowing will be cheaper
- *increase consumer spending* on items such as houses, cars and electrical equipment as the cost of borrowing is low
- *reduce the repayment burden of borrowers*
- *lead to inflation in house prices,* eroding the benefits to borrowers of lower mortgage rates
- *give people more disposable income,* which will ease the pressure on pay demands.

TAX

Taxes are a compulsory contribution of money to the Government. They are the principal source of finance for the state and are used to finance Government expenditure.

Businesses must pay the following taxes: income tax, VAT, corporation tax, capital gains tax, capital acquisitions tax, deposit interest retention tax (DIRT).

IMPACT OF TAXES ON BUSINESS

1. High personal taxes (PAYE) leave less disposable income and discourage the motivation to work and promotion.
2. The administrative costs involved in collecting tax increases business costs for employers.
3. Taxes discourage entrepreneurs from setting up, as they are an additional cost to be borne by the business.
4. High taxes lead to workers seeking increased wages.
5. VAT and excise duties increase the selling prices of goods, leading to reduced sales and higher inflation.
6. Customs duties increase the price of raw materials.
7. Corporation tax reduces the profit that can be paid out as dividends or retained by a business.
8. Capital gains tax discourages investment.
9. Low rates of tax stimulate enterprise and employment.

GRANTS AND SUBSIDIES

GRANTS

A grant is a non-repayable source of finance provided by the Government or the European Union to a business to promote enterprise and expansion. Grants are given for

- feasibility studies and market research
- capital expenditure (fixed assets)
- training and employment
- infrastructural development.

IMPACT OF GRANTS ON BUSINESS

1. They reduce the risk involved in setting up a business.
2. They are given to Irish firms by Enterprise Ireland to assist with start-up and development costs.
3. They are given to transnationals by IDA Ireland to attract them to the country.
4. They are given to companies to set up business in certain areas, for example Údarás na Gaeltachta areas.
5. Grants are given by the European Union for infrastructural developments.

SUBSIDIES

These are payment by the Government to producers of certain goods to reduce the costs of production and to enable firms to keep down prices. They are designed to increase production and exports.

UNEMPLOYMENT

Unemployment is the inability to find work though it is actively sought. The unemployed are those members of the labour force who are available for work but cannot find a job.

Unemployment is measured as a percentage of the registered labour force without a job.

IMPACT OF UNEMPLOYMENT ON BUSINESS

1. Revenue from direct and indirect taxes falls, while Government expenditure on social welfare increases.
2. There is a cost in helping the unemployed find a job and in the various training programmes in operation.
3. There is extra Government spending on health and law and order because of the social costs of poor health and the increased level of crime associated with unemployment. This money comes out of taxes, and there will be pressure on the Government to increase taxes, including business taxes.
4. Increased crime increases firms' security and insurance costs.
5. Unemployed people have less money to spend, which leads to less demand for goods and services, especially non-essential goods; the result is reduced sales and reduced profit.
6. Part of the country's available labour is not used, and there is a loss to the economy of potential output.

EXCHANGE RATES

These are the price of a country's currency expressed in terms of another country's currency.

IMPACT OF EXCHANGE RATES ON BUSINESS

Exchange rates have a significant impact on companies that export large amounts of their output and on companies that import large quantities of raw material.

If the value of the home currency rises in relation to the currency of the country to which it is exporting—that is, there is a strong home currency—the following occurs:

- goods and services being exported become more expensive, reducing their competitiveness, which results in loss of sales and profits and lost jobs
- imported raw materials will be cheaper, leading to increased importing of raw materials at the expense of home-produced goods.

If the value of the home currency falls in relation to the currency of the country to which it is exporting—that is, there is a weak home currency—the following occurs:

- goods and services become cheaper abroad and are easier to sell
- imported raw materials will become dearer.

The euro eliminates exchange rate difficulties within the euro zone.

Impact of business on the economy

Business, by providing goods and services, affects the economy in many ways. It affects

- employment
- tax revenue
- the environment.

IMPACT OF BUSINESS ON EMPLOYMENT

1. Business increases employment, which means less unemployment benefit and less social welfare.
2. People employed have an income in the form of wages, and therefore living standards are improved.
3. Increased production leads to reduced imports, increased exports, and the creation of more jobs.
4. A lot of profit is re-invested in businesses for expansion, eventually leading to more jobs and increased output.
5. There is increased demand for services, for example transport to deliver raw materials and to distribute finished goods; also banking, insurance, and other financial services.
6. There is increased demand for housing, leading to more jobs for builders, plumbers, carpenters, electricians, etc.
7. There is increased employment in local shops, pubs, cinemas and restaurants, because people have more disposable income.

IMPACT OF BUSINESS ON TAX REVENUE

1. There is an increase in tax revenue—in PAYE tax, because of the larger work force, and in VAT, because extra goods and services are bought. Some of this increased revenue is used for education, social welfare, and health.
2. There is an increase in corporation tax from business, as increased business leads to increased profits.

IMPACT OF BUSINESS ON THE ENVIRONMENT

The environmental costs associated with increased business activity include industrial pollution, water and air pollution.

The social costs associated with increased business activity include increased road traffic and delays, noise pollution, and health risks to workers.

Increased business also leads to parking problems, more litter, and fewer parks and green areas.

20. GOVERNMENT AND BUSINESS

The Government's role in business

1. It provides essential services: health, education, security, transport, communication.
2. It sets down rules and regulations to be observed by business and society.
3. It redistributes wealth by taxing people who can pay and transferring money to those in need, for example the unemployed.
4. It introduces legislation to protect consumers and those in employment, for example the Sale of Goods and Supply of Services Act (1980), Employment Equality Act (1998).
5. It monitors business growth through the Competition Authority.
6. It promotes enterprise and employment through many state agencies.

INDUSTRIAL POLICY

This is concerned with promoting industrial efficiency, competitiveness and expansion and the creation of employment opportunities. It includes making fiscal, monetary and foreign currency decisions in accordance with business needs.

The Government's role in encouraging business

Changes in Government policies have a significant impact on business.

REVENUE AND EXPENDITURE POLICIES

Changes in Government revenue and expenditure policies have the following effects on business:

Revenue policies

Personal taxes

A *decrease* in personal taxes means that

- employees have more disposable income; business activity increases
- employees will be more willing to work and will be encouraged to do overtime, leading to increased productivity.

An *increase* in personal taxes means that

- employees will have less disposable income; business sales and profits are reduced.

Corporation tax

A *decrease* in corporation tax encourages enterprise and increases the ability of firms to re-invest in the business, encouraging business growth and job creation. Favourable corporation tax rates encourage foreign investment and job creation.

An *increase* in corporation tax rates reduces the amount of money available for re-investment, restricting job creation.

Value-added tax (VAT)

A *decrease* in VAT may increase sales and profits. An *increase* in VAT may reduce sales and profits.

Expenditure policies

Capital expenditure

Government capital expenditure on schools, hospitals and roads improves the country's infrastructure and has a positive effect on many industries, including construction, transport, and tourism. It also encourages the growth of indigenous firms and attracts transnationals.

Current expenditure

This is day-to-day expenditure on goods and services to supply education, health, security etc. and to supply the Government with such items as stationery, computers, and cleaning. It increases the sales of firms producing those goods and services.

Government wages

Government spending on wages to employees and on social welfare payments such as unemployment benefit and retirement pensions is spent in local communities and has a significant impact on business locally.

INTEREST RATE POLICIES

If interest rates increase, it is expensive for individuals and firms to borrow money, leading to reduced spending and demand.

If interest rates decrease, individuals and firms can borrow money easily, leading to increased spending and demand.

GOVERNMENT PLANNING

The implementation of Government plans drawn up in conjunction with employers and the trade unions greatly affects all employees and businesses.

National agreements determine pay for all workers for a number of years, allowing businesses to plan accurately their future wage costs for the period with the hope that there will be no industrial relations problems during the period of the agreement.

INFRASTRUCTURAL DEVELOPMENT

The Government, through EU structural funds, has greatly transformed the country's infrastructure, with improved roads, railways, airports, harbours, and telecommunication services, all encouraging the future development of business.

GOVERNMENT DEPARTMENTS

Government departments that encourage business directly include:

Department of Agriculture and Food

- promotes agriculture and food, manages the Leader programme, and oversees the implementation of reforms in the Common Agricultural Policy.

Department of Enterprise, Trade and Employment

- promotes enterprise and job creation, encourages good industrial relations.

Department of the Environment, Heritage and Local Government

- encourages businesses to operate in a way that is responsible towards the environment.

AGENCIES THAT ENCOURAGE BUSINESS INCLUDE:

Forfás

- the policy, advisory and co-ordinating agency for industrial development and science and technology.

Enterprise Ireland

- encourages the development of indigenous industry.

IDA Ireland

- encourages transnational corporations to set up in Ireland.

FÁS

- operates training and employment services.

Fáilte Éireann

- responsible for the development of tourism and the promotion of Ireland as a tourist destination.

County enterprise boards

- assist entrepreneurs in setting up and developing business in local communities.

Leader programmes

- develop rural enterprises.

ENVIRONMENTAL PROTECTION AGENCY

- monitors environmental pollution and encourages environmentally responsible business.

TEAGASC

- the agriculture and food development authority, providing advisory, research, education and training services to agriculture and agri-food industries.

AN BORD BIA

- responsible for the promotion of Irish food and drink products.

SHANNON FREE AIRPORT DEVELOPMENT COMPANY

- responsible for the development of Shannon Airport and of small business in the Mid-West Region.

ÚDARÁS NA GAELTACHTA

- responsible for the development of business and job creation in Gaeltacht areas.

The Government's role in regulating business

The Government must regulate business in order to protect the environment and to ensure that employees' and consumers' rights are safeguarded. Regulation is achieved through legislation and state agencies.

COMPETITION AUTHORITY

- investigates proposed mergers and take-overs to examine their impact on consumers and the public
- investigates the abuse of a dominant position by businesses.

HEALTH AND SAFETY AUTHORITY

- deals with the health and safety of employees in the work-place
- enforces the Health and Safety Act
- has seven regional offices, whose inspectors can be contacted for advice on issues of health and safety.

OFFICE OF DIRECTOR OF CONSUMER AFFAIRS

- promotes high standards in advertising
- investigates complaints relating to false or misleading descriptions
- prosecutes offences under the Consumer Information Act (1978)
- monitors compliance with the Sale of Goods and Supply of Services Act (1980).

DATA PROTECTION AGENCY

- protects the public against the misuse of information stored on computers under the Data Protection Act (1988).

ENVIRONMENTAL PROTECTION AGENCY

- monitors businesses to ensure that they do not damage the environment
- advises firms on environmental protection
- prosecutes offenders.

Role of the Government as an employer

The Government provides direct employment through:

PUBLIC SECTOR WORK FORCE

- **the civil service**—those working in various Government departments
- **public servants**—those paid by the Government but who have a separate employer, for example nurses, teachers.

COMMERCIAL STATE BODIES

State bodies pay employees from income generated by the sale of goods or services, for example the ESB, CIÉ.

INDIRECT EMPLOYMENT

Indirect employment is provided by the Government through employing the services of other firms that supply goods and services to state bodies.

HOW THE GOVERNMENT AFFECTS THE LABOUR FORCE

The labour force is the total number of people in a country available to produce goods and services. The Government affects the labour force by helping to generate employment in the following ways:

(1) PERSONAL TAXES

Favourable rates of personal tax allow more disposable income. The demand for goods and services increases, with increased production and job creation.

(2) BUSINESS TAXES

Favourable rates of business tax stimulate enterprise and employment.

(3) LOW INTEREST RATES

Low interest rates stimulate enterprise and job creation.

(4) LOW INFLATION

Low inflation increases the sale of goods and services, with increased production and job creation.

(5) IMPROVED STATE INFRASTRUCTURE

Improved infrastructure stimulates business growth and job creation.

(6) PUBLIC SECTOR EMPLOYMENT

This is direct employment in the public sector and commercial state bodies.

(7) NATIONAL AGREEMENTS

The negotiation of national agreements allows businesses to plan for the future with greater certainty, with increased investment and job creation.

PRIVATISATION

This is the process of transferring a state business from the public sector (owned by the Government) to the private sector (owned by shareholders). This is done by offering shares to members of the public in a flotation on the stock exchange.

A number of large state enterprises have been privatised recently, including Irish Life Assurance Company, which became Irish Life PLC (1991), the Irish Sugar Company, which became Greencore PLC (1991), Telecom Éireann, now Eircom (1999) and Aer Lingus (2006).

OPPORTUNITIES OF PRIVATISATION

1. It is an important source of revenue for the state. The proceeds of the sale can be used to repay Government borrowing or can be spent on infrastructural projects.
2. Privatised companies can sell shares to members of the public to raise capital for expansion.
3. There is a reduction in Government expenditure and hence in the level of tax if an unprofitable state firm is privatised.
4. Privatised companies must become more efficient, competitive and profitable to be able to pay dividends to shareholders.
5. As privatised companies are profit-motivated, entrepreneurship and risk-taking are encouraged.

THREATS OF PRIVATISATION

1. Newly privatised companies can act freely to raise prices and reduce essential services beyond Government control in striving for profit.
2. There is a loss of future profits to the state.
3. Jobs are lost as companies strive to become more efficient and take on a commercial status.
4. It is generally the more profitable state companies that are sold off; loss-making companies are left in state ownership.
5. The shares of privatised companies can end up in the hands of foreign investors, which could have long-term implications.

21. THE SOCIAL RESPONSIBILITY OF BUSINESS

Business ethics

'Ethics' are standards or moral principles that govern the actions of people or groups of people.

In business, ethics are rules of conduct for those with whom the business comes into contact. They are concerned with issues of morality, that is, of right and wrong, honesty, and fairness.

An ethical decision means doing what is morally right: for example, a decision made on ethical grounds might reject the most profitable solution in favour of one of greater benefit to society.

CODE OF ETHICS FOR BUSINESS

This sets out the principles that govern how a business operates. It is a framework describing the principles and standards of behaviour expected of management and workers when decisions are being made.

Social responsibilities of business

Social responsibilities are a company's responsibilities to those with whom it comes into contact. It means conducting business activities in a way that is acceptable to society—acting truthfully, with justice, fairness and honesty.

A business has a responsibility to consider the effects of its decisions on the community and to act ethically for all its stakeholders, for example maintaining employment, obeying legislation, and minimising social costs.

BUSINESS STAKEHOLDERS

These are all those who have an interest in the behaviour of a business. Companies have a social responsibility to a wide number of stakeholders.

SHAREHOLDERS (INVESTORS)

- Ensuring that their investment is secure
- Providing the highest possible rate of return

EMPLOYEES

- Paying fair wages
- Creating reasonable working conditions
- Maintaining employment
- Creating a safe working environment

CUSTOMERS

- Producing safe and reliable products at fair prices
- Using advertising that is not misleading

SUPPLIERS

- Honouring contracts
- Paying bills on time

SOCIETY

- Minimising social costs (traffic congestion, noise, pollution)

GOVERNMENT

- Paying taxes
- Obeying legislation

THE ENVIRONMENT

- Producing environmentally responsible products

IMPACT OF BUSINESS ON THE ECONOMY, THE COMMUNITY, AND THE ENVIRONMENT

- Business provides the country with the goods and services it needs.
- It combines the factors of production to create wealth for the economy.
- Employment is created in the community.
- Income is created, and the standard of living is improved.
- There are social costs for this wealth created: pollution, traffic congestion, fewer green areas, litter problems, parking problems.
- Business makes a contribution to communities through the sponsorship of sports, art, and cultural events.
- This investment in the community improves the quality of life in that community.

WAYS IN WHICH BUSINESS CAN BECOME SOCIALLY RESPONSIBLE

- Keeping high standards of self-regulation: code of ethics
- Being aware of the public image (perception) of the company
- Working closely with the Environmental Protection Agency and obeying regulations regarding pollution etc.
- Getting involved in the community, for example by sponsoring clubs, providing facilities for schools, etc.

Environmental issues

ENVIRONMENTAL ISSUES AND BUSINESS

Business has a responsibility to the environment. The main environmental issues include:

POLLUTION

- Slurry and effluent seep into rivers and lakes.
- Chemicals and oil are dumped into water systems.
- Chemical emissions from industrial plants and car exhausts cause acid rain, which kills forests.
- The destruction of the ozone layer brings about an increasing risk of skin cancer.

ENERGY CONSUMPTION

- Fuels such as oil and gas are limited and will quickly be exhausted, unless they are conserved and used more efficiently.

SUSTAINABLE DEVELOPMENT

This means using an environmentally responsible approach when using natural resources to satisfy the needs of the present generation without damaging the environment for future generations, for example replacing non-renewable energy resources, such as oil and gas, with renewable energy resources, such as wind and solar power.

EXPLOITATION OF THE THIRD WORLD

Many countries in the Third World are being denuded of raw materials.

CHARACTERISTICS OF AN ENVIRONMENTALLY CONSCIOUS COMPANY

Sensitivity Being sensitive to all environmental issues in decision-making. This involves conducting a social audit, which is a check-list against which a business measures whether it is being socially responsible towards its stakeholders.

Openness Being open to developing and implementing new methods and ideas for dealing with environmental issues.

Honesty Being honest in all matters affecting the environment, even when things go wrong, for example not covering up industrial accidents.

Awareness Being aware of the importance of the environment, promoting environmental awareness among employees; awareness of the damage the firm can cause to the environment, and ensuring that the environment is protected.

Consultation Consulting all stakeholders when developing and implementing policies that affect the environment.

COSTS FOR BUSINESS OF BEING SOCIALLY RESPONSIBLE

The costs to a business of acting in a socially responsible manner are:

- increased cost of production—increased cost of raw materials, for example using recycled paper
- increased cost of equipment to reduce pollution and emissions
- increased cost of changing production methods to meet environmental demands
- adverse publicity—bad publicity and public image if it is seen that the firm is not acting in a socially responsible manner
- EPA regulations—the Environmental Protection Agency can bring offenders to court and seek fines or prison sentences
- new products—the cost of developing new environmentally responsible products
- other costs—the cost of the safe disposal of dangerous and toxic waste
- cost of developing codes of ethics and carrying out social audits to ensure that the firm is acting responsibly.

OPPORTUNITIES FOR A BUSINESS IN MEETING ITS ENVIRONMENTAL RESPONSIBILITIES

Socially responsible behaviour can pay off in the long run, even where it involves some short-term sacrifice of profit.

Cost reduction Using clean and safe technologies and production systems will reduce costs and insurance premiums, and the business will become more cost-effective.

New business possibilities Technologies and methods used in looking after environmental concerns may be turned into profitable business opportunities, for example recycling.

Better public image Socially responsible business can create a better public image. Ireland's 'green' image in the European Union is a valuable marketing tool.

Customers Socially responsible business attracts responsible customers, who may remain loyal to the business.

Employees Socially responsible firms treat employees fairly. They find it easy to recruit employees; and employees who are treated fairly will be more productive and motivated to work harder. There will be less industrial conflict, and labour turnover will be low.

Financial institutions Financial institutions are sensitive to environmental issues. A business with a good environmental control system will find it easier to obtain finance when required.

KEY TERMS

These are some of the more important terms introduced in unit 6:

articles of association	inflation
business ethics	interest rates
categories of industry	limited liability
community enterprise	memorandum
co-operatives	privatisation
exchange rates	public limited company (PLC)
grants and subsidies	sole trader
indigenous firms	state enterprise
industrial policy	

LEGISLATION DISCUSSED IN UNIT 6

Companies Act (1990) (as it relates to the formation of private limited companies only).

ON COMPLETION OF UNIT 6 YOU SHOULD BE ABLE TO

(1) recognise and illustrate the categories of industry and their contribution to the economy;
(2) recognise the types of business organisation;
(3) compare and contrast the different types of business organisation;
(4) explain why businesses change their organisational structure over time;
(5) identify the importance of community initiatives in the development of the local economy;
(6) explain the impact of the economy on business;
(7) explain the impact of business in the development of the economy;
(8) identify important environmental issues in business;
(9) list the ways in which the Government creates a suitable climate for business;
(10) explain the ways in which the Government affects the labour force;
(11) define ethical business practice;
(12) describe the characteristics of an environmentally conscious company;
(13) analyse the impact of environmental issues on business;
(14) discuss the social responsibilities of business;
(15) evaluate the effects on a firm's costs of meeting its ethical, social and environmental responsibilities.

Examination-style question and solution

Domestic environment

Mary and Paul Murphy, together with their daughter Fiona, are considering opening a family hotel in County Kerry, based on their combined hotel and catering skills.

(**A**) Explain why it is true to say that the proposed venture is both an indigenous and a service industry. **(15 marks)**

(**B**) Advise the Murphy family on the type of business organisation they should choose, giving reasons for the choice. **(25 marks)**

(**C**) Identify one community initiative that would assist the Murphys, and describe the benefits of this initiative to the business and to the community. **(20 marks)**

Suggested solution

(A) *This is an indigenous firm because it is a local business set up by local people in their own locality. It is a service industry because it is in the tertiary sector of the economy, providing a service rather than producing goods. The hotel provides a service both to local people and tourists in the form of food, drink, and accommodation.*

(B) *Choice: private limited company*

The Murphy family should choose a private limited company, for the following reasons:

1. *It will be a corporate body.*
2. *A company can act as a person in the eyes of the law.*
3. *A private limited company will have continuity of existence.*
4. *A company will remain in existence even if one director should die.*
5. *It will have access to greater amounts of capital.*
6. *A company can sell more equity.*
7. *A company enjoys greater creditworthiness.*
8. *A company finds it easier to borrow funds from banks than, for example, a sole trader.*
9. *The members of a company enjoy limited liability.*
10. *The maximum loss on the winding up of a company is the amount of capital invested.*

(C) *One community initiative that would assist the Murphys is a county enterprise board. These boards were set up by the Government to assist and to finance new and existing small enterprises and micro-enterprises in communities.*

The benefits of this initiative to the business are as follows:

1. *The CEB will provide a grant to allow the local initiative to undertake research on the feasibility of the project.*
2. *If the project seems to make financial sense, the CEB will advance it funds.*
3. *The benefits of this initiative to the community are as follows:*
   (a) *It will help to provide jobs in the community.*
   (b) *CEBs provide the essential encouragement and advice to potential entrepreneurs in the community to set up their own firms.*

Practice questions — Section 1

1. Define the term 'code of ethics' as applied to a business.

2. Outline two economic variables that affect the economy.
   (*a*)
   (*b*)

3. Inflation affects business by
   (i)
   (ii)

4. (*a*) Franchising is

   (*b*) List two examples of franchising in Ireland.
   (1) (2)

5. 'Socially responsible business' refers to

Revision question

Domestic and international environment

Businesses form an important part of the wider economic system in Ireland.

(A) Compare a private limited company with a partnership as desirable forms of business organisation. **(25 marks)**

(B) Name one community development organisation designed to help business enterprises in your locality. Describe the services provided by it. **(20 marks)**

(C) Illustrate the importance of socially responsible business practice for a business enterprise. **(15 marks)**

[60 marks]

Unit 7: The International Environment

Ireland is open to economic, social and cultural trends from abroad, and the international environment has a significant impact on Irish business. This section introduces the international trading environment and developments in international business. It also deals with Ireland's membership of the European Union.

Objective: To enable pupils to understand the opportunities and challenges facing Irish business in the international environment.

22. Introduction to the International Trading Environment

Ireland as an open economy

Ireland has an 'open economy', in which a significant proportion of its goods and services are traded internationally. This is because the economy is significantly dependent on foreign trade.

INTERNATIONAL TRADE

International trade refers to the exporting and importing of goods and services.

EXPORTING

This is the production of goods or services and selling them to another country.

Visible exports

These are goods that Ireland sells to other countries, for example butter produced in Ireland and sold in Britain.

Invisible exports

These are services that Ireland sells to other countries, for example Spanish students coming to Ireland to learn English during the summer. Foreign money comes to Ireland.

IMPORTING

This is the buying of goods or services from a foreign country to be used in the home market.

Visible imports

These are goods that Ireland buys from other countries, for example cars bought from Germany.

Invisible imports

These are services that Ireland buys in other countries, for example Irish pupils going abroad on a school tour. Irish money goes to a foreign country.

MEASURING INTERNATIONAL TRADE

International trade is measured by
(*a*) the balance of trade, and
(*b*) the balance of payments.

Balance of trade

This is the relationship between visible exports and visible imports.

Balance of trade = visible exports – visible imports

If visible exports are greater than visible imports there is a *surplus* in the balance of trade. If visible exports are less than visible imports there is a *deficit* in the balance of trade.

Balance of payments

This is the difference between all the money coming into the country (total exports) and all the money going out of the country (total imports).

Balance of payments = total exports – total imports

When total exports are greater than total imports there is a surplus in the balance of payments. This is good for a country, as it means it is earning more than it is spending.

When total exports are less than total imports there is a deficit in the balance of payments. This is not good for a country, as it is spending more than it is earning.

Example Visible exports: €950 million
Invisible exports: €280 million
Visible imports: €640 million
Invisible imports: €360 million

Solution

Balance of trade = *visible exports – visible imports*
= €950 million – €640 million
= €310 million balance of trade surplus

Balance of payments = *total exports – total imports*
= €1,230 million – €1,000 million
= €230 million balance of payment surplus

The significance of international trade for the Irish economy

Small home market
The Irish market is small, and if firms want to survive and grow they must export.

High dependence on exports
Ireland is very dependent on exports: exports account for two out of three jobs in the manufacturing sector. Seventy per cent of exports go to EU countries.

Excess production
Too much food is produced for domestic consumption, so the excess can be exported to avoid a glut on the home market.

Raw materials
Many raw materials required for production would not be available in Ireland without international trade.

Consumer tastes
Consumers' tastes would not be satisfied without international trade.

Employment
Many jobs in Ireland are dependent on exports.

Economies of scale
Irish firms could not avail of economies of scale without getting involved in international trade.

REASONS FOR INTERNATIONAL TRADE

- The climate is unsuitable for the production of certain products, for example oranges, bananas.
- Countries must import raw materials required for production that they cannot produce themselves, for example oil, coal.
- Consumers want variety—Italian shoes, French wines.
- Foreign currency is earned to pay for imports.
- The Irish market is too small: firms would have to go onto the export market to expand and increase sales.
- Surplus production can be sold, for example beef.
- Irish products are demanded by consumers abroad, for example Kerrygold butter.

BARRIERS TO TRADE

FREE TRADE

This means there are no barriers to the movement of goods and services between countries. Free trade exists between EU member-countries.

PROTECTION

This is the policy of erecting barriers to trade, such as quotas, tariffs, and embargoes, to protect home industry. Trade protection is used to protect industries against foreign competition and to help them to survive and to provide jobs.

BARRIERS TO TRADE INCLUDE:

Tariffs

- taxes or duties on goods imported to make them more expensive.

Quotas

- limits on the quantity of certain goods that can be imported.

Embargoes

- a ban on the importing of specified goods.

Regulations

- restricting international trade by governments delaying the issue of licences for importing goods.

Subsidies

- payments by governments to firms to reduce the costs of production, encouraging them to increase output and enabling them to sell goods at a lower price to compete with foreign competition.

Foreign trade restrictions

- limits set by a government on the amount of foreign currency available for buying imported goods.

DEREGULATION

Deregulation is the removal of regulations and trade barriers. It increases competition between firms internationally and increases the level of trade in the world.

The World Trade Organisation (WTO) was set up in 1995. Its function is to promote free trade through the reduction or elimination of trade barriers.

The changing nature of the international economy and its effects on business

Many changes are taking place in the world economy. The main changes and their effects on Irish business include:

GLOBALISATION

Global firms treat the world as a single market. They manufacture products for markets throughout the world. Their products are of a high standard and are bought throughout the world, for example Ford, Toyota, Coca-Cola.

INFORMATION TECHNOLOGY

Developments in technology mean that communication with all parts of the world is available at the touch of a button, for example the internet and e-mail. Technology has improved methods of production and has reduced costs.

Technology enables transport to be managed more effectively and easily. All methods of transport are more efficient, with reduced costs.

DEREGULATION

The removal of trade barriers provides more opportunities for Irish firms abroad, as they have access to foreign markets.

Deregulation has increased competitiveness in both domestic and international markets, improving quality and reducing prices.

THE DEVELOPMENT OF TRADING BLOCS

A distinctive feature of the world economy in recent years has been the growth of trading blocs, where a group of countries share free trade agreements with each other. The European Union is a trading bloc.

GROWTH OF THE 'PACIFIC RIM'

This is a name sometimes given to the economies of China, South Korea, Taiwan, Singapore, Indonesia, and Malaysia. The region offers opportunities for Irish exporters, but there is also the challenge of low-priced imports coming in from there.

SALES OPPORTUNITIES

Opportunities exist for Irish companies to develop overseas markets, which will increase sales and profits.

Opportunities and challenges in international trade

OPPORTUNITIES FOR IRISH BUSINESS IN INTERNATIONAL TRADE INCLUDE:

Free trade and markets

With the abolition of many trade restrictions and with access to both new and existing markets, there are huge opportunities for increased sales and profit.

Proximity to continental Europe

Because of Ireland's proximity to continental Europe there exist opportunities for transnationals to set up in Ireland, with easy access to EU markets.

Language and culture

English is an important trading language and gives Ireland an advantage when doing business internationally. Ireland's cultural heritage of art, music and literature gives us a marketing advantage internationally.

'Green' image

Ireland's food products have a healthy image, making it easy to market them abroad.

Educated work-force

A well-educated work-force is a huge resource for entrepreneurs establishing business in Ireland.

Developments in information technology

Developments in information technology have made instant global communication possible for new and existing businesses.

CHALLENGES IN INTERNATIONAL TRADE INCLUDE:

Competition

Irish firms face competition from foreign companies setting up here. They must improve quality and standards to survive in domestic and export markets.

Distribution costs

Because of Ireland's position on the edge of Europe, distribution costs for exports are high, making Irish products less competitive. A similar problem exists in relation to raw materials imported into Ireland.

High cost base

Labour and insurance costs are higher in Ireland than in the Pacific Rim or central Europe, making Irish products more expensive and less competitive on international markets.

Language and culture

Language difficulties can arise if firms lack specialists who can successfully negotiate in the buyer's language. Firms must also consider the customs and cultures of different countries when marketing products in foreign markets.

Payment difficulties

There can be problems in getting paid for exports and in ensuring that fluctuating exchange rate losses are minimised when dealing with customers outside the euro zone.

Economies of scale and product and service quality

Irish firms are small by the standards of other countries and cannot avail of the same economies of scale (where average costs are lower in large-scale operations) as foreign competitors. They may not be able to compete on price and so they must produce goods or services to the highest standards to compete on the export market and concentrate on filling niche markets.

Trading blocs and agreements

Trading blocs increase the level of international trade; however, they impose tariffs on imports from countries outside the bloc.

THE EUROPEAN UNION AS A TRADING BLOC

Irish firms have free access in selling goods and services to any country in the European Union, the largest market in the world, with nearly half a billion people.

The EU bloc is made up of twenty-seven countries, which have organised a free trade area in which

- there are no tariffs on the movement of goods and services within the bloc
- there is a common tariff on imports from outside the bloc
- there is free movement of capital and labour within the bloc.

Other trading blocs

- North American Free Trade Agreement (NAFTA)—United States, Canada, and Mexico.

- Asia-Pacific Economic Co-operation (APEC)—thirteen member-states in the 'Pacific Rim', including Australia, New Zealand, and Brazil.

The effects of trading blocs have been very significant. They lead to a growth in trade between members at a much faster rate than trade with countries outside the bloc.

WORLD TRADE ORGANISATION

The World Trade Organisation (WTO), set up in 1995, replaced the General Agreement on Tariffs and Trade (GATT).

OBJECTIVES

- Reducing or eliminating barriers to free trade (tariffs, quotas, etc.) and promoting fair trade among its members
- Eventually achieving global free trade, by negotiating with the governments of member-states to promote free trade
- Arbitrating on trade disputes between member-states
- Deregulating markets

MEMBERS OF THE WTO HAVE AGREED

- to reduce tariffs throughout the world
- to give to other members 'most favoured nation' treatment, that is, not to give any special trading advantages to another country or discriminate against it
- to reduce or eliminate subsidies to agriculture
- to remove restrictions on service industries, that is, to increase competition in services
- to recognise international copyright protection in relation to intellectual property, such as patents or inventions.

23. THE EUROPEAN UNION

Importance of the European Union

FREE TRADE AREA

The European Union is a trading bloc made up of twenty-seven countries that provide free trade in goods and services between member-states through the removal of tariffs, quotas, and other obstacles to trade. Irish firms have opportunities to expand.

FREE MOVEMENT OF CAPITAL AND LABOUR

It provides for the free movement of capital and labour across national boundaries.

ECONOMIES OF SCALE

It provides a huge market of nearly half a billion people in twenty-seven countries for the products of Irish firms. Its size offers possibilities of economies of scale.

EU SUPPORTS

Support to Irish agriculture has increased the standard of living of the farming community.

FOREIGN INVESTMENT

Foreign investment is encouraged. Companies from non-EU countries, such as Japan, have set up in Ireland because of easy access to EU markets, increasing employment and living standards.

CHOICE FOR CONSUMERS

Consumers have a wide choice of goods from among twenty-seven countries.

COMPETITION

There is greater competition for Irish firms, which increases efficiency and encourages innovation.

GRANTS AND LOANS

Ireland receives a lot of finance from the European Union in the form of grants and loans.

Decision-making process in the European Union

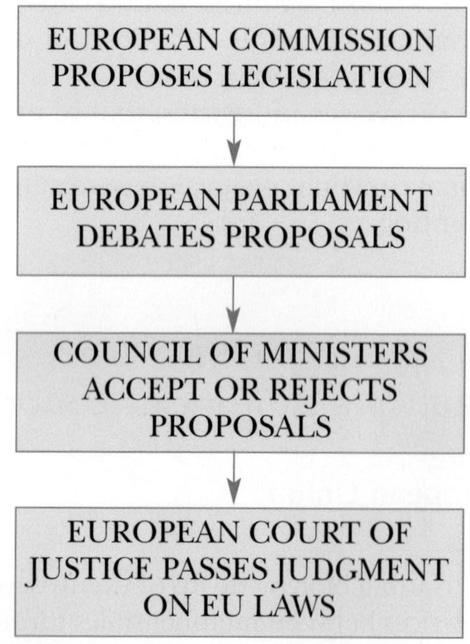

- The European Commission proposes legislation.
- The European Parliament expresses its opinions on the proposals, debates and possibly modifies them.
- The Council of Ministers makes decisions; it has power to reject, amend or adopt proposals, and only then does it become EU legislation.
- The European Court of Justice passes judgment on EU laws and treaties.

IMPLEMENTATION OF EU LAW

The Council of Ministers decides how laws should be implemented. EU law is implemented by the issue of

(1) REGULATIONS

- A regulation is applicable to all member-states.
- It does not need the national law of a member-state to ensure that it is adopted.
- If a regulation conflicts with national law, the regulation takes precedence.
- Regulations are binding on all member-states.

Examples of common policies that may be covered by regulations are some aspects of agriculture and fishing.

(2) DIRECTIVES

- A directive provides an outline to member-states of legislation to be achieved in a specific area and the date by which it is to be done.
- It requires member-states to alter their national laws to implement the directive.
- The member-state then decides how best to implement the legislation in its own situation.
- Directives are binding on member-states.

Examples: the directives on company law, misleading advertising directive, directive on health and safety at work.

(3) DECISIONS

- Decisions are binding agreements addressed to named member-states, organisations, or individuals.
- Decisions are binding only on the parties involved.

(4) RECOMMENDATIONS

- A recommendation is not binding on the groups involved.
- Generally, member-states accept recommendations.
- A recommendation is a decision reached by the Council of Ministers or the European Commission expressing an opinion on policy issues that have not reached directive or regulation stage.

EU institutions

(1) THE EUROPEAN COMMISSION

- The European Commission is based in Brussels. Members are nominated to the Commission by national governments who serve a five-year term of office.
- Members of the Commission must act independently of their national governments, concentrating on the interests of the European Union as a whole, not those of their own country.
- Specific responsibilities are allocated to each commissioner.

Role of the European Commission

The Commission represents the European Union at all international trade negotiations. Its role includes

- making proposals for EU legislation and ensuring that all EU treaties are enforced
- initiating proceedings against any member-state that does not uphold the treaties or EU policies
- imposing fines on individuals or companies when they act in breach of the European Union's competition rules
- ensuring that all laws passed by the European Union are implemented by member-states
- administering structural funds and programmes
- acting as legislator, observer, manager, enforcer of treaties and budget-maker within the European Union.

(2) THE EUROPEAN PARLIAMENT

This body meets one week each month in Strasbourg but holds most of its important meetings at its head office in Brussels. Members are elected by direct vote within the member-states for a five-year term of office.

Role of the European Parliament

- generating policy initiatives
- acting as a supervisory body over the activities of the European Commission and Council of Ministers
- adopting, amending or rejecting EU legislation proposed by the Commission, in consultation with the Council of Ministers
- giving its approval to international agreements binding on the European Union
- voting on the adoption of the annual budget and overseeing its implementation
- approving the nomination of the president of the Commission and subsequently of the entire Commission.

(3) THE COUNCIL OF MINISTERS

This body consists of government ministers from the member-states. Its meetings are attended by different ministers, depending on the agenda, for example education, agriculture, environment, finance, social affairs. Generally they meet in Brussels, but sometimes meetings are held in Luxembourg.

Role of the Council of Ministers

- It is the main decision-making body of the European Union.
- Proposals from the European Commission are examined by the Council of Ministers, and decisions are then taken, based on its findings. Decisions are made by majority voting, but unanimous decisions are required for important issues.

(4) EUROPEAN COURT OF JUSTICE

This is the most important court in the European Union. It is an independent body and its term of office is six years. One of the judges is elected president of the court.

ROLE OF THE COURT OF JUSTICE

- interpreting the laws of the European Union and deciding whether or not they are being applied correctly
- imposing fines on member-states if they break the laws
- ruling on disputes between other institutions; these rulings are final, and they take precedence over national laws.

(5) COURT OF AUDITORS

ROLE OF THE COURT OF AUDITORS

- auditing and checking all accounts of the European Union and related bodies
- supervising the financial management practices and budgets of the European Union
- making an annual report to the Council of Ministers and the European Parliament and preparing a statement of assurance that the accounts are reliable.

EU policies and their impact on business

EU policies set out strategies in many different areas. The most important policies are:

- the Common Agricultural Policy
- the Competition Policy
- the Common Fisheries Policy
- the Social Charter
- economic and monetary union
- the Single European market.

COMMON AGRICULTURAL POLICY

The Common Agricultural Policy (CAP) was introduced to make the European Union self-sufficient in food and to improve farm incomes.

PRINCIPLES OF THE CAP

- A single market: all agricultural produce to move freely in a single market.
- EU preference: products from the European Union to be given preference.
- Finance: the European Union will continue to finance the CAP.

THE COMMON AGRICULTURAL POLICY

- promoted a fair standard of living for European farmers
- stabilised agricultural markets and regulated prices
- assured farmers of a market at guaranteed prices for their output
- guaranteed consumers a steady supply and choice of high quality products at reasonable prices
- provided an opportunity for farmers to increase productivity—grants were available for farm improvements
- guaranteed farmers that surplus produce would be purchased by EU intervention
- increased productivity led to permanent surpluses—some exported with the help of subsidies, remainder had to be stored or disposed of within the EU;

dealing with these had a high cost in terms of subsidised exports and storage costs.

CAP reforms

1984: Milk quotas were introduced

1992: Major reform to the CAP. Moved away from a system of market support to direct payments to farmers. The reforms also included measures to encourage less intensive farming in the interests of the environment and provided an early retirement scheme for farmers over fifty-five years of age.

Agenda 2000: Reinforced the move from market supports to direct payments. It intensified the emphasis on food safety and the environment.

June 2003: Fundamental change in nature of support for farmers—full decoupling of direct payments from production from 1 January 2005. Subsidies are paid independently from the volume of production.

Decoupled payments known as the Single Payments Scheme are conditional on the farmer's compliance with a range of environmental, food safety and animal welfare standards.

Farmers are now free to focus on the market and the demands of the final consumer; breaking the link between subsidies and production makes EU farmers more competitive and market-oriented while providing the necessary income stability.

COMMON FISHERIES POLICY

The European Union Common Fisheries Policy manages fisheries for the benefit of both fishing communities and consumers. It sets out to

- conserve fish stocks
- protect the marine environment
- ensure the economic viability of the European fishing fleets
- provide good quality food for consumers.

New Common Fisheries Policy

- The Common Fisheries Policy needed to be reformed as it was not effective enough in doing what it had been created to do.
- Far too many fish had been taken from the sea by fishing leaving too few adult fish to reproduce and rebuild stocks. Such a situation has a significant negative effect on fishermen's income.
- Reform was necessary to achieve biologically, environmentally and economically sustainable fisheries.
- The New Common Fisheries Policy was introduced on 1 January 2003.

The main changes can be summarised as follows:

1. Long-term approach

Measures concerning fishing opportunities and related measures had been taken annually. They had prevented fishermen from planning ahead, and failed to conserve fish stock. Under the new Common Fisheries Policy long-term objectives for attaining and/or maintaining safe levels of adult fish in EU stocks are set, as well as the measures needed to reach these levels.

2. A new policy for fleets
The reform responded to the challenge posed by the over-capacity of the EU fleet by phasing out aid to private investors to help them renew or modernise fishing vessels.

3. Better application of the rules
Measures taken to develop co-operation among various authorities to strengthen the uniformity of controls and sanctions for rule breakers throughout the EU.

Inspectors' powers to ensure the equity and effectiveness of EU enforcement have been extended. The measures will help establish a level playing field throughout the EU.

COMPETITION POLICY

The aim is to ensure that consumers get quality goods at reasonable prices, by restricting anti-competitive practices. The policy protects consumers against:

The formation of cartels
The policy restricts anti-competitive cartels that
- fix prices at artificially high levels
- share markets between firms
- block new firms entering the market.

Dominant firms
Firms that abuse their dominant position to increase prices or to restrict smaller firms are in breach of EU competition rules.

Mergers and take-overs
The European Union has the power to prevent large mergers and take-overs if it believes they might restrict competition.

THE SOCIAL CHARTER

Its aim is to protect the rights of workers in the European Union. The social charter called the 'Community Charter of Fundamental Social Right of Workers' proclaims the following rights:

- freedom of movement—the right to work in the country of one's choice
- employment and remuneration: the right to a fair wage
- freedom of association and collective bargaining
- social protection—based on the rules and practices of each country
- vocational training
- equal treatment for men and women
- consultation and participation for workers: the right to participate and be consulted in decision-making
- health protection and safety in the work-place
- protection of children and adolescents

- protection of the elderly
- protection of the disabled.

The Social Charter is not law. It is the responsibility of individual member-states to implement these rights.

ECONOMIC AND MONETARY UNION (EMU)

This is a policy designed to
- introduce a single currency, called the euro
- create a single monetary policy for the European Union, to be implemented by the European Central Bank.

BENEFITS OF ECONOMIC AND MONETARY UNION FOR IRELAND

(1) *Economic stability* will be maintained through adherence to strict criteria.
(2) *Reduced business costs:* there will be no bank charges on foreign currency transactions; exchange rate risks in foreign trade will be eliminated.
(3) *Lower inflation:* price stability should lead to lower inflation.
(4) *Lower interest rates:* interest rates will be lower and less volatile.
(5) *Payments for exports:* exports to other euro countries will be paid for in euro.
(6) *Price comparisons:* all goods and services in EU member-states who use the euro will be priced in euro.
(7) *Increased tourism:* no currency conversion will be required for travel within the euro zone; travel will be cheaper.
(8) *Foreign investment:* Ireland's attractiveness for foreign investment will increase.
(9) *Currency fluctuation,* which distorted foreign trade, will be eliminated.

SINGLE EUROPEAN MARKET

The single European market came into effect on 1 January 1993. It implemented
- free movement of goods, services, labour and capital between member-states
- a common tariff on imports to the European Union from non-EU countries.

OPPORTUNITIES FOR IRISH BUSINESS AS A RESULT OF THE SINGLE EUROPEAN MARKET

(1) *Access to EU markets*: Irish firms have access to a huge export market of nearly half a billion people.
(2) *Economies of scale*: unit costs are reduced because of increased production.
(3) *Free movement of workers*: workers can travel and work in any EU country.
(4) *Free movement of capital*: money can be invested anywhere in the European Union—wherever it earns the highest profit. When borrowing, firms and individuals can shop around in the EU market for the cheapest finance available.
(5) *Harmonisation of taxes*: tax rates on goods and services will be standardised.
(6) *Government contracts*: Irish companies can tender for government contracts in any EU member-state.
(7) *Structural and Cohesion Fund*: money from the European Union is available to Ireland for infrastructural development.
(8) *Increased consumer choice*: consumers will have an increased choice of goods imported from the European Union.
(9) *Employment*: increased competition will encourage efficiency and employment opportunities.

CHALLENGE TO BUSINESS AS A RESULT OF THE SINGLE EUROPEAN MARKET

(1) Irish firms may have difficulty surviving against foreign competition and imports from other EU countries; firms may be forced to merge to survive.
(2) There is a risk that skilled workers will move to other EU countries to work.
(3) There will be higher costs of operating in a huge international market, for example travel costs, insurance costs, etc.
(4) Irish firms must produce top-quality goods to compete successfully abroad and with foreign products imported into the Irish market.

Role of special-interest groups in the decision-making process

The main role of special-interest groups is lobbying EU bodies to influence policy decisions that affect their members to ensure that their interests are considered and reflected in policy.

Some interest groups are permanent: they have representatives on the Economic and Social Committee and are consulted before decisions affecting their members are made.

Interest groups such as the Irish Farmers' Association and the Society of the Irish Motor Industry maintain offices close to the EU decision-making bodies and use many techniques to influence the decision-making process.

Techniques used by interest groups to achieve their aims include:

- *lobbying*—putting their viewpoint directly to decision-makers: contacting members of the European Parliament, EU commissioners, or relevant Government minister on the Council of Ministers
- *media pressure* (television, radio, newspapers)
- *demonstrations and marches*
- *petitions*
- *strikes.*

The main interest groups include:

- the Irish Business and Employers' Confederation and the Irish Congress of Trade Unions: they try to influence decisions in the area of industrial relations
- the Irish Farmers' Association: it tries to influence decisions in relation to agriculture and proposed changes in the Common Agricultural Policy.

24. INTERNATIONAL BUSINESS

Global marketing of products and services

GLOBAL MARKETING is the building of a product brand and a company image throughout the world. The marketing of the firm's products or services is not only for the domestic market but also for world markets. All marketing plans are organised globally.

GLOBAL BRANDS

These are branded products that are marketed successfully throughout the world. The key to globalisation is standardisation. A Big Mac should taste the same in Tokyo as in Dublin.

Examples of global marketing

- Cars: Ford, Toyota, Nissan, Volvo
- Soft drinks: Coca-Cola, Pepsi-Cola, Lucozade
- Computers: IBM, Dell, Apple
- Sports gear: Nike, Adidas, Umbro, Le Coq Sportif.

These companies use the same marketing mix in all countries.

FACTORS GIVING RISE TO GLOBAL COMPANIES

(1) **Saturation of own market**
To increase sales and profit, firms must expand internationally.

(2) **Economies of scale**
Exports will increase growth and sales. Growth will allow economies of scale to be achieved, reducing costs and increasing profit.

(3) **Advances in information and production technology**
These developments allow firms to operate globally.

(4) **Improvements in transport and communications**
Faster travel and improvements in communications make it easier for firms to operate throughout the world.

OPPORTUNITIES OF GLOBAL MARKETING FOR IRISH BUSINESS

(1) **Expansion**
Irish companies may expand into global companies to increase sales and achieve economies of scale if they employ TQM techniques and invest in new technologies.

(2) **Profitability**
Profitability should rise as a result of increased sales.

(3) **Supplying raw materials**
Opportunities exist for firms to supply local raw materials to global companies.

THREATS OF GLOBAL MARKETING FOR IRISH BUSINESS

(1) **Recognisable brand name**
Global firms have a globally recognisable brand name, which provides a threat to Irish industry.

(2) **Advertising**
Global firms can afford large-scale advertising.

(3) **Competitive prices**
Prices may be more competitive than those of Irish industry.

STANDARDISED OR ADAPTED PRODUCTS

STANDARDISED MARKETING MIX

- The same market mix is used throughout the world, that is, the product is promoted in exactly the same way in different markets.
- Slight adjustments may be made in some countries to cater for local needs.

ADAPTED PRODUCT MARKETING MIX

- The product is adapted for different markets.
- Methods of promotion and price are varied to take account of differences in language, culture, economics, legislation, and buyers' characteristics, for example right-hand drive cars in Ireland and Britain.
- This leads to additional production, advertising and packaging costs.

GLOBAL MARKETING MIX

Firms must adopt the four Ps when going global.

PRODUCT

This is the element of the marketing mix most likely to remain unchanged. The product may be adjusted to suit

- technical regulations in different countries
- life-style and cultural differences
- different uses the product might have in different countries.

PRICE

The price charged in different countries must take into consideration

- the standard of living in different countries
- the extra costs of transport and other marketing costs
- duties or tariffs that might have to be paid in different countries
- the prices charged by local firms.

PROMOTION

Promotion must change in different countries to take account of language, cultural differences, and legal regulations regarding advertising.

- Language may be used differently to promote products in different markets.
- Cultural differences arise in different countries.
- Different advertising laws regulate advertising: for example, in Ireland cigarette advertising is banned on television.
- Which medium to use?

PLACE

In global marketing, the channel of distribution is longer than in a domestic market and usually includes exporters and importers.

Lack of local market knowledge makes it imperative for a firm to use overseas sales agents and distributors to market their products.

THE ROLE OF INFORMATION TECHNOLOGY IN GLOBALISATION

Advances in information technology through applications such as electronic mail (e-mail), videoconferencing and electronic data interchange (EDI) allow global business to function efficiently.

Information technology helps global firms in the following ways:

(1) DECISION-MAKING
Managements can avail of up-to-date information from any part of the world for speedy decision-making by using e-mail or videoconferencing.

(2) TRANSMISSION OF INFORMATION
Suppliers and customers can be linked through EDI for stock ordering, invoicing, etc.

(3) MARKET INFORMATION
Managements must respond rapidly to changes in the market. Information technology allows global firms to respond faster than competitors when redesigning products.

(4) VIDEOCONFERENCING
Videoconferencing allows managers in different places to hold meetings as if they were in the same room, without the need of costly travel.

(5) THE INTERNET
Internet services such as e-mail and the worldwide web allow global companies access to up-to-date information on the size of populations or cultural differences, which helps in decision-making regarding individual markets.

DIFFERENCES BETWEEN GLOBAL COMPANIES AND TRANSNATIONAL COMPANIES

Global companies attempt to sell a standardised product in all countries in the same way. **Transnational companies** take the differences between countries into consideration, so the product is adapted for different markets.

Development and impact of transnational companies

TRANSNATIONAL COMPANIES ARE COMPANIES THAT

- are structured globally
- own production, sales and other income-generating assets in a number of countries outside the country in which they are established
- have their head office in one country and factories in different countries, for example IBM, Volkswagen, Siemens, Nestlé, Intel, Guinness.

DEVELOPMENT OF TRANSNATIONAL COMPANIES

Several reasons can be put forward for the remarkable growth of transnationals, including:

- *the relaxation of exchange controls*, allowing easier transfer of capital between countries
- *technology:* improvements in communications and travel have reduced difficulties in controlling the operations of overseas subsidiaries
- *import tariffs and restrictions:* manufacturing in other countries is a way of avoiding import tariffs and restrictions
- *increasing sales and profits* and achieving benefits of economies of scale
- *being powerful* enough to combat competition.

IMPACT OF TRANSNATIONAL COMPANIES

Transnational companies have the following positive impacts:

Employment
Transnationals buy raw materials and services from local firms, creating local employment and a better standard of living. Increased production leads to direct employment.

Balance of payments
Exports are increased by the overseas sales effort of transnationals. This has a positive effect on the balance of trade and balance of payments. Imports may be reduced, as goods that were not previously produced in the host country are now available to satisfy local demand.

Competition
Competition in the host country is stimulated, with beneficial effects on prices, efficiency, and innovation. Modern management and production techniques force domestic producers to improve their own standards of efficiency in order to survive.

Government finances
Transnationals are an important source of revenue for the Government through corporation tax on profits, VAT on purchases, and PAYE and PRSI paid by employees.

Job security
Transnationals are able to resist competition, so employees have job security.

TRANSNATIONAL COMPANIES HAVE THE FOLLOWING NEGATIVE IMPACTS:
Large grants are often required before they set up in a country.

Repatriation of profits
They may transfer all their profits to the home country.

Political pressure
Because of their size, transnationals have been known to exert political pressure on governments and politicians and may threaten to withdraw from a country if they do not get their own way on grants, taxes, etc.

Social implications
Transnationals operate in countries to earn a profit. If they become unprofitable they shut down without much notice and leave, with little consideration for stakeholders.

KEY TERMS
These are some of the more important terms introduced in unit 7:

Council of Ministers	global marketing
European Commission	imports
European Court of Justice	international marketing
EU directive	international trade
EU policy	single market
European Parliament	trading bloc
European Union	transnational company
exports	

ON COMPLETION OF UNIT 7 YOU SHOULD BE ABLE TO
(1) identify the effects of the single market on Irish business;
(2) describe the reasons for the development of transnational companies;
(3) explain the role of information technology in international trade;
(4) discuss the opportunities and challenges facing Irish business in developed and developing markets;
(5) explain the role of global marketing in international business;
(6) explain the purpose of the main EU policies and directives.

Examination-style question and solution

European Union—social responsibilities of business

Pat O'Brien owns a motor dealership and is a member of the Society of the Irish Motor Industry (SIMI). He is worried about a proposed EU directive on reducing the emission of lead from car exhausts.

(**A**) Outline how an EU directive is formulated and implemented. **(30 marks)**
(**B**) Explain how interest groups, such as SIMI, influence this process. **(10 marks)**
(**C**) Analyse the effects on the garage of meeting its ethical responsibilities. **(20 marks)**

Suggested solution

(A) *Formulation of a directive: A directive is a piece of EU law. All EU legislation is proposed or drafted by the European Commission and adopted by the Council of Ministers after getting the opinion of interested parties, for example the European Parliament.*

Implementation of a directive: A directive requires member-states of the European Union to alter national laws to implement its requirements. The directive is binding on each state within a required time but through the individual state's own laws.

(B) *The main objectives of interest groups are to influence policy decisions that affect their members and to ensure that their interests are considered during the policy-making procedure. In the European Union, interest groups such as SIMI or their representatives maintain offices close to the EU decision-making bodies and use techniques such as research, publications, lobbying the European Parliament and other bodies, holding conferences, applying pressure on the media, holding demonstrations, getting petitions signed, organising strikes and conducting advertising campaigns to influence the process.*

(C) *Ethical responsibilities are responsibilities concerned with moral principles that affect the action of a person or a group, in this case the garage-owner Pat O'Brien. The ethical responsibilities the business has include:*

—responsibilities to employees: the creation and maintenance of employment, fair wages and conditions of work, etc.

—responsibilities to customers: safe products, reasonable prices, honest advertising, etc.

—responsibilities to the Government: social duties such as planning, observing the law, paying taxes, etc.

—*responsibilities to the community: not engaging in pollution or dereliction, supporting the local economy, supporting local activities such as the arts, etc.*

By not meeting its responsibilities to these stakeholders a business may

—*lose out to competitors;*

—*be subject to unfavourable publicity;*

—*be forced to incorporate cost increases;*

—*suffer fines because of breaches of the law;*

—*be subject to delays from official sources that require ethical standards, such as the Environmental Protection Agency.*

Examination-style questions and solutions

European Union—social responsibilities of business

Recent news reports have upset the O'Brien household. John O'Brien, who runs the family farm, is a member of the Irish Farmers' Association. He is concerned about a proposed EU directive on environmental protection.

(**A**) Outline how an EU directive is formulated and implemented. **(30 marks)**
(**B**) Explain how interest groups such as the IFA influence this process. **(10 marks)**
(**C**) Analyse the effect on the farm of meeting its environmental responsibilities. **(20 marks)**

Suggested solution

(A) *Formulation of a directive: A directive is a piece of EU legislation. It is proposed or drafted by the European Commission and adopted by the Council of Ministers after getting the opinion of interested parties, for example the European Parliament.*

Implementation of a directive: A directive requires member-states to alter their national laws to implement its requirements. The rules of the directive are binding on each state within a required time but with the method of implementing the directive left to the individual state.

(B) *The main objectives of interest groups are to influence policy decisions that affect their members and to ensure that their interests are considered during the policy-making procedure. In the European Union, interest groups such as the IFA or its representatives maintain offices close to the EU decision-making bodies and use research, lobbying the European Parliament and other bodies, conferences, pressure on the media, demonstrations, petitions, strikes, advertising campaigns etc. to influence the process.*

(C) *Environmental responsibilities are those concerned with protecting the environment, which is a legacy for future generations. The business in this case is a family farm. The environmental responsibilities of the owners, and their effects, include:*

—*keeping production processes clean, quiet, and safe; while this increases production costs, it may also result in increased sales and farm income;*

—carefully maintaining the quality and fertility of the land; this may mean incurring increased costs for fertilisers and may not maximise output, because of crop rotation and leaving some fields fallow;

—ensuring that products are safe and healthy; this will avoid possible unfavourable publicity, a boycott of products by customers, and delays from official sources, which demand clean and careful farm production, practices, and products;

—safely and carefully disposing of animal and farm effluents, ensuring that they don't seep into rivers; the careful disposal of farm waste will ensure that the O'Brien family will not be fined or even imprisoned for damaging the environment.

Practice questions—Section 1

1. What is global marketing?

____

____

Name two global businesses.

(1) ______________________________

(2) ______________________________

2. List two challenges that face companies in the global marketing of their products, and give a one-sentence explanation of one of them.

(i) ______________________________

(ii) ______________________________

____

3. Describe the role of the European Court of Auditors.

____

____

4. What is the main purpose of European monetary union for business?

____

____

5. (i) Interest groups influence EU decisions by:

(*a*) ______________________________

(*b*) ______________________________

(ii) Give two examples of interest groups in the European Union.

(*a*) ______________________________

(*b*) ______________________________

Revision question

Domestic and international environment

(A) Outline the significance of international trade for Ireland. **(15 marks)**

(B) Explain the opportunities and challenges for Irish business as a result of the single European market. **(30 marks)**

(C) Analyse the impact of transnational companies on Ireland. **(15 marks)**

[60 marks]

25. Applied Business Questions

Higher level only
Compulsory question [80 marks]

ABQ describes a business situation facing a company. It will usually contain three paragraphs of text, with three questions based on the information given.

It contains 'outcome verbs', which are keywords in all questions, informing candidates about what is required in the answer: 'explain', 'describe', 'analyse', etc.

Pupils must have a thorough knowledge of the units of the syllabus on which the ABQ are based. (See 'Examination structure'.)

Questions will in general be based on the material contained in the question. The answers provided must link the information given to the text of the ABQ.

Examination structure

Leaving Certificate Business Higher level
400 marks
Three hours
Candidates must attempt all three sections.

Section 1—80 marks

Ten short-answer questions.

All questions carry equal marks.
Answer eight out of the ten questions.

This section is to be returned with the answer book.

Section 2—80 marks

One applied business question.

This question is based on the following units.

2007 Units	2008 Units	2009 Units	2010 Units
4	5	1	2
5	6	2	3
6	7	3	4

2011 Units	2012 Units	2013 Units	2014 Units
3	4	5	1
4	5	6	2
5	6	7	3

Section 3—240 marks

Seven structured questions.
All questions carry equal marks (60).
Four questions to be attempted.

NOTE: For the purposes of this section, the syllabus is divided into two parts.

Part 1: people in business (unit 1) and environment (units 6 and 7).

Part 2: enterprise (units 2, 3, 4, and 5).

ANSWER FOUR QUESTIONS.
Part 1 (three questions): answer **one** question.

Part 2 (four questions): answer **two** questions.

Answer the **fourth** question from either part 1 or part 2.

Examination structure

Leaving Certificate Business Ordinary level
400 marks
$2\frac{1}{2}$ hours
Candidates must attempt both sections.

SECTION 1—(100 MARKS)

Fifteen short-answer questions.

All questions carry equal marks.

Answer **ten** out of the fifteen questions.

This section is to be returned with the answer book.

SECTION 2—(300 MARKS)

Eight structured questions.

All questions carry equal marks **(75)**.

Four questions to be attempted.

NOTE: For the purposes of this section, the syllabus is divided into two parts.

Part 1: people in business (unit 1) and environment (units 6 and 7).

Part 2: enterprise (units 2, 3, 4, and 5).

Answer four questions

Part 1 (three questions): answer **one** question.

Part 2 (five questions): answer **two** questions.

Answer the **fourth** question from either part 1 or part 2.

Time plan

Leaving Certificate Business Higher level
400 marks
Three hours
Candidates must attempt all three sections.

A good exam depends on good timing.

SECTION 1—(80 MARKS)	SECTION 2—(80 MARKS)	SECTION 3—(240 MARKS)
20% of examination Answer **8** out of **10** questions.	**20% of examination** **1** applied business question	**60% of examination** **7** Structured questions at **60** marks **Four** questions to be attempted
Exam technique Time: **36** minutes Reading time: **4** minutes **8** questions at **4** minutes	*Exam technique* Time: **36** minutes Reading time: **8** minutes **1** question at **28** minutes	*Exam technique* Time: **108** minutes Reading time: **8** minutes **4** questions at **25** minutes

Leaving Certificate examination
Business
Ordinary level
400 Marks
$2\frac{1}{2}$ hours
Candidates must attempt two sections

SECTION 1—(100 MARKS)	SECTION 2—(300 MARKS)
25% of examination	**75% of examination**
15 short-answer questions	**8** structured questions at **75** marks
Answer **10** out of **15** questions	**Four** questions to be attempted
Exam technique Time: **38** minutes Reading time: **8** minutes **10** questions at **3** minutes	*Exam technique* Time: **112** minutes Reading time: **8** minutes **4** questions at **26** minutes

Business syllabus

Outcome verbs

analyse (HL): study a problem in detail by breaking it down into various parts and examining possible relationships.
apply (HL): bring knowledge or skill into use, for example use for a particular purpose.
calculate: find out or ascertain by using numerical data, ratios, etc.
compare (HL): examine two or more things so as to discover their similarities or differences.
contrast: place in opposition so as to show the differences between.
define: state the precise meaning of a term or concept.
demonstrate: explain or describe by showing examples, charts, diagrams, graphs, etc.
describe: give an account of a person, relationship, event, institution, etc.
differentiate (HL): distinguish between; develop separate characteristics.
discuss (HL): examine or consider, suggesting a detailed and careful investigation; it may require debating both sides of an argument.
distinguish: recognise something as distinct from other things, that is, to point out the differences.
draft: draw up an outline in writing—document, letter, etc.—or a sketch, diagram, etc.
evaluate (HL): find or determine the worth, value, amount or significance of something.
explain: make clear in a detailed manner.
identify: show that you recognise something.
illustrate: make clear by means of examples, charts, diagrams, graphs, etc.
interpret: give or explain the meaning of; derive a particular understanding of.
list: write down a number of names or things having something in common.
outline: give a short summary of the general principles or chief elements, omitting details.
recognise: identify something known or perceived before.
understand: grasp something as distinct from other things; point out the differences.

LEAVING CERTIFICATE EXAMINATION, 2007

BUSINESS – HIGHER LEVEL
(400 Marks)

CANDIDATES ARE REQUIRED TO ANSWER
(A) Eight questions from SECTION 1
AND
(B) The Applied Business Question in SECTION 2
AND
(C) Four questions from SECTION 3 as follows:
One question from Part 1,
Two questions from Part 2
and One other question from either Part 1 or Part 2.
All questions carry equal marks.

Please note allocation of marks per question.
Calculators may be used.

SECTION 1
SHORT ANSWER QUESTIONS
(80 marks)

This section is compulsory. Answer eight questions. Each question carries 10 marks.

1. **Column 1** is a list of business terms. **Column 2** is a list of possible explanations for these terms. (*One explanation does not refer to any of the terms.*)

Column 1 – Terms	Column 2 – Explanations
1. Arbitration	**A.** Protection against an event that might happen
2. Agenda	**B.** A review of an employee's job performance
3. Assurance	**C.** One enterprise purchases another enterprise
4. Acquisition	**D.** The referral of a dispute to an independent body for settlement
5. Appraisal	**E.** The details of business to be transacted at a meeting
	F. Protection against an event that will happen

Match the two lists by placing the letter of the correct explanation under the relevant number below:

1.	2.	3.	4.	5.

2. (a) What do the letters SWOT stand for? ______________________________

____

(b) Explain its use in business: ______________________________

____

____

3. An EU directive is ______________________________

____

4. Draft and label a matrix structure for a manufacturing organisation:

5. In a legal context, consideration means ______________________________

____

6. (a) What is a trading bloc? ______________________________

____

(b) Give **two** examples: (i) ______________________________

(ii) ______________________________

7. Maslow identified, in his hierarchical model, 'self-actualisation' as a human need.
(a) Self-actualisation means ______________________________

____

(b) Name **two** other human needs he also identified:

(i) ____________________ (ii) ____________________

8. Identify **two** parties in business and describe a competitive relationship between them:

____

____

____

9. Below is a diagram used in business. In the answer box beside this diagram, name the diagram and insert the appropriate labels for the numbered lines in the diagram:

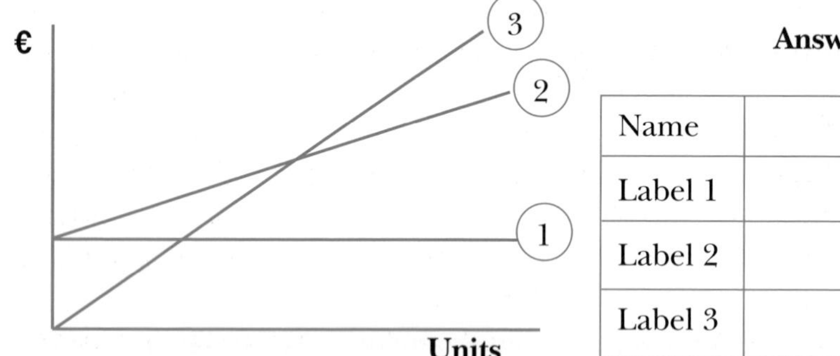

Answer Box

Name	
Label 1	
Label 2	
Label 3	

10. (a) Name a state-owned enterprise in the 'production' category:

____

(b) Explain **two** reasons for state involvement in this category:

____

____

____

SECTION 2

(80 marks)

This is a compulsory question based on Units 4, 5 and 6.

Applied Business Question

McGComputers

McGComputers was founded in 1986 by Jason McGinley. It is an independent firm specialising in the sale and repair of computers, operating from a premises fronting onto the main street of a large town. Jason had worked a standard five-day week in his previous job, as a qualified engineer, with a transnational computer company. The new venture forced him to adjust to working long and irregular hours, and to manage with limited financial resources. The change also meant a review of his commitments to health and life plans, and the provision of his home as security. While his formal bookkeeping skills were limited, he maintained details of all customers and their transactions.

Responding to published official forecasts and trade publications, Jason recruited sales people and qualified technicians to serve the client base and expand the product range of the firm. He encouraged the staff to engage with customers and to note their reactions to new ideas and products. His reliance on trust in the staff has been successful in that only one employee has had to be dismissed for theft. McGComputers is now well established with twelve full-time employees and five service vehicles on the road. It regularly hosts product presentations and demonstrations on its premises for representative sections of its customer base.

Siobhán, Jason's daughter, a recent business graduate has joined the firm. Siobhán would like to add other services such as website design and maintenance, training and consultancy, and has held focused discussions with groups of customers. This has led Jason to consider reorganising the firm and leaving the day-to-day running with Siobhán. Overall policy control would rest with him, supported by a limited number of reward-seeking investors.

(A) Discuss the methods of market research currently used in the business and how these could be developed. (20 marks)

(B) Describe the types of insurance appropriate to the context described above. (30 marks)

(C) Evaluate McGComputers as a type of business organisation with appropriate recommendations. (30 marks)

(80 marks)

SECTION 3
(240 marks)

Answer four questions from Section 3 as follows:
One question from Part 1, Two questions from Part 2 and One other question from either Part 1 or Part 2. All questions carry equal marks.

PART 1
PEOPLE IN BUSINESS/BUSINESS ENVIRONMENT

People in Business

Question 1

(A) Under the terms of the Industrial Relations Act 1990, (i) define a legitimate trade dispute and (ii) explain the role of the Labour Relations Commission. (20 marks)

(B) Describe the provisions of the Sale of Goods and Supply of Services Act 1980 and evaluate its effectiveness. (30 marks)

(C) *Specific Performance* is a term used in contract law. Explain what it is and when it would be used. (10 marks)

(60 marks)

Domestic/International Environment

Question 2

(A) Discuss the importance of the categories of industry to the current Irish economy. (20 marks)

(B) Name **three** examples of community development organisations and describe the services provided by **one** of them. (20 marks)

(C) (i) Define code of ethics.
(ii) Outline the effects on a firm's costs of meeting its ethical and social responsibilities. (20 marks)

(60 marks)

Domestic/International Environment

Question 3

The Irish economy is an open economy and is greatly affected by economic influences from abroad. These influences create both opportunities and challenges for Irish business.

(A) Discuss the opportunities provided by international trade for Irish business. (25 marks)

(B) Explain the term 'global marketing' and its role in international business. (25 marks)

(C) Outline, using an example, the role of 'interest groups' in the European Union. (10 marks)

(60 marks)

SECTION 3

PART 2
ENTERPRISE

Enterprise/Managing

Question 4

(A) Describe **three** enterprise skills required of an entrepreneur. (15 marks)

(B) Discuss the importance of good communication between the levels in an organisation. (20 marks)

(C) The Data Protection Act 1988 sets out the following:

(i) The rights of Data Subjects
(ii) The obligations of Data Controllers and
(iii) The functions of the Data Protection Commissioner

Explain any **two** of the above. (25 marks)

(60 marks)

Managing

Question 5

(A) Distinguish between the following taxation forms: *Form P21* and *Form P60.* (20 marks)

(B) From the following information, calculate the net annual take-home pay of Ms. Joan McCormack.

Joan McCormack is an employee of Lynch Printers Ltd and earns a gross annual salary of €84,000.

She is allowed the following tax credits: Single Person credit of €1,760 and PAYE credit of €1,760. The income tax rates are: 20% on the first €34,000 (standard rate cut-off point) and 41% on the balance. The employee PRSI rate (including the health levy) is: 6% on the first €48,800 and 2% on the balance. (20 marks)

(C) Explain the term TQM and describe how it can be of benefit to an organisation. (20 marks)

(60 marks)

Business in Action/Managing

Question 6

(A) (i) Explain, using a diagram, the stages in the product life cycle.
(ii) In the case of **each** stage, describe the implications for the cash flow of a business.

(20 marks)

(B) Balden Ltd prepared the following cash flow forecast:

2007	July €	August €	September €	Total €
Receipts	70,000	55,000	80,000	205,000
Payments	80,000	45,000	55,000	180,000
Net Cash	(10,000)	10,000	25,000	25,000
Opening Cash	3,000	(7,000)	3,000	3,000
Closing Cash	(7,000)	3,000	28,000	28,000

(i) Why would this cash flow forecast be prepared by Balden Ltd?
(ii) How might management deal with the financial issue highlighted in this forecast?

(20 marks)

(C) Liquidity ratios are used to assist in managing a business. Name **two** of these ratios and describe their respective benefits.

(20 marks)
(60 marks)

Business in Action

Question 7

(A) Explain **four** pricing policies that businesses can adopt as part of their marketing strategy and apply **one** of them to a product of your choice. (30 marks)

(B) (i) What is a marketing plan?
(ii) Evaluate the role such a plan can have for a business. (20 marks)

(C) Outline and illustrate the term 'niche market'. (10 marks)

(60 marks)

LEAVING CERTIFICATE EXAMINATION, 2007

BUSINESS – ORDINARY LEVEL
(400 marks)

ANSWER
(A) Ten questions from SECTION 1

AND

(B) Four questions from SECTION 2 as follows:

One question from Part 1 and
Two questions from Part 2 and
One other question from either Part 1 or Part 2.

All questions carry equal marks.

Calculators may be used.

SECTION 1
(100 marks)
SHORT ANSWER QUESTIONS

Answer 10 questions. Each question carries 10 marks. Please return this question paper with your answer book.

1. What do the following letters stand for? (Write each answer in the space provided.)

(i) PRO	
(ii) ATM	
(iii) PRSI	

2. List **four** methods of written communication used in business:

(i) ____________________

(ii) ____________________

(iii) ____________________

(iv) ____________________

3. Explain the term 'producer' and give **two** examples:

Examples: (i) ____________________

(ii) ____________________

4. Distinguish between employer's liability insurance and public liability insurance:

(i) Employer's liability insurance

(ii) Public liability insurance

5. Draw a bar chart below to illustrate the following information for FLYNN MOTORS Ltd:

Year	**2002**	**2003**	**2004**	**2005**	**2006**
No. of Employees	**25**	**30**	**40**	**35**	**20**

No. of Employees

Year

6. Explain the term 'transnational company' and give **one** example:

____

____

____

Example:____________________________________

7. (i) Write in **three** items to complete the following Agenda for the AGM of Newtown Golf Club:

Newtown Golf Club
Agenda for the AGM

1. Minutes of the last meeting
2. ____________________________________
3. ____________________________________
4. ____________________________________
5. A.O.B.

(ii) What do the letters A.O.B. stand for?

Answer: ____________________________________

8. **Column 1** is a list of six business terms. **Column 2** is a list of seven possible explanations for these terms. (One explanation has no match.)

Column 1: Terms	**Column 2**: Explanations
1 Credit Rating	A Payment of part of a company's profits to its owners
2 Utmost Good Faith	B A long-term source of finance with a fixed rate of interest and a fixed date of repayment
3 Paypath	C A medium-term source of finance
4 Dividend	D A method of payment from a bank account at regular intervals
5 Direct Debit	E Payment of wages directly into an employee's bank account
6 Leasing	F The applicant must tell the truth and disclose all material facts when seeking insurance
	G An assessment of a person's creditworthiness

Match the two lists by placing the letter of the correct explanation under the relevant number in the box below: (One answer has already been provided.)

1	2	3	4	5	6
G					

9. Explain the term 'prototype development': ______________________

____

10. List **three** of the main headings in a Business Plan: (Example: *Production*)
(i) ______________________
(ii) ______________________
(iii) ______________________

11. The following information is taken from the final accounts of S.K. Ltd on 31/05/2007.

Sales € 500,000
Gross Profit € 100,000
Net Profit € 37,500

Calculate:
(i) the Gross Profit Margin.
Answer: ______________________

(ii) the Net Profit Margin.
Answer: ______________________

WORKINGS

12. Explain the term 'quality control': ________________________________

____

____

13. Indicate, by means of a tick (✔), the category to which each good or service belongs:

	Category			
	Visible Exports	**Visible Imports**	**Invisible Exports**	**Invisible Imports**
Irish beef sold abroad				
Foreign music bands on tour in Ireland				
French fans coming to a match in Dublin				
Japanese cars sold in Ireland				

14. Explain each of the following types of training offered to employees:
(i) On-the-job training ________________________________

____

(ii) Off-the-job training ________________________________

____

15. Outline **two** benefits which business can bring to a local community:
(i) ____

____

(ii) ____

____

SECTION 2
(300 marks)

Answer four questions from SECTION 2 as follows:
One question from Part 1 and
Two questions from Part 2 and
One other question from either Part 1 or Part 2.

PART 1

PEOPLE IN BUSINESS

QUESTION 1

Study the information supplied and answer the questions which follow:

James and Emer O'Brien ordered paving slabs for their garden patio from Healy's Garden Centre Ltd. They selected the paving slabs from samples shown to them at the garden centre. When the paving slabs were delivered, they were not the same as the sample they had chosen. The O'Briens were not happy but the sales assistant told them that they must pay for the goods delivered.

(A) (i) Name the law that protects the O'Briens in this case. (10 marks)
(ii) Outline **one** non-legislative method of solving the above problem. (10 marks)
(iii) Explain the legal rights of the O'Briens and the duties of Healy's Garden Centre Ltd. (20 marks)

The Employment Equality Act 1998 aims to prevent discrimination in the workplace.

(B) (i) Describe **two** grounds on which discrimination is unlawful under this Act. (20 marks)
(ii) Outline the role of a Rights Commissioner. (15 marks)

(75 marks)

DOMESTIC/INTERNATIONAL ENVIRONMENT

QUESTION 2

Study the information supplied and answer the questions which follow:

Goodfoods Ltd is an indigenous company set up by sisters Una and Jane O'Sullivan and it has 14 full-time employees. As a company, it benefits from limited liability.
The company prepares readymade meals for the home market and is currently considering exporting to foreign markets.
The owners have drafted a code of ethics for the business believing that decisions made should be guided by what is morally right, honest and fair.

(A) Explain the term 'limited liability'. (10 marks)

(B) What is meant by the term 'indigenous company'? (10 marks)

(C) Outline **three** challenges Goodfoods Ltd may face when exporting to foreign markets. (15 marks)

(D) Describe **two** environmental responsibilities of Goodfoods Ltd. (20 marks)

(E) Using examples, describe how Goodfoods Ltd can behave ethically towards (i) its employees and (ii) its customers. (20 marks)

(75 marks)

DOMESTIC/INTERNATIONAL ENVIRONMENT

QUESTION 3

Study the information supplied and answer the questions which follow:

Unemployment in Ireland is less than 5% but some economists are concerned because interest rates have risen and are forecast to increase.

(A) Outline **three** benefits of low unemployment to the Irish economy. (15 marks)

(B) Outline **three** effects of increasing interest rates on Irish business. (15 marks)

(C) Describe **two** ways in which the Irish Government assists business. (20 marks)

(D) Discuss **two** opportunities and **two** challenges for Irish business arising from the enlarged European Union. (25 marks)

(75 marks)

PART 2

MANAGING

QUESTION 4

Study the information supplied and answer the questions which follow:

Cathal and Joan Lyons and their three school-going children live in Cork city. Their household income totals €3,000 a month. They regularly prepare a household budget to help them manage their finances.

Lyons Household Budget (Summary)			
	July	**August**	**September**
	€	**€**	**€**
A. Income	3,000	3,000	3,000
B. Expenditure	2,100	2,900	4,800
Net Cash (A-B)	900	100	(1,800)
Opening Cash	100	1,000	1,100
Closing Cash	1,000	1,100	(700)

(A) Explain **three** benefits to a household of preparing a budget. (15 marks)

(B) (i) Identify **three** items that could be included in the 'Income' section of the household budget.

(ii) Suggest **two** ways in which the Lyons household could overcome the expected deficit in September. (25 marks)

(C) In the context of banking, explain **three** features of a current account. (15 marks)

(D) Name **two** types of insurance that are important for a household to have and explain **one** of them. (20 marks)

(75 marks)

ENTERPRISE/MANAGING/BUSINESS IN ACTION

QUESTION 5

Study the information supplied and answer the questions which follow:

Andrew Roche, a qualified plumber, has recently set up his own business. He provides services for households and small businesses in his local area. He has rented premises and is considering the purchase of a van. He intends to employ other staff as his business expands and knows that this may require focus on the area of human resource management.

(A) Describe **three** enterprising skills/characteristics that Andrew has as an entrepreneur. (15 marks)

(B) Explain **two** appropriate sources of finance that Andrew may use to purchase the van. (20 marks)

(C) Outline **three** disadvantages of Andrew setting up his own business. (15 marks)

(D) Outline **two** suitable methods that Andrew could use to promote his new business. (10 marks)

(E) (i) Explain the term 'human resource management'.
(ii) Identify and explain **two** functions of a Human Resources Manager. (15 marks)

(75 marks)

MANAGING

QUESTION 6

Study the information supplied and answer the questions which follow:

The Shareholders and Managing Director fulfil important roles in a company. Leadership and Motivation are two management skills. Technology and modern developments in technology have changed the role of management.

(A) Explain the role of Shareholders in a company. (10 marks)

(B) Describe **two** functions of the Managing Director of a company. (15 marks)

(C) Autocratic, Democratic and Laissez-faire are three styles of leadership. Describe the characteristics of **two** of these leadership styles. (20 marks)

(D) Describe **one** of the following theories of motivation;
(i) Maslow's Hierarchy of Needs <u>or</u> (ii) McGregor's Theory X and Theory Y. (15 marks)

(E) Using examples, describe **three** ways in which technology has changed the role of management. (15 marks)

(75 marks)

BUSINESS IN ACTION/MANAGING

QUESTION 7

Study the information supplied and answer the questions which follow:

Michael Brennan has recently completed his degree in Administration and Marketing. He has started his first job as overall Marketing Manager with Stewart Chemists Ltd, a national franchise of chemist shops. His first task is to carry out market research for the business. He is looking forward to both the financial and non-financial rewards of his position.

(A) Explain the term 'franchise'. (10 marks)
(B) Outline **three** reasons why businesses carry out market research. (15 marks)
(C) Using examples, explain the terms (i) field research and (ii) desk research. (20 marks)
(D) Outline **one** financial reward and **one** non-financial reward that Michael may receive in his job. (10 marks)
(E) Form P21, Form P60 and Form P45 are three forms used in PAYE taxation. Outline the purpose of **two** of these forms. (20 marks)

(75 marks)

BUSINESS IN ACTION

QUESTION 8

Study the information supplied and answer the questions which follow:

Milltown Bakery Co-operative was set up in 1998 by a group of workers who had been made redundant when a national bakery closed its base in the town. The co-operative has been very successful and uses a system of batch production to produce different kinds of breads, cakes and pastries which it sells nationwide.
The co-operative is considering expanding the business and the management committee has discussed the idea of becoming a limited company.

(A) Outline **two** differences between a co-operative and a limited company. (10 marks)
(B) (i) Apart from batch production, name **two** other types of production used in business.
(ii) Outline **three** features of batch production. (15 marks)
(C) Identify **four** factors that Milltown Bakery Co-operative should consider when deciding the price of its products. (20 marks)
(D) Describe **three** reasons why Milltown Bakery Co-operative would consider expanding the business. (15 marks)
(E) Outline **three** advantages to Milltown Bakery Co-operative of having a brand name. (15 marks)

(75 marks)

LEAVING CERTIFICATE EXAMINATION, 2008

BUSINESS – HIGHER LEVEL
(400 Marks)

2.00 p.m. to 5.00 p.m.

CANDIDATES ARE REQUIRED TO ANSWER:
(A) Eight questions from SECTION 1
AND
(B) The Applied Business Question in SECTION 2
AND
(C) Four questions from SECTION 3 as follows:
One question from Part 1,
Two questions from Part 2
and One other question from either Part 1 or Part 2.
All questions carry equal marks.

Please note allocation of marks per question. Calculators may be used.

SECTION 1
(80 marks)
SHORT ANSWER QUESTIONS

This section is compulsory. Answer eight questions. Each question carries 10 marks. Remember to return this question paper with your answer book.

1. (a) Intrapreneurship is:

____

____

____

____

(b) State **two** examples of intrapreneurship:

(i) ______________________________

____

(ii) ______________________________

____

2. In relation to the law of contract distinguish between the terms 'offer' and 'invitation to treat'.

3. Differentiate between Working Capital and Equity Capital.

4. (a) Explain what is meant by the term 'Open Economy'.

(b) Outline its possible impact on Ireland's economic development.

5. Draft a typical Agenda for the AGM of a Private Limited Company.

Agenda

1.

2.

3.

4.

5.

6. Distinguish between Strategic Planning and Tactical Planning. Give **one** example in each case.

7. (a) Identify a suitable source of finance for the purchase of a delivery van in a new business enterprise.

(b) Give **two** reasons for your choice.

(i)

(ii)

8. (a) Outline **two** benefits of community initiatives in the development of a local community.

(i)

(ii)

(b) State **two** functions of either FÁS **OR** the County Enterprise Boards (CEBs).

(i)

(ii)

9. List **five** grounds under which **employment discrimination** is outlawed in Ireland.

(i)

(ii)

(iii)

(iv)

(v)

10. (a) John O'Neill owned a house worth €350,000 and had insured it for €300,000 when a fire caused a partial loss of €63,000. Calculate the amount the insurance company will pay. **(Show your workings.)**

Workings

(b) Name the principle of insurance that applies in (a) above.

SECTION 2
(80 Marks)

This is a compulsory question based on Units 5, 6, and 7

Applied Business Question

FRUIT FIRST LTD

Fruit First Ltd produces a range of 'smoothies', a fruit drink made from crushed fruit. Mary Ryan, a food scientist in the food industry, identified a gap in the market for an Irish supplier of natural fruit drinks. In her spare time she produced a batch of smoothies, supplying samples to local shops. Encouraged by the favourable responses, she left her job and set up Fruit First Ltd in 2001.

The business, based in the midlands, sources fresh fruit locally and from abroad. Bringing new investors on board in 2006 enabled Fruit First to invest in larger premises, doubling its production capacity. Profits are approaching €1million and the business now employs thirty full-time workers. The chilled drink products come in attractively designed cartons of different sizes, supplied by a local firm. Fruit First vans deliver the products to retail outlets, nutrition shops and fitness centres nationwide. Mary's focus on producing a quality product has allowed her command a higher price than her competitors. Annual investment in research and development has led to a widening of the product range and development of a green image for the business. Initially Mary used local supermarkets to encourage consumers to taste the products. Over time Fruit First's marketing strategies expanded and the brand has now become associated with 'National Healthy Heart Day'.

As the leading Irish supplier of smoothies, further expansion in the small Irish market is unlikely. Mary sees the potential to grow the business and she is considering entering the UK market initially and subsequently the wider EU market. While recognising the high cost base in Ireland and the perishable nature of the product, Mary has begun developing an export strategy. Fruit First is in discussion with a leading food retailing chain in relation to supplying shops throughout the UK. Mary views this as an opportunity and a necessary step before entering the wider EU marketplace.

(A) Evaluate the elements of the marketing mix for Fruit First Ltd. (30 marks)

(B) Discuss how Fruit First Ltd benefits the local **and** national economy. Refer to the above text in your answer. (25 marks)

(C) You have been appointed to advise Fruit First Ltd on entering international markets.

Outline your analysis of the opportunities **and** challenges facing Fruit First Ltd and make an appropriate recommendation.

(25 marks)
(80 marks)

SECTION 3
(240 marks)

Answer four questions from Section 3 as follows:
One question from Part 1, Two questions from Part 2 and One other question from either Part 1 or Part 2. All questions carry equal marks.

Part 1
People in Business / Business Environment

People in Business

Question 1

The quality of the relationship between stakeholders determines the success of any enterprise.

(A) Describe a competitive relationship and a co-operative relationship between two producers in the same line of business. Use appropriate examples to support your answer. (15 marks)

(B) (i) Illustrate the circumstances where retailers would be in breach of the Sale of Goods and Supply of Services Act 1980.

(ii) Outline remedies available to consumers for breaches of the Act.

(25 marks)

(C) Evaluate the role of the Labour Court in dealing with industrial disputes.

(20 marks)
(60 marks)

Domestic / International Environment

Question 2

(A) (i) Explain the term 'Transnational Company' (TNC).
(ii) Discuss the reasons for the development of transnational companies in Ireland. (20 marks)

(B) "As global warming becomes a reality for the world, there is an increasing concern for the protection of the environment".
Illustrate how businesses in Ireland today could become more environmentally responsible. (20 marks)

(C) Evaluate, using examples, the arguments in favour **OR** against the privatisation of commercial state enterprises in Ireland. (20 marks)

(60 marks)

Domestic / International Environment

Question 3

(A) Discuss the impact of the Single European Market (SEM) on Irish business. (25 marks)

(B) Explain the functions of any **two** of the following European institutions.

(i) The European Parliament
(ii) The Council of Ministers
(iii) The European Commission

(20 marks)

(C) (i) In the context of the European Union (EU) distinguish between a Directive and a Regulation.

(ii) Choose **one** example of either and describe its purpose.

(15 marks)

(60 marks)

SECTION 3
Part 2
Enterprise

Enterprise / Managing

Question 4

(A) "Being decisive, creative and being prepared to take risks are personal characteristics often associated with entrepreneurs".
Discuss these characteristics and support your answer with examples.
(15 marks)

(B) Describe the barriers to effective communication in a business enterprise and suggest methods a business might consider to overcome **two** of these barriers.
(25 marks)

(C) Evaluate the contributions that Stock Control and Credit Control make to the successful management of a business. Use examples in your answer.
(20 marks)
(60 marks)

Managing

Question 5

People are at the heart of every successful business.

(A) Performance Appraisal, Training & Development and Managing Employer and Employee Relationships are important functions of a Human Resource Manager.

Explain the functions underlined above and analyse the benefits of **two** of the functions for the business organisation. (25 marks)

(B) Outline the different methods of reward used to motivate employees in a business.
(15 marks)

(C) Describe **two** strategies that a business organisation can use to manage change. Use examples to support your answer. (20 marks)
(60 marks)

Business in Action

Question 6

(A) "Managing a business is similar to managing a household in the areas of finance and taxation."
Discuss this statement, using examples to support your answer.
(20 marks)

(B) (i) Explain the term 'risk management'.
(ii) Illustrate **three** methods that can be used to reduce risk in a business.
(20 marks)

(C) Illustrate the impact of new technologies on business opportunities.
(20 marks)
(60 marks)

Business in Action

Question 7

(A) Outline the benefits for a new business of preparing a Business Plan. (15 marks)

(B) Motor Manufacturing Ltd. is considering the introduction of a new product. The business has provided the following figures:

Fixed Costs	*€200,000*
Variable Cost per	*Unit €5*
Selling Price	*€15*
Forecast Output (Sales)	*30,000 Units*

(i) Illustrate by means of a break-even chart:

(a) The Break – Even Point.

(b) Profit at forecast output.

(c) The Margin of Safety at forecast output.

(ii) Explain 'Margin of Safety'. (30 marks)

(C) Evaluate the importance of 'Feasibility Study' and 'Prototype Development' in the development process of a new product of your choice.
(15 marks)
(60 marks)

LEAVING CERTIFICATE EXAMINATION, 2008

BUSINESS – ORDINARY LEVEL
(400 marks)

ANSWER
(A) Ten questions from SECTION 1
AND
(B) Four questions from SECTION 2 as follows:
<u>One</u> question from Part 1 and
<u>Two</u> questions from Part 2 and
<u>One</u> other question from either Part 1 or Part 2.
All questions carry equal marks.
Calculators may be used.

SECTION 1
(100 marks)
SHORT ANSWER QUESTIONS

Answer 10 questions. Each question carries 10 marks. Please return this question paper with your answer book.

1. What do the following letters stand for? (Write each answer in the space provided.)

PLC	
AGM	
R & D	
MD	

2. List **three** elements of a valid contract.

(i) ____________________

(ii) ____________________

(iii) ____________________

3. Outline **two** characteristics/skills of an entrepreneur.

(i) ______________________________

____

(ii) ______________________________

____

4. Distinguish between Gross Pay and Net Pay.

Gross Pay: ______________________________

____

Net Pay: ______________________________

____

____

5. Draw a line graph to illustrate the following information for O'Malley Furniture Ltd.

Year	2003	2004	2005	2006	2007
Wage costs €	150,000	160,000	180,000	200,000	190,000

Wage Costs €

Year

6. Outline **two** reasons why goods are imported into Ireland and give **two** examples of such imports.

Reason 1: ______________________________

____

Reason 2: ______________________________

____

Examples: 1. ______________________________

2. ______________________________

7. Explain the term 'target market' and give **one** example to illustrate your answer.

____

____

____

Example: ______________________________

8. Write TRUE or FALSE after each of these sentences:

Sentence		True or False
1.	A strategic plan is a short term plan.	
2.	Conducting a survey in the marketplace is an example of Field Research.	
3.	The Balance Sheet is a statement of assets and liabilities.	
4.	A Curriculum Vitae is a document used for loan applications.	
5.	Prototype Development involves making a mock-up or first sample of a product.	

9. People whose personal information is kept on a computer have rights under the Data Protection Act 1988.

   Outline **two** of these rights.

   (i) ______________________________

   ____

   (ii) ______________________________

   ____

10. Explain the term 'induction training':

   ____

   ____

   ____

   ____

11. Outline **one** social responsibility of a business to **each** of the following stakeholders.

   (i) Local Community: ______________________________

   ____

   (ii) Suppliers: ______________________________

   ____

12. What is a SWOT analysis?

   ____

   ____

   ____

   ____

13. Name **one** state-owned enterprise/state agency involved in each of the following areas.

	Name of state-owned enterprise/state agency
(i) Production	
(ii) Transport	
(iii) Training	
(iv) Marketing	

14. Explain the term 'global marketing':

15. Outline **two** benefits of teamwork to an organisation.

(i)

(ii)

SECTION 2
(300 marks)

Answer four questions from SECTION 2 as follows:
One question from Part 1 and
Two questions from Part 2 and
One other question from either Part 1 or Part 2.

PART 1

PEOPLE IN BUSINESS

QUESTION 1

Study the information supplied and answer the questions which follow:

Martina bought a pair of boots costing €100 from Reilly's Footwear Ltd. After one week the heel came off one of the boots. She returned to the shop with the receipt but they refused to take the boots back.

Martina is considering taking her case to the Small Claims Court.

(A) (i) Name the law that protects Martina in this case. (10 marks)

(ii) Explain Martina's legal rights **and** the duties of Reilly's Footwear Ltd. (20 marks)

(iii) Explain **two** advantages to Martina of taking her case to the Small Claims Court. (10 marks)

A Trade Dispute can be explained as a dispute between an employer and the employees.

(B) (i) Outline **three** reasons/causes of trade disputes. (20 marks)

(ii) Describe any **two** functions of a Trade Union. (15 marks)

(75 marks)

DOMESTIC ENVIRONMENT

QUESTION 2

Study the information supplied and answer the questions which follow:

The secondary sector of the economy includes the manufacturing and construction industries.

(A) Outline **three** benefits that the growth in the construction industry in recent years has brought to the Irish economy. (15 marks)

(B) Explain **two** challenges faced by manufacturing industries in Ireland. (15 marks)

(C) (i) What is a Credit Union?
(ii) Briefly explain **two** services of a Credit Union to its members. (20 marks)

(D) (i) Explain what is meant by the term 'partnership'.
(ii) Give **three** advantages of a partnership as a type of business organisation. (25 marks)

(75 marks)

DOMESTIC / INTERNATIONAL ENVIRONMENT

QUESTION 3

Study the information supplied and answer the questions which follow:

Ireland has been a member of the EU since 1973. EU membership has had a significant effect on Irish economic growth and development.

(A) Outline **three** advantages to Irish business of European Union membership. (15 marks)

(B) (i) Name **two** EU institutions.
(ii) Explain the role of **one** of them. (20 marks)

(C) Outline **two** effects of rising unemployment on the Irish economy. (20 marks)

(D) Outline, using examples, **two** ways in which Information Technology helps Irish firms involved in international trade. (20 marks)
(75 marks)

PART 2

MANAGING

QUESTION 4

Study the information supplied and answer the questions which follow:

It is important that a business identifies, assesses and tries to reduce risks before taking out insurance.

(A) Outline **four** different types of insurance policies you would expect a <u>factory</u> to have. (20 marks)

(B) Outline **three** ways in which a manager can reduce risks in a factory. (20 marks)

(C) Name and explain the functions of **two** documents commonly used in insurance. (15 marks)

(D) Explain the following **three** principles of insurance. Give **one** example in each case to illustrate your answer.

(i) Insurable Interest
(ii) Utmost Good Faith
(iii) Indemnity. (20 marks)

(75 marks)

ENTERPRISE / MANAGING / BUSINESS IN ACTION

QUESTION 5

Study the information supplied and answer the questions which follow:

Sinéad has been working for a number of years in a busy department store in Dublin, a distance of 50 kilometres from her home.

Sinéad would like to set up a business in her home town and has employed a consultant to advise her on matters relating to finance, taxation and the recruitment and selection of employees.

(A) Identify **two** risks and **two** rewards for Sinéad if she sets up her own business. (20 marks)

(B) Outline **three** sources of new business ideas for Sinéad. (15 marks)

(C) Outline **three** methods Sinéad could use to recruit employees for her business. (15 marks)

(D) Name **two** taxes Sinéad would expect to pay. (10 marks)

(E) Name **two** long term sources of finance Sinéad could use to start her business and explain **one** of them. (15 marks)

(75 marks)

MANAGING

QUESTION 6

Study the information supplied and answer the questions which follow:

A vacancy has arisen in LMN Ltd for the position of Office Manager.
John Muldoon is the Human Resource Manager and he wants to fill this position internally.

(A) Draft, using today's date, a Memorandum (memo) from John Muldoon to all staff reminding them that the closing date for job applications is the 20th June, 2008.
(15 marks)

(B) Apart from memos, name **three** other methods of internal communication. (15 marks)

(C) Identify and explain **three** factors that affect the choice of methods of communication in business. (20 marks)

(D) Outline **two** advantages for LMN Ltd of recruiting internally. (10 marks)

(E) Explain the following terms:
(i) Stock Control.
(ii) Financial Control. (15 marks)
(75 marks)

MANAGING

QUESTION 7

Answer all parts of this question:

(A) Outline **three** items of information that a bank manager would require when considering an application for a business loan. (15 marks)

(B) Explain **two** reasons why a business would prepare a cash flow forecast. (10 marks)

(C) Explain the term 'bank overdraft'. (10 marks)

(D) The following information is extracted from the accounts of Sweeney Sports Ltd.

BALANCE SHEET (Extract) as on 31 December		
	2007	**2006**
	€	€
Current Assets	300,000	290,000
Current Liabilities	200,000	145,000

(i) Identify **two** items that could be included under the 'Current Assets' section of the Balance Sheet of Sweeney Sports Ltd. (15 marks)

(ii) Calculate the **Working Capital Ratio** for 2006 and 2007 and comment on the trend.
(Show the formula and all your workings.) (25 marks)
(75 marks)

BUSINESS IN ACTION

QUESTION 8

Study the information supplied and answer the questions which follow:

Promotion by a business is necessary to bring its products to the market's attention and to encourage consumers to purchase.

(A) Promotion is one of the four elements of the Marketing Mix. Name the other **three** elements and explain **one** of them. (20 marks)

(B) (i) List **three** methods (media) of advertising and give an advantage of **each** one. (15 marks)

(ii) Outline **three** functions of advertising. (15 marks)

(C) Draft and label a Product Life Cycle diagram. (15 marks)

(D) Outline **two** examples of Public Relations (PR) methods used by business. (10 marks)
(75 marks)

INDEX